Intelligent Cities

By the same author:

- *Theory of Urbanity* (Athens: Synchrona Themata, 1986)
- *Capitalist Development and Crisis Theory: Accumulation, regulation and spatial restructuring* (eds with M. Gottdiener, London: Macmillan, 1989)
- *Technocities and Development Strategies in Europe* (Athens: Gutenberg, 1993)
- *The Innovative Region: The regional technology plan of Central Macedonia* (Athens: Gutenberg, 1998)
- *Innovation Development Technologies in Regions and Production Complexes* (eds with L. Kyrgiafini and E. Sefertzi, Athens: Gutenberg, 2001)

Other titles of interest:

- *Innovative Cities*, ed. James Simmie (London: Spon, 2001)
- *Urban Future 21: A global agenda for twenty-first century cities*, Peter Hall and Ulrich Pfeiffer (London: Spon, 2000)
- *Making of the European Spatial Development Perspective*, Andreas Faludi and Bas Waterhout (London: Spon, 2002)

Intelligent Cities

Innovation, Knowledge Systems and Digital Spaces

Nicos Komninos

London and New York

First published 2002 by Spon Press
11 New Fetter Lane, London EC4P 4EE

Simultaneously published in the USA and Canada
by Spon Press
29 West 35th Street, New York, NY 10001

Spon Press is an imprint of the Taylor & Francis Group

Typeset in 10 on 12½pt Sabon by Wearset Ltd, Boldon, Tyne and Wear
Printed and bound in Great Britain by Biddles Ltd, Guildford and King's Lynn

British Library Cataloguing in Publication Data
A catalogue record for this book is available from the British Library

Library of Congress Cataloging in Publication Data
A catalog record for this book has been requested

ISBN 0-415-27717-5 (HB)
ISBN 0-415-27718-3 (PB)

In memory of my mother Olga
and my father Ioannis Komninos

Contents

Contents

Acknowledgements

I have benefited enormously from the assistance I received from colleagues involved in research related to this work and I wish to take this opportunity to thank them for their support. Yannis Bakouros, Theo Chadjipandelis, Lina Kyrgiafini, Dimitris Milossis, Bernard Musyck, Alasdair Reid, Elena Sefertzi, Voula Tarani, Panos Tsarchopoulos, Sotiris Zygiaris for their participation in projects at the URENIO Research Unit. Andrea Tosi at the Politecnico di Milano and Daniel Mercier at the Université Catholique de Louvain for their genuine contribution in technopolitan planning projects in southern Europe. Apostolos Apostolou, Philippe Delavergne, Eusebio Gainza, Fotis Kitsios, Vassilis Kelesides, Martin Rishiart, Gareth Roberts, Christos Skiadas, George Strogylopoulos, Meirion Thomas, and Kostas Tramantzas for their involvement in projects on technology dissemination and virtual innovation environments. Mikel Landabaso at the DG REGIO of the European Commission and Mark Gottdiener at the University of Buffalo, US who strongly encouraged this work.

This book includes certain pieces that were written as articles and presentations to conferences that have been substantially revised and rewritten. Bits and pieces of empirical material and research in Chapters 1, 2, 4, and 5 are to be found in my articles published in: Andrikopoulou, E. and Kafkalas, G. (eds) (2000) *The New European Space*, Athens: Themelio; Morgan, K. and Neuwelaers, C. (eds) (1999) *Regional Innovation Strategies; The challenge for less-favoured regions*, London: The Stationery Office; Simmie, J. (ed.) (1997) *Innovation, Networks and Learning Regions*, London: Jessica Kingsley; Dunford, M. and Kafkalas, G. (eds) (1992) *Cities and Regions in the New Europe*, London: Belhaven. All these pieces have been further elaborated and developed for this book.

Permissions are gratefully acknowledged from the following: The Stationery Office Limited, UK, for part of Section 2, Chapter 5; Office for Official Publications of the European Communities for Map 1 and Map 5.1; Andalusia Technology Park for Map 3.1; Smart Communities US for Figure 8.1; European Digital Cities for Figure 8.2; International Business Machines Corporation for Table 8.1; Elsevier Publishers for Figure 9.1.

INTRODUCTION
Origins, Structure and Contents

In 1953, relying on the experiments and photographs of X-ray diffraction made by Rosalind E. Franklin and given away by the laboratory head without her knowledge, J. D. Watson and F. H. Crick claimed that DNA consists of two nucleotide chains that form a double helix. This model was able to interpret the reproduction of DNA and the preservation of its characteristics and was thus immediately adopted by the scientific community.

In 1962, Watson and Crick were awarded the Nobel Prize for Physiology and Medicine. In the meantime, Franklin had passed away and her contribution was ignored.

(I. Asimov, *Chronology of Science and Discovery*)

During the last decades of the twentieth century, some cities and regions in Europe, Japan, and the US, displayed an exceptional capacity to incubate and develop new knowledge and innovations. The favourable environment for research, technology, and innovation created in these areas, was not immediately obvious, yet, it was of great significance for a development based on knowledge, technology, and learning. It is these areas of technological innovation and the favourable environment for learning and technology dissemination, on which this book focuses. It summarizes more than ten years of research conducted by URENIO[1] and funded by the R&D Framework Programmes of the European Commission and the Innovative Actions of the ERDF.[2]

We will deal with the relationship between knowledge and innovation that transfers knowledge to everyday life, and the environment of innovation. More specifically, what interests us is the contribution of the environment of innovation to the creation of new knowledge, the transfer of technology, and to knowledge-based development. The great majority of information and knowledge that we possess was created in the past. This knowledge can be stored in books and libraries, or in electronic databases, in order to be referred to when we need it. Yet human society's progress depends on the creation of new knowledge, knowledge that we acquire from the environment with the help of human intelligence and the appropriate tools. The value of this new knowledge is commensurate with the difficulty experienced in creating it and also to its usefulness. In any case, the value of new knowledge today seems to be significantly greater than that of the assimilated knowledge of the past. But how much does the social and technological environment contribute, and in what way, to the creation of new knowledge and the transfer of this knowledge to production? This is a question encountered throughout the book. A question that acted as a steady drive towards the completion of this book.

The arguments we present are developed along two dimensions. The first dimension concerns the *areas of technological innovation* and describes characteristic cases of such areas, demonstrating the evolution of their typology and their planning models. In other words, it focuses on cities and regions whose development relies on research and technology, communities, technological innovation processes, high-tech firms, technological cooperation networks and infrastructure. We believe that these areas create a favourable environment through which science, technology, and innovation fertilize each other and grow unhindered. It should be noted that the terms 'areas of technological innovation' and 'areas of knowledge-based development' are more or less equivalent, given that they describe the same urban and regional development processes. Both describe the polarization of technological innovations in certain cities and regions where favourable conditions promote the transfer of knowledge to the sphere of production, which in turn promotes development and prosperity in the specific region.

The second dimension of this book concerns *intelligent cities and regions*, the newest development in areas of technological innovation from a theoretical as well as a practical perspective. These are 'islands' where the innovation processes meet the digital world and the applications of the information society. This digital environment provides the particular human community of the island with additional capabilities in handling knowledge and new tools for problem solving. It therefore broadens its scope of knowledge and its ability to solve problems; in other words, it increases the community's intelligence.

Areas of Technological Innovation

Interest in the contribution of technological innovation to urban and regional development peaked after 1980. It was further aroused by economic geography research conducted in the industrial districts of central Italy and the west coast of the USA, and the planning of large technopolises in Japan. These new industrial and technological complexes, situated on the outskirts of cities or in entirely new locations, brought to light a series of parameters that were of particular significance for development at the end of the twentieth century; parameters such as, the geographical polarization of innovation, production flexibility, research and technology dynamics, spin-offs, just-in-time delivery systems and productive co-operation networks. Since then, technology, and more specifically techno-logical innovation, has been a fixed point of reference in the analysis and planning of cities and regions, with rapid developments not only in the theoretical field (regional innovation systems, learning regions, intelligent cities) but also in the field of regional policy and urban and regional planning.

Allen Scott's classic article on flexible production systems and regional development links the changes in the industrial systems of America and western Europe with the rise of new industrial spaces and new forms of industrial organization inspired by the flexible specialization paradigm (Scott 1988b). He examines the relative decline in the importance of Fordist mass production centres and the enormous expansion of manufac-turing activities based on less rigid and more flexible technological and institutional structures. An impressive characteristic of the new, flexible capitalism is its differentiation from the old mass production centres. The new centres of growth appear as islands of innovation either situated inside older industrial areas or in a series of areas formerly on the geo-graphical borders of post-war mass production. Their economies relied on agriculture, trade, and small industry, in many cases family owned, but actually they represent highly innovative and dynamic localities. Best known cases of such areas are: Orange County and Silicon Valley (the two leading high-technology production complexes), Route 128 in the western suburbs of Boston in the United States, the design-intensive industrial dis-tricts of Emilia-Romana, Marche, Tuscany and Veneto in Italy, the periph-eral cities of Montpellier, Sophia-Antipolis, Grenoble and Toulouse, in France, the scientific city of southern Paris, the M4 corridor between London and Reading, and the Cambridge University city in Britain, Bavaria and Baden-Württemberg in southern Germany, the Jura region of Switzerland, north-eastern Spain, and central Portugal.

Recent research in the European Union has validated the role of innova-tion in regional development, as well as the geographical polarization of research and technology, leading to the creation of islands of innovation. The 6th Periodic Report on the social and economic situation and develop-ment of the regions of the European Union contains a very interesting chapter titled 'Introduction to competitiveness' (European Commission 1999b). Competitiveness is defined as the capacity for production of prod-ucts and services that acquire the approval of international markets, while sustaining high and durable levels of income. In other words, it is the capacity of companies, industries, and regions, to generate relatively high levels of income and employment, while being exposed to international competition. A major indicator of competitiveness is GDP per head, of which two components are labour productivity (GDP/Employees) and employment intensity (Employees/Population).

Indicator of competitiveness:
GDP/Population = GDP/Employees × Employees/Population

A competitive region has to combine high growth levels of labour productivity and employment intensity. The growth rate of GDP per head in a region reflects the sum of the growth rates in productivity and employment.

Based on this simple model, the 6th Periodic Report retraces the changes in competitiveness of the European regions. In the post-war period, their development was based mainly on increases in productivity, rather than in employment size. During 1986–96, an annual growth of GDP per head of 2.2 per cent was observed, which was due to an annual increase in productivity of 1.8 per cent and to an increase in the number of employees of 0.4 per cent. The healthiest European regions, located across the 'blue banana' strip, are characterized by high labour productivity (GDP/Employees). In the periphery of Europe, the situation is more complex. In Ireland both the components of competitiveness have higher scores than the European average; the regions of Portugal and southern Italy are catching up on the basis of a higher annual change in productivity than the European average; the regions of Greece show an annual change in productivity that is lower than the European average, combined with an annual change in employment higher than the average. Convergence, in this case, is slower.

An analysis made by Cambridge Econometrics explains this regional variation of competitiveness and GDP per head in the EU with respect to four factors most closely connected with it. These factors are:

- The structure of economic activity, measured by the distribution of employment in agriculture, manufacturing, construction, market services, and non-market services. The regions with a higher GDP per head tend to have a higher employment ratio in market services and/or manufacturing.

- The regional accessibility, measured by a composite accessibility indicator.

- The innovation activity in the region, measured by the number of applications for patent.

- The skills of the labour force, measured by the level of education of the population between 25 and 59 years.

These four factors (and the corresponding indicators) explain more than 65 per cent of the variation of GDP per head among the European regions. However, this relationship has to be cautiously interpreted, given that many regions have relatively high competitiveness, but low scores in one or more indicators. The most interesting feature of this interpretation is the quantitative documentation and highlighting of technological innovation as the main variable in the growth and prosperity of European cities and regions. Two of the four factors that explain regional differentiation in competitiveness (patents and level of education of the active population) express the basic dimensions of technological innovation.

Furthermore, it has been found that R&D laboratories and companies involved in research and technological development in the European Union are to a great extent concentrated in a few 'islands of innovation'. It is calculated that three-quarters of all public research contracts, including those funded by the EU, are concentrated in only twelve regions, namely London, Rotterdam, Amsterdam, the Ile de France region, Ruhr, Frankfurt, Stuttgart, Munich, Lyon, Grenoble, Turin, and Milan. These regions of 'Archipelago Europe' are mainly urban, with a concentrated network of businesses and research centres working together to develop new products and production processes. The farther one travels from these islands of innovation, the more the collaborating laboratories tend to outnumber the businesses, while the research projects are on a smaller scale and of a more specialized nature (European Commission 1994c; 1999b).

In this environment created by high-technology industrial clusters, technopoles, and islands of innovation, there is a significant improvement in the capability of established organizations, which learn to adopt technologies, to conduct original research, and to develop new products. This social and institutional environment enhances the capacity for handling information and knowledge and possesses mechanisms for acquiring and developing technology and innovation. Many examples can be mentioned to illustrate that in an innovative region, a technology park or industrial district, the performance of small firms is higher compared with similar firms outside the innovation island, both in terms of competitiveness and know-how to develop and market new products and technologies.

The above mentioned developments in urban and regional theory and the empirical analysis on the dynamic regions in the European Union highlight a major contradiction between technological innovation and the regions, with significant consequences:

- On the one hand, knowledge-intensive activities, new industrial sectors and technological innovation are recognized as central factors in the development of cities and regions. Each city or region, aiming at high rates of growth and prosperity, is turning towards the forces of knowledge and technological innovation and sets in training mechanisms to reinforce its endogenous technological capabilities. This is now recognized as a rule and dominant model.

- On the other hand, the development of technology and innovation are highly geographically concentrated and polarized (European Commission 1994f). The basic entities in technology-based development are the

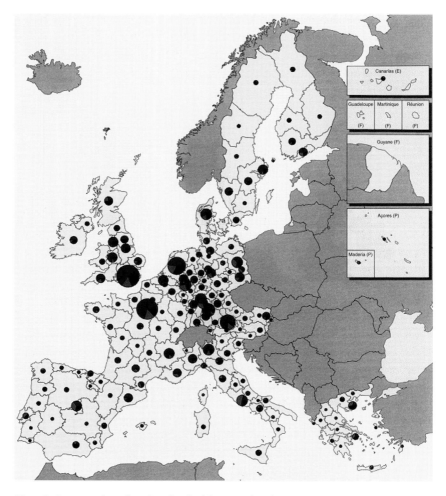

Map 1 Geography of technological innovation in Europe
Source: European Commission (1999a).

islands of innovation (industrial complexes, technopoles, knowledge-intensive clusters, innovative regions) where relations of spatial integration, institutional regulation of know-how, and informational infrastructure, support the dissemination of innovation and technological development.[3]

Urban and regional development at the beginning of the twenty-first century is characterized by a shift towards technology, innovation, and selective urban development, similar to the shift, immediately after the Second World War, towards mass industrialization and intensive urbanization. This change of direction is marked by the geographical polarization of technological development into islands of innovation, and the establishment of relationships of local integration and collaboration between research and production. The contradiction between the role of technological innovation and its geographical polarization sustains the gap between core and peripheral regions, and guides the contemporary efforts of regional policy and planning.

Three Theories on the Environment of Innovation

Intensive research on the regions and the environment for innovation led to the creation of a new theoretical paradigm on innovative development, where economics of innovation, industrial geography, management of technology, urban and regional development and planning converge.

Today, 25 years after the first research was conducted on communities and system-areas of Third Italy, we can distinguish three major directions of theoretical thinking on innovative development, which were formed with reference to the theories of: (1) the industrial district, (2) the learning region, and (3) the digital/intelligent city. These paradigms were spread rapidly by the academic community to political bodies and inspired the efforts for technological development on a regional level. Planning models were accordingly defined in order to facilitate the processes of innovation and technology development, including models for science parks, technopolises, regional innovation strategies, digital islands, and virtual innovation environments.

Industrial districts and high-tech clusters exert a long-term influence on

Table 1 Urban and regional technological development: Theories and planning models

Theoretical paradigms	Planning/policy models
Industrial District	<ul><li>Flexible industrial districts</li><li>Tertiary clusters of knowledge-intensive activities</li><li>Technopoles, science and technology parks</li><li>Technopolis programmes</li></ul>
Learning Region	<ul><li>EU innovating regions: RTP, RITTS, RIS, RIS+</li><li>Regional innovation strategies</li><li>Regional systems of innovation</li><li>Trans-regional innovation projects</li></ul>
Digital City	<ul><li>Smart cities</li><li>Intelligent cities and regions</li><li>Virtual innovation islands: virtual districts, technology poles, and regional innovation systems</li><li>Telematics and online innovation/knowledge management</li></ul>

the planning of technological growth. The June 1999 issue of the *Journal of Regional Studies*, one of the most influential journals on regional development and policy, is devoted to clusters, and shows the continuing impact that this concept and the associated theoretical paradigm continue to have (Regional Studies 1999).

For Marshall, the founder of the industrial district theory, the importance of the localization of production within industrial districts is that it creates an environment more favourable to the success of individual companies. This environment stems from the geographical proximity of firms rather than any institutional structuring. Close proximity between producers within a particular industrial location provides opportunities for entrepreneurs to specialize and cooperate (Marshall 1920).

High-technology industries (consumer electronics, electronic equipment, computers and components, telecommunications and broadcast-receiving equipment, aerospace, pharmaceuticals) show a tendency to cluster in specific localities. But industrial districts are not necessarily based on high-technology sectors and firms only. Most of the districts in central Italy and southern Europe, for instance, specialize in traditional activities, such as textiles, clothing, leather goods, metal goods, mechanical engineering, and ceramics (Hall *et al.* 1987; Amin 1989a).

Spatial proximity is considered as a major factor in effective technology development and transfer. Based on the analysis of the transfer of process technologies developed by German firms to Canadian users-firms, for example, Gentler (1996) notes that extended interaction between user and producer is indeed a key ingredient of successful technology development and transfer. Whenever user-firms invest in leading edge, best practice or state-of-the-art technologies, which originate from sources that are geographically distant, they can expect serious implementation difficulties to arise. It seems clear that the technology transfer process is indeed strongly subject to spatial limits, and that the positive externalities arising from inter-firm interaction are also geographically determined.

Inter-firm cooperation is the key factor in the favourable environment created by the spatial proximity of producers within the district. The literature identifies two main aspects of cooperation among local producers. The first is the provision of collective goods and services, such as training and education, research and development; the second concerns reciprocity in sharing technical information, refraining from wage competition, selecting subcontractors, etc. (Lawson and Lorenz 1999). However, the literature on industrial districts does not offer a detailed account of the innovation and knowledge processes that create the favourable environment of the district and the competitive advantage of the regionally clustered firms. In recent studies on clusters, more emphasis is given to the collective culture of the industrial milieu and the institutional basis of inter-firm cooperation.

A number of planning and policy models were based on the industrial district theory, looking to create a physical space that can reproduce the favourable conditions of the district in terms of inter-firm cooperation and technology development. These attempts include: (1) providing support for clusters in traditional or new industries, (2) creating knowledge-intensive clusters in central-city areas that host producer services, financial services, company headquarters, new tertiary activities like software and multimedia, (3) constructing science and technology parks that host R&D institutes, innovative firms, and technology transfer organizations, and (4) supporting more extensive technopolises combining science and technology parks, industrial districts, and clusters of producer services (Komninos 1993). These spaces favour the spatial agglomeration of technology-based companies, R&D institutes, and other facilities, and provide a good environment for networking and technology cooperation. However, as the understanding of the spatial dynamics of innovation is enriched, so are these technology poles and agglomerations of technology-driven activities enriched with innovation support institutions and knowledge diffusion mechanisms.

Regional innovation systems and *learning regions* were a next major step in the understanding of the dynamics of technology-driven agglomerations and regions (Morgan 1997; Simmie 1997a). This theory, inspired partly by evolutionary economics and the pioneer work of Freeman, Lundvall, and Nelson, identifies at the regional level, the institutional arrangements and actions that sustain the dynamics of innovation (Freeman 1990; Lundvall 1992; Nelson 1993).

A regional system of innovation is a multilevel system of institutions supporting knowledge and learning processes. The main components of the regional innovation system are the organizations for: (1) research and development, (2) technology transfer, (3) the use of technology, (4) innovation funding, and (5) the provision of technological information. The fundamental institutions of technology production and use (labs, R&D institutes, companies, and producer services) are found at the base of the system. At a higher level is the operation of more complex institutions for technology cooperation, and networking among agencies of production, transfer, and knowledge application. This institutional edifice supports the processes of technological development and learning, which take shape through joint projects, infrastructures, institutions, networks, and financial agreements. The main function, however, of an effective regional innovation system is to sustain the creation of new technology-based firms, knowledge-intensive start-ups, and spin-offs (Komninos 1998).

The positive influence of the regional innovation systems on the technological capacity of businesses is derived from collective learning procedures. Landabaso *et al.* (1999) point out that the innovative capacity of the regional firm is directly related to the 'learning' ability of a region. A step forward, the innovative capacity and the learning ability of a region are associated with the density and quality of networking within the regional productive environment (Debresson and Amesse 1991; Camagni 1991; Cooke and Morgan 1993). Inter-firm and public–private cooperation, and the institutional framework within which these relationships take place, form the substance of a regional environment favourable to innovation; innovation is the end product, whereas regional 'learning' dependent on the quality and density of the above relationships is the process.

This theoretical model supported the particularly successful European policy of Regional Innovation Strategies (RITTS, RIS). As Landabaso points out,

RIS are an instrument to create and/or strengthen regional innovation systems in less favoured regions, in terms of the coherence of the systems, of inter- and intra-regional co-operation networks, and of the amount and quality of innovation related public spending.

(Landabaso 1999)

Regional Innovation Strategies began in 1994 with pilot exercises in a small number of European regions (Wales, Limbourg, Lorraine, Castille-Leon, Central Macedonia) and were extended through successive second and third generation programmes to more than 100 regions across the European Union. Their influence lies in the dissemination of the culture of innovation, the drawing up of projects of technological development in each region, but mainly in the orientation of the EU structural funds support to activities designed to foster technological innovation and development.

Digital cities, virtual innovation islands and *intelligent cities* have opened a third important strand in the theoretical thinking on the environment and policy of innovation. This is mainly due to the meeting of innovation with information technologies and the World Wide Web. The fact that basic innovation processes and functions can be carried out in a digital space has actualized the creation of a series of virtual innovation environments. The result is not a theoretical paradigm in the conventional sense of the term, so much as a group of approaches and concepts and an extremely rich literature, focusing on the procedures of innovation and their digital transcription. Here, the interest lies in how fundamental processes of innovation can be actualized at a virtual space and be used by the most distant company and technology user. Innovation is conceived not that much as a communication process or institution, but as a combination of knowledge, management tools, telematics for learning, and virtual spaces for interaction and experimentation. The understanding of the internal sequence in these processes allows for the creation of virtual islands, based on the non-material factors and mechanisms for the dissemination of knowledge and innovation (Caves and Walshok 1999; Downey and McGuigan 1999; Demachak *et al.* 2000).

Certain characteristic processes of technological development – for example those involving spin-offs and the transfer of technology, networks and technological integration, reverse learning, technology lock-in avoidance, tacit knowledge, the development of creativity and creative thinking, as well as innovation management techniques and methods – can all be actualized in a virtual space. This enables virtual islands of innovation to be created in relation to non-material factors for the dissemination of knowledge and innovation. In turn, a virtual innovation environment can be combined with real islands of innovation, such as industrial districts and technology parks, in order to create a highly intelligent innovation support framework.

This course of events also promotes the exceptionally fertile meeting of innovation with telematics, the information society, and information technologies. The construction of a virtual innovation environment and intelligent cities is a captivating prospect, in which an environment of digital networks and software tools increases the creativity and effectiveness of a real community of researchers and producers.

Intelligent Cities and Regions

The second dimension of the book is about intelligent cities and regions. The term 'intelligent cities/regions' has been used with two different meanings. In the project *Intelligent Region*, the regions with high institutional capacity for technological innovation and development – which emerge from relationships of cooperation between regional development agencies and the universities – are characterized as intelligent (Morgan 1998; Kafkalas *et al.* 1998). A different interpretation is found in many publications on digital cities, which characterize intelligent (smart) cities as those that have applied information technologies and virtual spaces to urban functions and activities (Caves and Walshok 1999; Downey and McGuigan 1999; Mahizhnan 1999).

Our interpretation combines both points of view. Intelligent cities are those spatial entities that, on the one hand, offer a real environment for technological innovation based on clusters and institutions for R&D, and product and process innovation. And on the other hand, intelligent cities are endowed with a digital capacity to manage and diffuse knowledge and technology. This may be a technology park that has developed an information technology interface to sustain technology transfer (such as the Kyoto Technology Park); or it may be an industrial district with infrastructure supporting virtual relationships and inter-firm transactions (such as the city of Prato in Italy). It may also be a technopolis or a regional innovation system in which certain functions are transferred to digital or virtual spaces. In this sense, an intelligent city is an environment of learning and innovation, on real and virtual levels:

- At the real level, intelligence is linked to communication and institutional interaction of a community of people for learning, experimentation, knowledge, and technological development.

- At the virtual level, it is the capacity of the same community for knowledge management, technology diffusion, and communication based on a digital interaction.

Intelligent cities capture the innovation-friendly environment that can be formed upon knowledge-intensive localities and communities of people. With the help of information and communication technologies, any innovation island may be transformed into an intelligent community.

Intelligent cities also highlight the emerging character of cities as centres of knowledge, information management, technology, and innovation. They represent a major component in the process towards a knowledge-based society and economy, in which development and welfare depend on clusters of knowledge and networks among the producers of knowledge. There are numerous indications that leading industrial countries are accumulating scientific knowledge and technologies to accelerate and extend this process through the multiplication of virtual spaces. A major transition has started with the transfer of urban functions from a physical space to a digital one, allowing some functions related to cities (mainly transactions) to be realized virtually. This change is sustained by an economic rationality. A determining factor has been the rise of a new international division of labour, in which the competitiveness of the European Union and the US relies mainly on their capacity to generate and use knowledge, with the aid of their respective labour forces, scientific and technological infrastructure (European Commission 1995b).

The two aspects of this book, namely the analysis of the theories and planning models for innovative regions, and virtual cities and digital applications for innovation dissemination, are complementary. Intelligent cities and the virtual innovation islands present a contemporary extension of the theories on the environment of innovation, which provide the next paradigm of technological innovation, the de-materialization of basic processes, and their digital transcription.

The book has a simple structure. The introduction and the first chapter deal with innovation as an environmental condition, and with the geography and typology of islands of innovation.

In the next three Parts, the focus is on the theoretical paradigms and the planning models of the industrial district, the learning region, and the intelligent city, which offer three alternative ways to create an environment of innovation. However, this arrangement must not be viewed as a linear evolution and replacement of theories and planning models. On the contrary, it is in fact a continuous enrichment of the theory on the environment of innovation, beginning from spatial proximity to which are added an institutional dimension and, following that, the dimension of virtual spaces and digital tools.

Part I is about *technology districts*, *technopoles* and *science parks*, and includes three chapters that present the evolution of the theory, and the link between theory and political practice, which guides the planning of science and technology parks. The transcription of district theory to technopolitan planning is the central issue of these chapters.

Chapter 2 focuses on a theoretical perspective on districts and technopoles and analyses the contribution of technology parks and technopoles in the transfer and use of the industrial district theory as policy and planning model.

Chapter 3 presents the adaptation of planning models for technology parks in the less favoured regions. We examine three cases of technology parks in Spain, Italy, and Greece, and discuss the double challenge that these regions are facing in the creation of an environment of innovation: the competition that comes from traditional industries and low labour cost countries outside the European Union, and the competition from high-technology regions and industries located inside the Union.

Chapter 4 is a critique of the innovation and technology transfer concepts that are associated with technopoles and science parks, characterized by the limited institutional power for knowledge management and technology transfer. Recent developments in technology transfer policy are examined, and new tools for research–industry cooperation that diffuse innovations through network structures and decentralized institutions are discussed.

Part II focuses on *learning regions* and *regional innovation strategies*, the new innovation policy of the European Commission, implemented through RTP, RITTS, and RIS projects.

Two chapters (5 and 6) deal with regional innovation strategies, and the relation between regional and national innovation strategy. A case study is presented, the Regional Technology Plan of Central Macedonia, Greece, which was one of the first pilot projects of Innovating Regions' initiatives in Europe.

Regional innovation strategies attempt to bring to the surface the main factors behind the region's system of innovation and its structural deficits: the archaic character of the small and medium-sized businesses, the inadequacies of its mechanisms for the diffusion of technology, the latent character of demand for technology and innovation services. They adopt an integrated view of dealing with innovation, a systemic model of interaction between technology supply, demand, transfer, and finance. Basic differences between this strategy and the strategies of technology poles and industrial districts are in the promotion of an institutions-based regional innovation system, the exploitation of the existing industrial and research capability of the region, as well as the emphasis on the demand side of the innovation process.

Chapter 7 is an original approach on technology intelligence methods suitable for regional innovation strategies. The theoretical discussion on regional technological development gives no satisfactory answer to the question of the technologies that should be prioritized at the regional level. There are many references to 'new technologies', but this is not an adequate definition of the best science and technology areas for regional technological development. Regional authorities are not adequately informed which technologies they should promote through regional incentives, which technologies accelerate more regional development, and which are the emerging technologies for the coming years. With respect to these questions, we discuss the procedures that allow for the creation of technology intelligence that can guide the decisions of the regions in technology investments, technology attraction, technology training and learning. Technological priorities found in the European R&D programmes, the technology priorities suitable for the less favoured regions are reviewed and some major technology foresight studies on critical technologies are examined including the tools for undertaking regional technology intelligence exercises.

Part III is about *intelligent cities* and includes three chapters that discuss the concept and creation procedures of an intelligent city.

Chapter 8 starts with the experiments developed in the framework of the Smart Communities movement in the US and the European Digital Cities programme. This chapter ends with the description of the components of an intelligent city, and the integration of real and virtual innovation environments in such a place.

Chapters 9 and 10 are particularly significant with respect to the novel approach on intelligent cities being promoted. These chapters describe the conclusions and findings from two research projects of the European Commission concerning the creation of real–virtual innovation environments. The first titled 'Virtual Network of European Technology Parks', concerns the development of virtual technology transfer functions in technology parks, and the digital environment that is subsequently created over a technology park. The second is a large innovation development and dissemination project, titled 'Innovative Region', and concerns the creation of virtual applications upon regional innovation systems capable of supporting the dissemination of innovation development technologies. In both cases, the methodological basis for developing intelligent environments is the same. It is based, on the one hand, on the capabilities provided by telematic tools for online innovation development and knowledge management, and on the other hand, on the integration between the real and the digital environment of innovation of a learning human community.

The book is based on more than ten years of research in different regions of the European Union, in Finland, Germany, Greece, Italy, Portugal, Spain, and the UK, and includes results from research projects on clusters and networks, science and technology park planning, the design and implementation of regional technology plans and regional innovation strategies, and on knowledge management and online innovation tools. Most of these projects were realized by trans-regional research teams in the framework of European R&D programmes, mainly the Sprint and Innovation Programme, the Recite Programme, and the Innovative Actions of the European Regional Development Fund.

The central reasoning is that innovative regions and the environment of innovation evolve from relatively simple structures, such as those of the industrial district and the science park, to more complex ones, where institutional arrangements and digital (non-material) procedures of learning and knowledge diffusion take over. During the past five years we have had the opportunity to witness this development, not only in the arena of theoretical thought but also in political practice and in planning innovation support systems.

1   Innovation is an Island

Over the past twenty years industrial countries have put considerable effort into research and technological development in order to meet the challenges of globalization. Since the Western world has chosen technological innovation as the basic competitive advantage in the global economy, it has led to extensive mobilization of scientific and technological knowledge in the search for solutions to problems of production and development. However, despite the pre-eminent position of technological innovation in the contemporary world, our knowledge of its processes and mechanisms is largely axiomatic and empirical. It is based, on the one hand, on the concept of innovation as the commercial and productive exploitation of science and technology, and on the other, on best practice and examples of organizations that have developed successful technological innovations.

In this chapter we argue that technological innovation is an environmental condition. Innovation flows from an environment rich in factors and mechanisms facilitating the conversion of scientific knowledge into products and services. Such a favourable environment for technological innovation has been created in a whole series of areas, including industrial districts, technopoles, innovative regions, and intelligent cities, in which conditions of collaboration and collective ingenuity reinforce the capabilities of established organizations and enterprises. The environment of innovation is characterized by specific functions, among which research and development, technology transfer, networking, and technological cooperation dominate.

Innovation and the R&D Lab

The term 'innovation', notes the *Green Paper on Innovation*, is somewhat equivocal, for it designates both a process and its result. It signifies the transformation of scientific and technological knowledge into products and services, and in this sense the term describes a process (European Commission 1996a). However, when the word innovation designates a new product, then the emphasis is on the result of the process. This double meaning is a source of misunderstandings, the most common of which is confusion between the factors that promote innovation, such as research and development (R&D), technology purchase, international technological cooperation, funding, and their result, that is, a new product, a new method, a new service.

In some surveys, for instance, the enterprises that buy or sell technology are considered innovative, a definition that creates confusion between a cause (purchase of technology) and its result (the renewal of products and processes, being innovative).[1] The same perplexity is found in assessments of the regional technology gap, measuring the intensity of efforts devoted to R&D and technology, although these efforts do not necessarily mean that a region or organization spending more on research is by definition more innovative. This indeed is the criticism of the linear model of innovation. It is not sufficient to increase the intensity of R&D in order to trigger the process and increase the potential for innovation. Many experiences from regional innovation strategies show that a critical parameter in the innovation process is not the size of the regional research budget, but the institutional and social web permitting the transformation of scientific knowledge into new products and processes.

It is important to remember at this point that technological innovation is the transformation within an organization (enterprise, service organization, research laboratory) of:

- *Production processes* (through information technology, automation, energy saving systems);

- *Products* (new products and services, new product models, improved quality, shorter life cycle of products); and

- *Organization* (flexibility, just-in-time delivery systems, lean production, networks, optimization of producer-supplier relations, etc.).

The renewal of products and production processes can be radical or incremental. It is radical when it has to do with the development of a new technology or the initial commercial exploitation of a new product, and it is incremental when it concerns the adoption of a technology that is considered 'good practice' and that is already being implemented in more advanced segments within a productive sector or region. In the first instance we have a generic innovation, whereas the second is innovation on the level of the specific organization. This distinction opens the door of innovation to all those organizations that improve their production up to the level of the best practice. Innovation does not concern only the best enterprises and organizations that carry out original research and develop original products, but includes technology transfer and dissemination, in addition to the development of new products and technologies.

With the globalization of economies and competition, innovation has become the most important factor in development, employment, and prosperity. Innovation in methods and processes permits increased productivity, energy saving, ergonomic optimization, better efficiency and reliability in production. Innovation in products and services permits differentiation from competing products, opens new markets, and improves the competitiveness of the company. Innovation in organizations permits the better use of human resources, flexibility, and it is usually a precondition for the successful implementation of new products and processes. Despite this logical systematization, innovation is difficult to measure. If, for example, one organization develops one new product a year and another develops three in that year, does that mean the second is more innovative than the first? Probably not. Innovation is not only about the number of new products. We have to measure the effort made to develop them and the results in terms of growth and employment. This goes back to expenditure on R&D, to the precondition rather than the result of the innovation. But as mentioned, expenditure on R&D does not always lead to a successful innovation. Without a global theory of the innovation process, this vicious circle among causes and results just goes on repeating itself.

The R&D Lab

In the rapid change and innovation of products, production technologies, and management methods, a number of factors come into play. Critical among them is research and development, and the use of scientific and technical knowledge for commercial purposes. Research capacity, however, is not sufficient for innovation. The latter also requires appropriate managerial support, funding, market promotion, and the collaboration with technology providers, suppliers, and other producers.

Until the 1980s, the process of innovation had been mainly conceived within the framework of the research laboratory of a large company (Alison 1969). Let us assume, for example, writes Donald Schon, that a researcher or engineer working in a lab discovers a new quality in some material or describes a new mechanical set-up (Schon 1969).

- The next step is to announce the discovery to his director and secure approval for further research. Now he will look into the question of intellectual property, to see whether an existing patent covers his discovery, and analyse in greater detail the problems of production and the probable market for the new product. Up to this point the investment in time and resources is relatively small.

- If this first enquiry has a positive result, the head of the R&D division will present the results to the senior management of the company, and secure approval for funding for a full-scale development plan.

- The technical characteristics and manufacturing problems of the new product are studied in detail on the basis of this plan, and a market research study will be carried out into sectors related to the expected product. The company will proceed with its full-scale research into patent rights and will explore the possibility of later competition from similar products. This stage may last up to six months, requires considerable outlays and concludes with the manufacture of the prototype.

- Now the company can submit detailed plans for patenting and organize a pilot production line. Here a new series of problems will appear, relating to large-scale production, and the technical characteristics of the product will be modified accordingly. On account of the size of the pilot application, changes in the production process are more costly. The quality of the product is checked, and selected users chosen to test and evaluate it.

- Everything is now ready for full-scale production, combined with marketing strategy. Mass production starts up, with numerous associated problems of reliability and quality, which will be solved in the course of production and in future improvements to the model.

It is obvious that the example describes in simplified form, the innovation process in the large (usually multinational) mass production companies that flourished in the second half of the twentieth century. It outlines the several stages in the innovation process: its origin in the R&D division, the securing of a budget from the administration, the support from the marketing division, the manufacture of prototypes and the pilot production and quality test run (Table 1.1). At each step, the innovation plan risks being dropped if cost, market, and technical problems appear to be insuperable.

Innovation, however, is not a linear process that begins with research and ends with a new product. On the contrary, a complex web of interactive relationships characterizes the transformation of scientific and technical knowledge into new production processes, products and services. The activation of the innovation cycle does not necessarily begin with research. Studies by the European Innovation Monitoring System show that, in many companies, the spark usually comes from benchmarking of competing companies and from suggestions from suppliers and customers (Cordis Focus 1997). This does not refute, however, the essential role of research,

Table 1.1 New product development stages

---
1 *Development of an idea*: Product architecture, design, target market
2 *Product planning*: Model, small-scale control, funding
3 *Product/process engineering*: Detailed design, manufacture of prototypes
4 *Pilot production programme*: Testing of production volume, initiation of laboratory process of adapting production to commercial purposes
5 *Production*: Preservation of models, continuous improvement

---

Source: Adapted from Best and Forrant (1998: 110).

which provides the necessary knowledge, capacities, and technologies that open new roads to production and products.

Interpretation

What we know about the factors involved in and the path of innovation is mainly axiomatic and empirical, arising out of the definition of innovation and the observation of innovating organizations. It is doubtful whether a general theory of innovation can be formulated, since the prediction capacity implied in the theory would destroy the possibility of innovation itself. What sort of innovation could there be in the automotive industry when a predictive theory could determine the next round of discoveries in motor and safety technologies and direct all manufacturers towards the same objectives?

Up until the 1970s, two theoretical constructions defined our understanding of innovation. The first was based on the concept of uncertainty, probability, and the necessity to come through the actual state-of-the-art. Nylon, for example, was apparently discovered by chance, when a lab technician at Dupont, accidentally left a flame alight and came back to find polymerized fibres (Drucker 1985). From this perspective Goldman points out that:

Research is like a giant poker game. In the final analysis, everything in our world – including the world of physics – is statistics and probabilities. You are playing with the laws of probability. But in order to maximize your chances you have to assess three important components at the same time. The first is chance. But along with chance there is the ability to understand the probabilities. How you can use the probabilities to your own benefit, how you can profit from the unusual. And finally there is the non-material component of psychology, your assessment of what the others are thinking and doing. Using these components you can maximize your winnings in the R&D game.

(Goldman 1969)

A long interval of time and considerable investment, sometimes in the development of new knowledge in basic sectors of the science in question, occur between the initial discovery of a new product and its final launching. Part of the total process can be interpreted in terms of entrepreneurship and investment. The global process however does not follow a clear model, at least in so far as the technical aspect of the problem is concerned.

If innovation is going beyond the state-of-the-art of a given technology, the effort required to exceed this level cannot be calculated, in terms of the knowledge needed and the series of technical problems that have to be resolved. The R&D division usually presumes that it is very close to getting past the state-of-the-art, without that necessarily being the case and without any guarantee that it will. This means that the most difficult and

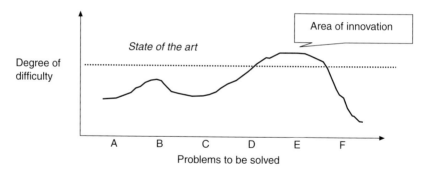

Figure 1.1 Innovation and state-of-the-art technology

crucial problems, which require more knowledge than is currently available, have to be dealt with first, with the solution of less complicated problems coming later.

The second theoretical description concerned the framework, the environment of innovation. It is easy to assume from what has already been said that this environment was the industrial R&D lab and the large company. Large companies could throw money and human resources at a problem and persist for long periods of time in the development of an innovation, without putting its own existence on the line. But this positive situation went hand in hand with the limited horizon of exploitation of such discoveries. The industrial research lab had only one chance to secure funding, since it could only turn to the senior management in its own company. If it failed to convince the top brass, then the innovation project it was promoting was doomed.

The industrial R&D lab environment posed a great deal of restrictions. Cohen described the case of an automotive electronics manufacturer in Toulouse that lost 40 engineers, who, when the management refused to proceed with the development of a new product, left the company to found their own firm and to continue their research and development work (Cohen 1988). Roussel *et al.* (1991) analysed a new entrepreneurial R&D culture (third generation R&D) where the industrial lab can look outside the company for backing and funding for technological innovation. However, neither path eliminates the difficulties inherent in the development of innovation in the environment of the R&D lab of a large company.

By the end of the 1970s a new environment of innovation was beginning to appear. It was no longer the large company, but rather a complex of smaller firms that in the framework of the industrial district developed and applied technological innovations and new product development through specialization and flexible collaboration.

Islands of Innovation: Technology goes out of Labs

In the 1980s it became clear that certain regions provided a particularly favourable environment for the development and dissemination of technological innovation. In California's Silicon Valley, in Japan's decentralized Technopolises, in Cambridge, in the Ile de France Science City, in Sophia-Antipolis, Montpellier, Grenoble and Toulouse in the south of France, in southern Bavaria and Baden-Württemberg, in Turin and the industrial districts in central Italy, the local environment has served as an incubator for the development of new industrial sectors, new products and innovative production processes (Castells and Hall 1994; Komninos 1993; Radovic and Auriol 1999; Scott 1988a; Simmie 1998; Tatsumo 1986).

These areas constitute *islands of innovation* within wider regions of more traditional activities. The islands reflect an historic process of new industrial activities formation, created as each new activity appears as a distinctive entity within established practices. The islands also express a new spatial division of production and labour, in the sense that the new technology-based activities need special socio-economic conditions to emerge and take root.

Empirical data show that we can distinguish five large categories of islands of innovation, each of which fosters innovation in a different way. These are: (1) flexible specialization industrial districts, (2) clusters of business services in metropolitan centres, (3) science and technology parks, (4) technopolises, and (5) innovating regions. To these particular categories we can add 'intangible islands of innovation' and the 'intelligent cities', which combine telematic applications over poles of technological creativity such as research labs, science parks, and industrial districts.

Flexible specialization industrial districts, in central Italy, were the first areas where the contribution of the local environment to the recent development of innovation and new industrial practices became evident. The innovation mechanisms activated within these districts emerge from *specialization* and the *multiplicity of possible collaborations* between producers. In the district, each production unit is sufficiently specialized to be near the state-of-the-art in its corresponding technologies, design, and industrial practice. This facilitates innovation. Further, the final product results from variable combinations of collaboration between producers, and this favours innovation in products that appear from new combinations. Becattini (1989) has given a fairly accurate description of the industrial district as a creative environment, and outlined three factors that contribute to the making of this environment:

- The first concerns the concentration in the industrial district of many and diverse skills, covering various fields of knowledge and production. Even in cases where the whole district focuses on a single industrial sector, the multiplicity of skills comes from specialization within different stages of the production process.

- The second factor is the capacity for alternative collaborations between the productive units in the district. These combinations produce innovations, since many new products are the result of the inventive way in which earlier qualities were put together. In order for alternative combinations to be possible, there has to be a minimum number of productive units in each district. In certain surveys, the presence of at least 100 productive units has been considered as the threshold for the definition of a production complex as a district.[2]

- The third factor concerns the presence of 'catalysts' that facilitate combinations among the many and diverse skills and units. The function of the catalyst, at Prato in Italy, for example, is ensured by the *impannatori*, who constantly reorganize the productive processes of the district in relation to orders. The catalysts mediate between skills and ensure an intensity of combination much higher than that created by spontaneous market and exchange relations only.

When an industrial cluster lacks the above characteristics of specialization, rich internal relationships, and catalysts, then it is just a spatial concentration of producers, without the properties of flexibility and innovation. By contrast, the innovation environment is reinforced where the district is technologically active as well. As Storper points out:

In technology districts, agglomeration seems to be tied to all three of the principal dimensions of technological change: technological (lock-in vs flexibility), economic (cost-minimization, knowledge spillovers and externalities), and behavioural (transactions and learning).

(Storper 1993)

In these areas, the agglomeration acquires all the dimensions of a dynamic innovation system, on the technological, economic, and behavioural levels.

The tertiary sector related to cultural and financial activities developing in metropolitan centres creates *knowledge intensive districts* of producer services that enhance the development of new products and processes. Central city knowledge intensive areas rely on activities such as financing, mass media, product design, marketing, market research, technology transfer, software development, and consulting. Well-known cases are the City of London financial district, the software production cluster in Athens, the film makers in Los Angeles, and the media in New York, indicative of a new tertiarization that have received substantial dimensions in many metropolitan areas. This corresponds to the plethora of urban renewal projects for reshaping the centres of European cities, attempting to create suitable localities for the new tertiary sector that flourishes with the multiplication of business services and the externalization of manufacturing services. In these cases, the favourable environment for innovation is due to the wealth of skills and specializations relating to the development of new products. Here innovation does not presuppose R&D, but is based on the exploitation of research results, the transfer of technology from consultants to companies, new product design, and specialized work by technicians and artists (Scott 2000). The Community Innovation Survey tabulates a large number of small and medium-sized firms that declare that they innovate in processes and products without having any R&D activity. The paradox is explained by the fact that innovation in this case is based on producer services, technology transfer, and technology dissemination, which replace the input from the R&D departments of the companies.

Equally well known to the industrial districts, *science and technology parks* have developed rapidly in all the countries in the European Union and created a phenomenon of significant magnitude and expectations. The first stage of this development, in the early 1970s, was largely experimental, and was the affair of a handful of cases in Cambridge and Heriot-Watt University in Great Britain, Haasrode in Belgium and Sophia-Antipolis in southern France. A second and more intense wave of development began in the 1980s, when the technopolitan development attained significant dimensions with the creation of more than 100 science and technology parks throughout the EU. These parks were associated with the wider restructuring of production, and the rise of small firms in electronic, computer, and information technologies. Despite differences from country to country, the basic model includes a relatively small area (a pole) which houses university laboratories and research institutes, processing and business service companies, and technology transfer units (Gibb 1985; Monck *et al.* 1998; Komninos 1992b).

The environment of innovation created in science and technology parks rests on four types of technology intermediation:

- Collaboration between universities and businesses relating to the use of university research facilities, exploitation of research results, mobility of personnel and information.

- Business networking, and development of strategic supplier–producer alliances and collaborations.

- Financing and supporting of spin-offs for the creation of new technology-intensive companies.

- Attracting innovative organizations and companies, spread and dissemination of research and technology from larger to small companies.

The technology transfer mechanisms of the parks are reinforced by relationships of localization and exploitation of real estate. The potential for revenue from the land permits the financing of technology transfer, which in turn promotes the park as an active technology site and contributes to the rise in demand for space there. This cycle constitutes a self-feeding mechanism between real estate, technology financing, and technology transfer.

Technopolises or *Technopolis* programmes represent an extension of the science park model on a bigger scale. The logic of a Technopolis is to reinforce the factors that contribute to innovation, including flexibility in production, technology development and transfer, collaboration between academia and industry, as well as the culture of innovation, but on the level of an entire city or region (Douglass 1988).

The application of Technopolis programmes has been rather limited in Europe. Most of the larger technopoles are found in France (Montpellier, Ile de France, Toulouse, Nantes, etc.), Spain, and Italy. A representative case of this development is the Technopolis of Montpellier. The environment of innovation is created by a number of science parks, industrial districts, renewed areas for business services in the city centre, and technology diffusion networks, and is coordinated by technology institutions and local development authorities. A less typical but equally interesting case is Technocity of Turin, which is the only project based on a private initiative. Technocity covers a triangle in the centre of Piedmont, marked by the cities of Turin, Ivrea, and Novara. It is a region that combines the characteristics of an industrial district, specializing in the manufacturing of machinery, electronics and textiles, and of a science park characterized by the high concentration of universities and R&D activities.

The environment of innovation in a Technopolis is based on a multi-pole system composed of industrial districts, areas of business services, and science parks. Networks of collaboration, communication, and coordination ensure the cohesion and synergy among the individual poles. The emphasis on networks and the search for technological integration on an urban scale can be considered as the distinctive characteristic of the innovation environment created in technopolises (Smilor *et al.* 1988).

The relatively low expansion of large-scale technopoles in Europe is partly due to the rise of an alternative planning model based on learning regions and regional innovation systems. *Innovating regions* highlight a strategy for the creation of innovative environments, developed in the framework of the European regional policy, aiming to support the less favoured regions of the EU through improvement of their capacity for technology and innovation. The strategy was drafted with a small number of pilot projects in 1995, through Regional Technology Plans (RTPs), and was subsequently implemented on a grand scale in approximately 100 European regions through Regional Innovation Strategies (RIS), and Regional Innovation and Technology Transfer Strategy and Infrastructure (RITTS) projects.

In RIS regions, the environment of innovation is created from the establishment and activation of institutions that make up part of the regional innovation system. This system links and integrates organizations producing technology, organizations using technology, organizations active in technology transfer, innovation funding, and the dissemination of know-how. The theory of innovative regions and regional innovation systems is, however, quite different from innovation systems based on flexible districts and technopoles. Here, innovation emerges from the cohesion and coordination between technology supply and demand. The elements of cohesion are the institutions for consensus and knowledge management that operate on the regional level, and the networks for collaboration, information, on-going education and training that orient the action of each individual organization in relation to the needs of the others.

Finally, *intangible innovation islands* that are formed upon research centres, technology parks, and industrial clusters, create a rather new type of environment of innovation. Such islands represent a phenomenon with exceptionally important consequences, as it reinforces the non-material components of the innovation process (information systems, spin-offs, human skills) and limits the pressure for conventional hard innovation infrastructures (parks, technopoles, clusters, renewal projects). An important push to the creation of intangible islands of innovation was given by communication and information technologies. The term 'Intelligent Region' (intelligent cities, intelligent parks) highlights here the application of information technologies and telematics in support of the functions of a real innovation island. IT is used for the promotion of scientific and research activities, for technology transfer and exchange between industry, government and academic bodies, and for round-the-clock distance business support services.[3]

An example of such an environment is the design of the virtual innovation island at the European Commission's Joint Research Centre (JRC). The JRC is made up of seven research institutes established in five different EU member states, and is charged with supporting technology transfer and contributing effectively to the synergy between research and industry in Europe (European Commission 1998a). Initially, a study examined the feasibility of creating a technology park at the headquarters of the JRC in Ispra, Italy. This solution, however, was considered not the best way to ensure the direct contribution of the JRC to the practical problems of Europe's industrial and research community. Thus, in the place of a conventional technology park it was decided to create an intangible innovation island, with flexible mechanisms providing access to the stock of research results and knowledge.

This environment includes five mechanisms for technology transfer and collaborative research and is expected to have a major impact throughout the entire European Union (Joint Research Centre 1998):

- An open-door policy providing access to the large and complex research facilities of the JRC, since the Centre has unique installations and laboratories that with the proper technical support can be used by companies and other external organizations.

- A fund to facilitate technology transfer in conjunction with (but not exclusively) the Centre's own research programmes. This fund will cover start-ups and technology transfers to small and medium-sized businesses.

- A virtual technology park operating on the European scale, exploring new means of technology transfer and supporting joint research. To this end it will make use of the latest developments in telecommunications, virtual applications for technology information, funding possibilities and technology collaboration.

- An incubator to support newly established businesses and research groups working with the Centre; and finally

- An education and training initiative that provides the possibility for industrial employees to work for short periods in research labs, training in technology areas in which the JRC has particular competence, and courses in the field of innovation for research on the doctoral and post-doctoral level.

This virtual innovation environment is being realized gradually, starting in 1998, on the basis of benchmarks, pilot actions and trial-and-error methods. This orientation is a milestone and clear expression of a change in European policy direction towards intangible actions and experiments that began with the Sprint and Innovation programmes.

The aforementioned six categories of innovation islands and the corresponding environments illustrate the complexity of the trajectories, and the multiplicity of the factors that contribute to the process of innovation. The creation of such environments has radically changed the entire landscape of innovation. The framework is no longer exclusively that of the large company and the industrial research laboratory. New factors have now acquired importance, including territorial innovation systems, flexible specialization clusters, collaboration networks, technology transfer and business services areas and organizations. These factors interact dynamically along non-linear relationships giving a more spontaneous and non-predictable character to the overall innovation process.

These recent experiences on the creation of territorial innovation systems have opened new ways in the understanding of innovation and the practical ways to interfere with the process. If we cannot predict innovation, we can however create environments where there is a higher probability that innovation will occur.

Environment of Innovation: Turning Knowledge into Products

The major added value of technological innovation areas is that they have radically changed the conditions and rules of innovation. A process hermetically sealed within the research lab of the large company has been transformed into a system that covers an entire city involving participants from the finance, technological, and production communities. In innovative cities and regions, established organizations improve their capacity to develop new products and services as proper mechanisms and networks are activated increasing their potential to develop and assimilate technologies.

In company research labs, innovation follows a linear trajectory from laboratory research to production. Feedback loops – return to the lab for further research, for example – are limited, and a predetermined succession of stages is almost obligatory (Figure 1.2).

By contrast, in territorial systems of innovation this path is enriched with new functions, it is extended beyond the R&D, and linked to the activity of a large number of organizations within the innovation island. Conti and Spriano counted 11 basic factors that shape the innovative capacity of a region. These include the presence of: (1) large industrial complexes, (2) innovative firms, (3) universities, (4) technology services and institutes, (5) international linkage infrastructures, (6) information mechanisms, (7) venture capital funds, (8) business services, (9) innovation support programmes, (10) access mechanisms to education and research facilities, and (11) high quality residential spaces (Conti and Spriano 1991).

A particularly interesting study on the same subject is that of James Simmie who looked at the factors that contributed to the development of innovation in the Hertfordshire region during the period 1985–95. Simmie (1997b) started from Michael Porter's Diamond Figure and defined four categories of characteristics that influence innovation capacity: (1) supply factors, such as land, infrastructure, investment and labour, (2) demand factors, such as existing and potential demand, needs, local and international markets, (3) industrial support activities, such as suppliers, collaboration networks, supply chains, business services, and (4) business strategies and structures, such as production, product and employment

Figure 1.2 Innovation within the company: From R&D to production
Source: Adapted from Arundel (1997: 6).

strategies and flexibility.[4] Studying the Innovation Award-winning businesses in Hertfordshire he identified factors that contribute positively to innovation as human resources, knowledge and information and funding, on the supply side, and information, international market identification capacity and the input of local technical skills, on the demand side. The interesting finding of the survey is that it shies away from the widely accepted conviction that collaboration networks and supply chains are the most important factors in technological innovation. It points out that innovation activity is far more chaotic than is described by available theories on networking, local industrial organization and institutional regulation. Upstream and downstream networks and links cannot interpret innovation in the Hertfordshire region, since it seems that the latter arises out of a fluid system in which the critical factors are scientific knowledge, the availability of capital, and access to international markets.

The different types and models of territorial systems of innovation discussed in the previous section highlight the multiplicity of conditions affecting innovation and the difficulty in defining a single set of factors that shape the innovation capacity of an area. What is true for Hertfordshire is not necessarily true for the industrial districts of Third Italy or the French technopoles.

A common base, however, of all territorial systems of innovation is the geographical concentration of knowledge-intensive activities and institutions involved in knowledge management that create a favourable environment of product/process renewal. Figure 1.3 shows some basic components of the innovation environment created in territorial systems of innovation, the organizations that take part and shape this environment, and the multiple trajectories for the actualization of innovation. Research results and scientific knowledge feeding the cycle of innovation are transformed into products with the support of innovation funding, technology transfer, and product development services. No doubt, this process represents a further advancement in the social division of labour. As the process of innovation has gone out of the research lab, a large number of organizations from the public and private sectors have become involved in it. In many cases this widening of innovation-related activities has led to the creation of new functions that have assumed the organizations of funding (through venture capital), intermediation (through technology transfer institutions) and collaboration (through networks and digital infrastructures).

When fully developed, an innovation environment embraces all five functions: research and technology development, innovation funding, technology transfer and adaptation, product development, networking and technology collaboration. This rich brew of technology resources is what characterizes technopoles and innovative regions, while a somewhat less rich mix of resources characterizes industrial districts, clusters of business services in city centres, and science parks.

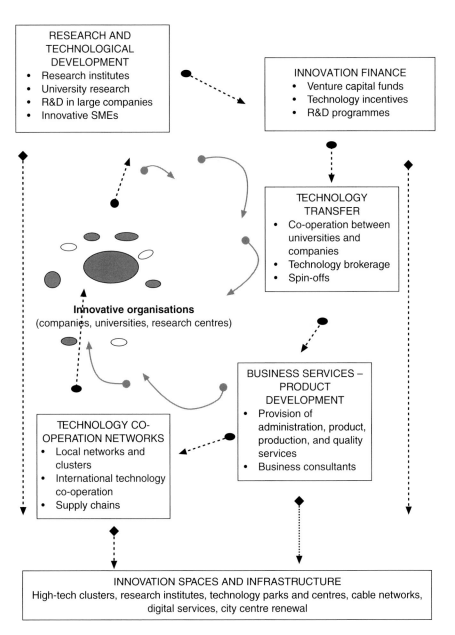

Figure 1.3 Innovation environment: Turning knowledge into products

Technology learning, interaction networks between the functions, and cooperation between the organizations of innovation are key elements in the construction of the environment of innovation. Learning and interaction are broadly accepted as key elements in the process of technological innovation. Learning permits the creation of a serious competitive advantage, while interaction is a social behaviour that allows certain economic agents to exploit information better than others (Storper 1997). These ideas go back to the original work on the 'innovation system' developed by Freeman and Lundvall. Freeman's definition stresses the institutional side of the innovation system, considering it as a network of institutions in the public and private sphere whose activities and interactions introduce, modify and disseminate new technologies (Freeman 1987). Lundvall does not give a precise definition of the innovation system, but focuses on the socio-cultural context, everyday relationships and tacit knowledge (Lundvall 1988). The importance of the networks is also due to other factors. In technologically dynamic systems where technologies are exceptionally uncertain and change very rapidly, the need to avoid 'lock-in', leads companies to the adoption of network forms of production. Networks allow companies to retain their flexibility on a technological trajectory whose boundaries cannot be fully defined at the outset (Nelson and Winters 1982). Similar assessments of the importance of networks emerge from observations of technology fusion in mechatronics and fibre electronics, where innovations are created from the fragmentation of the boundaries of established technologies and the interaction between technologies of different types (Kodama 1995).

In such an environment, the routes to innovation are neither unique nor predetermined, as two characteristics shape the synergy between the functions and organizations.

- The first characteristic of the environment of innovation concerns the '*condensation*' between the functions of the system. We call 'condensation' the merging or overlapping of individual functions that take part in the innovation process. A usual overlap, for instance, is between R&D and technology transfer. Many organizations have access to research results not through research, but through intermediary consultants or technology transfer agents diffusing research results from R&D institutions. In this case, the R&D function is assumed through technology transfer organizations.

- The second concerns the '*multiple activation*' of innovation, which can originate from any part of the overall process. Research is a permanent stimulus for innovation, but equally important are specialized funding, technology transfer, and business services facilitating the development of new products and services. For small businesses it has been observed, for instance, that business services and technology transfer are even more important than R&D and direct cooperation with research organizations.

The differences in the routes and processes of innovation emerge from the particular territorial system and innovation environment, each of which offers a different combination of resources and support functions.

- An *R&D-orientated environment* characterizes innovation in large companies, with the main emphasis on in-house development of research and its transfer to other departments of the company in the form of new products and processes.

- A *cooperative environment* characterizes industrial districts and technopoles, formed by the agglomeration of specialized firms in the manufacturing and/or tertiary sector, with the main emphasis on new product development.

- An *intermediation environment*, characteristic of science and technology parks, innovation centres, innovation relay centres, and industrial liaison offices, is composed of technology transfer mechanisms and institutions.

- An *institutional environment*, characteristic of innovating regions, includes mechanisms that activate the components of a regional innovation system, such as R&D, innovation funding, technology transfer, business support, and networking.

We witness therefore an exceptionally complex system of actors, relationships, and results, leading to different innovation trajectories. As innovation moved out of research labs, new functions were developed. This explains the diversity of the conditions and factors promoting innovation and the difficulty of formulating a single model correlating factors and results. The particular models of territorial systems and innovation environments link causes and effects in different ways. It seems that there is no single connection between input factors and innovation output, but rather a number of different trajectories and innovation development paths dependent on the external environment and conditions.

Components of the Innovation Environment

We have so far described the process of innovation and a series of innovation islands that provide a favourable environment for its development and dissemination. In this section we shall be looking at the contribution and role of the specific components constituting the environment of innovation and the innovation process. We will base this analysis on the findings of the first Community Innovation Survey (CIS), which is the major source of knowledge about technological innovation in the European Union (Arundel 1997). The first CIS provided valuable information about the innovation environment in the European Union, and the contribution of the particular factors affecting innovation. It gives statistical evidence and makes clear the weight and role of R&D, funding, technology transfer, and collaboration networks. In this sense it offers a useful platform to check the role of the functions and components of the innovation environment described in the previous section and highlighted in Figure 1.3.

The first CIS was carried out in 1993, simultaneously in all twelve member states and in Norway. It was based on a common questionnaire, which was prepared by Eurostat in conjunction with the OECD and a panel of experts from the member states. It made use of OECD's expertise to collect and interpret data on technological innovation, in particular the 1992 Oslo Manual. The survey, designed and coordinated by Eurostat and DG XIII, resulted in the creation of a vast database, including 40,000 companies and 200 variables for each (European Commission 1997b; 1998a).

The measurement method and indicators used in the CIS focused on the subject innovating (the firm) and described several aspects of its activity, including sources of information for innovation, the goals of the innovation, R&D activity, technology transfer, innovation costs, and inhibiting factors. By contrast, the basic indicators for measuring results (innovation output) were sales and exports from technologically improved and/or new products.

By way of parenthesis, let it be noted that innovation measuring methods and indicators can be classified into three main categories (Coombs *et al.* 1996):

- The first, 'subject-based' method studies the innovating organization; this is usually a company, but can equally well be a university or research centre. It generally uses R&D expenditure and its various subcategories (GERD, BERD, etc.)[5] as an index to characterize the innovating organization and the input of resources for innovation.

- The second, 'object-based' method studies the progress in specific technological innovations. It uses, as indicators, the announcements of new products or services in commercial or technical journals, inventions, royalty payments, and sales of new products. These indicators are constructed from data available in journals, technical literature, major innovation databases, patent offices, etc. This category may also include techno metrics, methods that monitor the development and dissemination of specific technologies.

- However, the above two orientations and the corresponding indicators give a rather static picture, and are unable to reflect interactions during the production of innovations. By contrast, process indicators, measuring the flows, links and mutual impact of the factors that participate in the innovation process, can show such interactions.

The CIS tried to enrich the first (subject-based) method with new concepts of the dynamics of innovation, drawn from the non-linear model of innovation, the evolutionary theories of innovation, and the functioning of national and regional innovation systems (Smith 1997). However, it was not always feasible to express these orientations through specific measurable indicators.

The concept of innovation in the CIS refers to the introduction of new products or technological processes. There are many valid approaches to the definition of an innovative business, which can be identified by research and development activity and by the acquisition or use of patents. The first CIS defined as innovative those businesses that developed or introduced at least one new product or production process in the three-year period prior to the survey. 'New product or process' does not mean a change in design, installation of a new machine or use of a new raw material, but implies a radical change to and an enrichment of the firm's system of knowledge. Even so, the above definition of innovative businesses still encompasses more firms than a definition based on R&D activity (Figure 1.4).

In total, 53 per cent of the European manufacturing firms that took part in the first CIS introduced one technologically new product or process in the period 1990–2, and were thus characterized as innovative. The proportion increases with size, from 45 per cent in small firms to 90 per cent in large ones. This is, then, a phenomenon of size, covering half of small industry and most of large industry.

Overall, the relative importance of the *individual components* of the innovation environment is reflected in the structure of the cost of innovation, that is, the total expenditure of the firm on the development of new

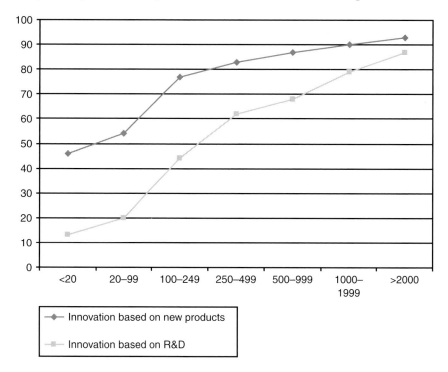

Figure 1.4 Innovative firms in the European Union (% of the total in each category/size of firm)
Source: Adapted from Arundel (1997: 6).

products and processes. The total cost of innovation in companies fluctuates between 8 and 11 per cent of sales. There is, however, no clear correlation between the size of expenditure and the size of the company, which means that innovating companies spend about the same proportion of sales on innovation, regardless of their size (Evangelista *et al.* 1997).

Table 1.2 shows that the major share of this expenditure goes on the acquisition and transfer of technology, mainly through the purchase of technological equipment, which covers more than 50 per cent of the resources poured into innovation, followed by research and development (20 per cent of the costs), product development services (13 per cent), and productive collaboration with third parties (11 per cent). Expenditure on the acquisition of inventions and the payment of royalties and for market research is very small. This means that technology transfer, achieved through the purchase of equipment, is by far the most important factor to innovation, followed by R&D, product development support, and production networking that takes the last place.

The contribution of *research and development* activity, and especially that of public R&D, is found in the creation of new ideas rather than in the solution of a company's immediate problems. For radical innovations, public and academic R&D is the most important source of ideas, and its contribution mainly affects companies competing on the world market. The findings of the CIS show that there is a positive correlation between the intensity of innovation (R&D and total innovation costs) and the performance of the company. In other words, industries with high expenditures on R&D and other innovation-related inputs also have higher sales of new and technologically advanced products. A very important issue, however, is the in-house R&D activity of a company, which influences its overall capability to acquire technology and manage the innovation process.

Table 1.2 Distribution of cost of innovation

Acquisition and transfer of technology	52%
▪ Purchase of equipment and machinery (50%)	
▪ Patents, licences (2%)	
Research and Development	20%
Product development services	13%
▪ Product design (10%)	
▪ Market research (3%)	
Contracting out	11%
Other expenditures	4%
Total	100%

Source: Adapted from Evangelista *et al.* (1997: 110).

The findings of the CIS also confirm the major significance of *funding*. The three most important obstacles of innovation are related to funding, and concern the high cost of innovation, the lack of finance, and the long period before the innovation investment begins to pay off (Table 1.3). This may explain the high demand for friendly innovation funding schemes by the companies, and the priority of funding in the public policies supporting innovation.

With regard to *technology transfer*, the CIS shows that the most usual method of acquisition of technology is through the purchase of equipment, while the most common method of technology transfer is through networks of communication with experts and collaboration with other firms. Although the geographical origin of technology varies, domestic sources of technology are more important than European sources, especially for small firms. Small countries, too, acquire technology from the domestic base to a greater degree. A detailed study of patents shows that Germany remains the driving force in this field, despite the significant progress made by France.

The survey explored the contribution of 13 *sources of information on innovation*, including: (1) sources within the company and the company group, (2) outside sources from suppliers, customers, competitors, consultants, (3) educational and research institutions, universities, government

Table 1.3 Importance of innovation barriers

Type of barrier	Non-innovator	Innovator
Costs too high	36	38
Lack of finance	29	34
Payoff too long	28	33
Legislation	14	21
Risk too high	17	21
Lack of clients	16	20
Copying too easy	15	20
Cost control	13	19
Lack of skilled staff	18	18
Lack of innovation potential	13	17
Uncertain timing	13	12
Lack of market information	9	12
Lack of cooperation opportunities	13	10
Lack of external services	7	10
Lack of technology opportunities	6	5
Lack of technology information	6	5
Resistance to change	6	4
No need	5	3

Results for 36,000 CIS firms. Percentage of firms that find each barrier to be 'very important' or 'crucial'. Different behaviour between non-innovator and innovator firms.
Source: Adapted from Smith (1997: 105).

research laboratories, technology institutes, (4) generally available information from patents, professional symposia and exhibitions. Regardless of the size of the company, outside sources were considered the most important, followed by sources within the firm and company group. The lowest rating (but still representing a substantial figure – 21 per cent for small and 32 per cent for large firms) went to universities, public research laboratories, and technology institutes.

The above findings of the CIS, and in particular the priority of technology transfer and external sources of information on innovation, confirm a series of perceptions associated with the 'environmental model' of innovation, that is, the geographically discontinuous development of innovation, by poles and islands. It confirms among other things:

- The significant contribution of small firms, proving that innovation intensity and outflow decrease as the size of the company increases.

- The important contribution of factors unrelated to R&D, such as technology transfer, information, and productive collaboration.

- The broad network of factors and functions outside the enterprise that are related to the development and dissemination of technology and information.

- The non-continuous character of innovation, which assumes special characteristics in relation to the type of company, the industrial sector and the geographical area.

In conclusion, the findings of the first Community Innovation Survey tend to confirm our understanding of the environmental conditions, basic functions and components of innovation. However, the most important finding concerns the role of external factors and the external environment of innovation. This is clearly reflected in Figure 1.4, showing that many companies innovate without having their own R&D departments, and in Table 1.2, showing that the expenditure for innovation goes mainly to external organizations in order to acquire technology, equipment, and services. The conclusion about the critical role of the external environment to innovation, together with the geographical concentration of the innovation resources, validates our view of innovation as environmental conditions structured in geographically discrete areas.

PART I

Technopoles and Science Parks

Innovation as Spatial Proximity

2 Districts and Technopoles in Europe

The emergence of the medieval urban community as a legal corporation occurred only by degrees. Still in 1313, according to Hatschek, English cities were not able to obtain the franchise because, speaking in modern terms, they had no 'legal personality'. It was only under Edward I that cities acquired the status of corporations.

It should be noted that guilds were by no means the only type of civic corporation. Besides professionally neutral religious associations there appear also purely economic, professionally staffed corporations. Movements towards religious unification and the creation of *confraternitates* accompany guild-political and purely economic movements, intersect with each other in manifold manner. They even played a significant though varying role among the handworkers. The fact that the oldest demonstrable corporation of handworkers in Germany, the Bed-Blanket Weavers in Cologne (1180) is older than the corresponding weavers' association does not demonstrate the priority of the professional aims for the origin of the associations but rather their basic character. However, the development of the weavers' guild permits the supposition that unions of free handworkers, at least outside Italy, established the authoritative form of association with handworkers as members and the master at the top.

(M. Weber, *The City*)

Districts and Technopoles: Concepts and Theories

During the last 20 years of the twentieth century, new concepts of urban and regional development were gradually shaped, based on the rise of new growth centres and the leading role of innovation in development. The focus of the new theories, which appeared in parallel in Europe and the United States of America, was the post-Fordist industrial organization, the flexible firm, and the coordination through the market, as phenomena that form the character of contemporary cities and regions (Chapman and Walker 1991). Theoretical thinking on the new growth centres, taking into account the innovations in the sphere of production and the new development conditions, followed five successive stages. The starting point was the understanding of mechanisms that sustain the dynamism of cities and regions in central Italy, known as system-areas.

System-areas and Industrial Districts

The theoretical foundations of system-areas can be traced back to 1977, when Bagnasco published his study on the Third Italy (Bagnasco 1977). He focused on small cities and communities of central Italy, which during the 1960s and 1970s proved very successful on the world markets and flourished on the basis of small company clusters belonging to the same industry. The social and economic structure of these areas was substantially different from the structures of the industrialized triangle of Milan-Turin-Genoa or the persistent backwardness of the Mezzogiorno. Their distinctive characteristic was the segmentation of the productive tissue into small firms, and the division of the different phases of the production process between the firms, each of which specialized in one or a few phases of production. Inter-firm alliances and institutional regulation assured the coordination and integration of the different production segments (Brusco 1982; Garofoli 1992).

Becattini reminded us that this industrial organization was already described in the concept of the 'industrial district' developed by Alfred Marshall in the early twentieth century. Furthermore, Becattini characterized the industrial district as a 'creative milieu', an environment of targeted creativity, which allows the tiny firm to develop an innovation capacity and to adapt the production process and products to rapid market changes. The main components of the creative milieu were the coexistence of multiple competences and professional skills, the existence of linking agencies (the buyers or *impannatori*) that acted as a catalyst for a flexible combination of professional skills and formal or informal institutions (for information exchange and coordination) enabling the competences to interact dynamically. The district ends up functioning like a machine that allows random skill factors to shower continuously on to solidified forms of competence (Becattini 1979 and 1991; Marshall 1920).

Flexible Specialization

A more coherent theoretical construction on these new development conditions came from the other side of the Atlantic. Michael Piore and Charles Sabel published the *Second Industrial Divide* in New York, in which they interpreted the success of some industrial districts as a particular case of a much wider tendency concerning the appearance of a new development model, that of 'Flexible Specialization' (Piore and Sabel 1984; Piore 1986).

Piore and Sabel argued that flexible specialization was the response to the rigidities of established production and consumption practices based on mass production and Keynesian regulation. The production rupture occurs at many levels, but it is mainly related to innovation, including new product design, product and process innovation, production decentralization and technology diffusion between producer and supplier, labour market flexibility and rapid change of skills. New competition strategies are based on product quality rather than price, new telecommunication and information technology infrastructure, automation and computer integrated manufacturing.

Piore and Sabel described the shift in strategy, organization, and technology as a necessary response to new conditions of international competition. Flexible specialization has major implications in that the shift towards greater flexibility requires greater technological sophistication. Firms have to develop technology strategies based upon new ways of cutting the costs of customized production. One of the main characteristics of flexible specialized industries is the production of a wide range of products for global and differentiated markets. This can be achieved by developing flexible and multiple purpose technologies rather than large dedicated machine systems, so that product innovation is not held back by massive capital investments in machinery and poorly qualified workers. Future prosperity, Piore and Sabel argued, depends on the development of flexible technologies, flexible organization of the production process, trained human resources, and economies of scope rather than scale. Firms have to choose either to invest in new flexible technologies or to externalize the risk of technological investment through subcontracting and network forms of organizations. The latter seems preferable, as it minimizes risk and opens a window to technology cooperation and transfer (see also Murray 1987 and 1991; Starkey and Barnatt 1997).

Flexible specialization was not a spatial concept. However, the spatial form of the model was the urban industrial agglomeration of the late twentieth century, and the industrial district in particular. Industrial organization in districts reflects the main principles of flexible specialization and the indefatigable search for production flexibility, networking, new products, short product cycles, and advanced professional and technological skills.

Innovative Environments

A separate theoretical strand dealing with innovative environments and local development appeared in France with the creation, in 1984, of GREMI (Groupe de Recherches Européens sur les Milieux Innovateurs) by Philippe Aydalot. Founding GREMI, Aydalot was probably not aware of the work of Bagnasco, Brusco, Piore, and Sabel on flexible specialization and industrial districts.[1] However, he arrived at similar concepts (the creative and innovative local environment) through a different path of analysis: the study of industrial location and the localization principles of high-technology firms in particular.

A central concern of GREMI was to understand the firm in its local and regional context, and to define what external conditions to the company are necessary both for the creation of new firms and the adoption of innovations by existing ones. The firms, and the innovating firm, were not viewed as pre-existing in or separate from the local environment, but as being products of it. Local milieus were regarded as the nurseries, the incubators, of innovations and innovative firms. Innovative behaviour is as much dependent on variables defined at the local level, such as access to technological know-how, availability of local industrial linkages and inputs, market proximity, and availability of qualified labour. All these are innovation support factors, which define the ability of an area for greater or lesser innovative activity. An individual firm is not an independent agent freely choosing its location from a range of alternatives; it is rather a direct product of its own particular local environment (Aydalot 1980 and 1986; Aydalot and Keeble 1988).

The sudden death of Aydalot, in April 1987, deprived GREMI of its most creative researcher. However, at this period the same theoretical considerations were pushed forward by geographers at the University of California Los Angeles, under the framework concept of 'new industrial spaces'.

New Industrial Spaces

Allen Scott, Michael Storper and Richard Walker were interested in the development of high technology and flexible production agglomerations in the USA, Europe, and South East Asia. Storper and Scott (1988) produced a synthesis of flexible specialization theory and industrial district approaches, establishing a theory for the contemporary technology-driven urban agglomeration. They focused on the analysis of horizontal and vertical disintegration of production activities, and the substitution of internal by external economies, and economies of scale by economies of scope. The small specialized company develops external linkages and networks to a higher degree, and acquires all the necessary technology and skill inputs from the agglomeration, which is also composed of specialized small businesses. The spatial form of this complex is the 'district' because there transactions costs are minimized. The district and the agglomeration composed of districts are considered as the dominant spatial form of flexible specialization.

Scott introduced the concept 'new industrial spaces' (NIS) to characterize a variety of agglomerations and regions sharing the same industrial structure: Los Angeles, Orange County, Silicon Valley, Route 128 in

Boston, in the USA; West London, the M4 corridor, and Cambridge in England; Montpellier, Toulouse, Grenoble and Sophia-Antipolis in France; south Bayer and Stuttgart in Germany; Carpi, Prato, Bologne, Sassuolo in Italy (Scott 1988a). He argued that new industrial spaces were the spatial manifestation of flexible production and flexible specialization strategies. NIS may take various forms, such as new high-technology and Sunbelt agglomerations in the periphery of mass production centres, internal zones of revived artisan and manufacturing activities in metropolitan agglomerations, and clusters of traditional manufacturing activity in peripheral semi-agricultural regions.

The United States high-technology industry revolves mainly around the rise of the aforementioned high-technology districts in Silicon Valley, Route 128, and elsewhere which comprise dense networks of small firms and other technology-based organizations (Larsen and Rogers 1984; Sigismund 2000; Soja 1992; Toedtling 1994; Winner 1992). The challenges of this form of industrial organization were discussed by Florida and Kenney, who pointed out that despite its tremendous innovative capabilities, this pattern generates significant costs (high turnover of labour, chronic entrepreneurship, emphasis on breakthrough innovations at the expense of manufactured products) which are not sufficiently recognized by the proponents of the flexible specialization or the 'simple flexibility' thesis. By contrast, the Japanese approach is one of 'structured flexibility' where large corporations perform important 'system governance' functions in the linking of manufacturing and innovations and act as focal points in just-in-time complexes. This overcomes many of the limitations of high-technology organizations in the USA (Florida and Kenney 1990a).

Krugman argues that the creation of high-technology clusters may be explained with respect to three processes: (1) labour market pooling which benefits both companies and employees because of the interaction of increasing returns and uncertainty, (2) intermediary and non-traded inputs, including the availability of specialized services, the rich web of suppliers, subcontractors, and technology providers, and (3) technological spillovers and knowledge flows between nearby firms or between the firms and nearby universities or research institutions (Krugman 1997). Highlighting the meaning of spillovers, Krugman goes back to Marshall's description of the evolutionary chain of ideas within the cluster that generate innovations: 'if one man starts a new idea, it is taken up by others and combined with suggestions of their own; and thus becomes the source of further new ideas' (Marshall 1920). However, thinking of districts in terms of the above three processes may fall easily into reductionism and create a great deal of misunderstanding. A series of monographs on high-technology districts, and the Silicon Valley in particular, demonstrate the role of quite new factors, such as university–industry relations, R&D and patents, active technology brokering and transfer, venture capital, working

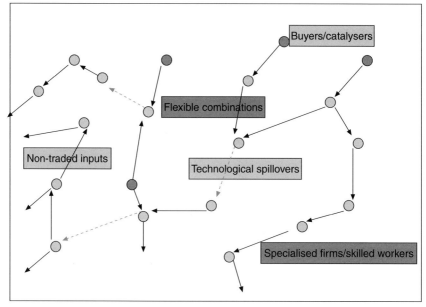

Basic elements:
• Specialized firms/skilled workers
• Buyers/catalysers

Structuring elements:
• Flexible combinations
• Non-traded inputs
• Technological spillovers

Figure 2.1 Five key elements of a flexible industrial district

and lifestyle patterns (Larsen and Rogers 1984; Saxenian 1990; Sigismund 2000; Winner 1992). Krugman admits that he became very unpopular with the engineers for suggesting that some very non-technological seeming clusters were in economic terms not so different from high tech.

Technopolitan Planning

There was a systematic effort to translate the theoretical thinking on industrial districts, flexible specialization and new industrial spaces into concrete political action for urban and regional development. Between different planning and policy initiatives, technopolitan planning was the most successful attempt. Major contributions came from Japan, which launched a large-scale Technopolis Programme in 1983, from the USA with the Research Triangle Park in North Carolina, the Stanford Research Park and many other similar, though smaller, projects, and from Europe with the creation of more than 100 Science and Technology Parks (Deog-Seong 1995; Luger and Goldstein 1991; Komninos 1993).

Technopolitan planning includes three main components. First, the public undertaking of part of the R&D and transaction costs due to external R&D and technology transfer. There is a wide range of public intervention in technology transfer, based on: (1) the development of incentive programmes and the subsidization of private R&D, and (2) the regional distribution of technology and consultant intermediaries (technology transfer institutes, science and technology parks) which can provide direct technology transfer and producer services to small firms. The second component is the public spending on urban regeneration programmes related to new tertiary activities (producer services, headquarters, etc.). The result of these projects is to make areas attractive to residents and external companies, to make inner city areas safe and attractive to live and work in, and to encourage enterprises to locate in particular cities and regions; thus, to sustain the position of cities and regions within the international mobility of skills and investments. The third component is the effort to stimulate new industry, system-areas and districts, through local integration, networks and inter-firm alliances.

All technopoles and science parks are not the same: small incubators, technology transfer oriented parks, and R&D department-based parks, are inserted differently into the regional economy and the processes of innovative growth. The literature on new industrial spaces, local innovative growth, and sunrise industrial strategies provides a framework for understanding the relationship and contribution of the small technology pole constituted by a park, and wider innovative processes on a regional scale. Technopoles start from different initial conditions. However, as technology parks grow and mature, the initial conditions become less apparent since all parks evolve towards the same model, that of a spatial cluster composed of R&D, technology transfer, and innovative production activities. At this later stage, the differences of start conditions are reduced to differences in the size of parks and the scale of their operation.

Innovation within Flexible Production Complexes

In Europe since the 1980s, a number of areas have attracted attention as centres of neo-industrialization, flexible specialization, and innovative development. While the traditional centres of heavy industry have gone into decline,[2] new dynamic areas have arisen, taking advantage of information technology and new production practices. Neo-industrialization and innovative growth have not been limited to core regions. A number of cities and regions in less developed areas have successfully undergone current industrial change and innovative development (Benko and Dunford 1991a and b; Cooke 1988; Cooke and Morgan 1997; Castells and Hall 1994; Dunford 1991; Hall and Markusen 1983; Komninos 1992a; Saxenian 1990; Scott 1988a and b). It seems that a new macro-economic cycle has opened, redefining 'core' and 'peripheral' regions, in which the critical factors are innovation, technology transfer, industrial clustering, and the internationalization of local productive systems (Gottdiener and Komninos 1989; Dunford and Kafkalas 1992; European Commission 1994c).

Well-known cases of this re- and neo-industrialization are the cities of Cambridge, Milton Keynes, Crawley and Bracknell, which are considered as models of a new flexible capitalism in England; the cities of Toulouse, Grenoble, Montpellier, Sophia-Antipolis, and the new towns in south Paris (Evry, Melun Senart, Saint-Quentin en Yvelines) in France; the industrial districts in Lombardy, Emiglia-Romana, Tuscany, Veneto, Marche, in Italy; and the regions of Baden-Württemberg and southern Bavaria, in Germany. Many of these areas were insignificant provincial cities, with no industrial tradition, but have actually become centres for new high-technology industries. Small and medium-sized enterprises flourished in highly competitive international markets, and new products were produced which were characterized by design quality and short life cycles.

There are important differences between these new centres of innovative growth; differences in form and formation processes, in the trajectories that were followed, in the role of the state, markets, and the cooperative networks that have sustained their development. In our opinion, three major trajectories towards neo-industrialization and innovative development appeared, each of which combines distinctive geographical features and strategic approach.

- A *neo-Taylorist development path* was outlined in a number of cities and metropolitan areas of Taylorist or Fordist tradition (Turin, Milan, Barcelona, northern Greece, etc.) where larger companies, multinationals, or large national companies lead the development. As these firms adopt flexible forms of internal organization, they introduce flexible labour markets and polarize the workforce with mass production technologies and neo-Taylorist work organization and automation. The labour market and the social structure in these areas are fragmented, and competitive strategies dominate inter-firm relations. The traditional industrial sectors, decentralization, and market forces drive this type of development (Aydalot and Keeble 1988; Breheny *et al.* 1985; Kratke 1992).

- A *sunrise development path* was outlined in the new centres of R&D and high-tech industry (Cambridge and Milton Keynes in England; Sophia-Antipolis, Montpellier, Grenoble and Toulouse in southern France; and Malaga and Seville in southern Spain). In these areas, new industries, R&D institutions, universities, and smaller businesses make the core of a flourishing local productive system. The roles of the state and local authorities, and other public institutions of education and R&D were crucial for the creation of the initial nucleus and the setting up of conditions for high-tech development (Crang and Martin 1989; Gilly 1992; Komninos 1993).

- A *corporatist development path* is seen in cities and communities of flexible specialization, such as the Marshallian Industrial Districts in central Italy, in Spain, and elsewhere (Amin 1989a and b; Pyke *et al.* 1990; Sforzi 1989). Bagnasco and Becattini clearly describe the industrial district as a socio-economic territorial entity based on a corporatist social contract. The district is more than an industrial cluster (Enright 2000). It is characterized by the active coexistence of an open community of people and a segmented population of firms. Production activities and daily life overlap. The firms specialize in one or more phases of the process of production. Inter-firm alliances and institutional regulation provide for the coordination and integration of the segmented production. Although by definition the presence of big firms in the district is not ruled out, the community prevents large firms from polarizing the overall process of production causing small firms to go bankrupt or be taken over (Bagnasco 1977; Becattini 1989).

Many of the areas of new growth were peripheral to the established post-war centres of development. They include regions with no industrial tradition, agricultural regions, and new agglomerations of industry chiefly on the margins of Fordist industrialization. These peripheral developments are bound up in the specificities of flexible production, and their *raison d'être* lies either in the structure of labour in the established Fordist industrial centres or in the competitive pressures within the areas of new industrialization, which has led to the spatial disaggregating of the internal functions of the firm and their dispersal over different territories (Scott 1987 and 1988a; Krugman 1997).

All these new growth centres are more or less linked to the rise of flexible production that permits a more efficient use of resources (capital, labour, stocks, etc.) and greater market competitiveness. What should be noted is that in all types of development, and beside the differences, the needs for R&D, technology transfer, and innovation were particularly intense. This was due to the character of flexible production itself and the day-to-day needs for technology and innovation inputs. Table 2.1 indicates some critical dimensions of flexible production, and alternative forms of organization at the levels of production, product innovation and R&D, inter-firm relations, and the labour market. On the left-hand side, we have noted the critical issues with which flexible production strategies are concerned and on the right-hand side we have listed some of the forms these strategies assumed.

Those flexible production strategies that are centred on technological

49

learning and product innovation involve high levels of expenditure on R&D and producer services (fundamental research, applied research, engineering consultancy, market research, advertising and information services). The need for these services is not just a once and for all need, but increases as product cycles become shorter and shorter: whenever a new product is introduced, a new niche market is created or customized goods are produced, a new round of research and producer service activities is set in motion. In a comparison of three different new industrial spaces, in South-East England, Scotland, and the San Francisco Bay, Oakey and Cooper stress that in these areas R&D and skills required to develop and produce high-technology products are high throughout the life cycle of the product. Moreover, because product life cycles are frequently short, the scope for long standardized phases of production, with standardized materials and unskilled labour, is rather minimal (Oakey and Cooper 1989).

To some degree, the rising needs for R&D and skilled labour may also explain the importance of economies of scope vis-à-vis the economies of scale. It does not follow that scale is not important. But, as product diversification increases and product life cycles decrease, economies within a firm are centred on the intensive use of skills and know-how in the production of different products rather than on the size of individual production runs.

With the emergence of these strategies there were significant moves towards greater vertical disintegration and growth of the small firm sector. Start-up mania, 'me-too start-ups', copycat companies, horizontal fragmentation and less and less vertical integration all contributed to a new industrial landscape (Florida and Kenney 1990b).

More analytically there were three major processes that sustained productive disintegration and the growth of the small firm sector.

- Larger firms pursued multiple forms of structural fragmentation. Included were: (1) the synchronic fragmentation of production of different products and in different localities, and the extension of the subcontracting system; (2) the diachronic fragmentation of production associated with shorter product life cycles and the rapid succession of different products and models; and (3) the introduction of tendering arrangements so that, for example, R&D departments were required to compete for work with outside contractors to ensure that in-house R&D was cost effective (Roussel *et al.* 1991).

- There was an externalization of activities by larger firms. All tertiary activities without strategic importance were contracted out, and this restructuring led to a wave of new small firms. These firms work in low risk environments, demand low entry costs and have high rates of turnover of capital.

Table 2.1 Flexible production strategies and forms of appearance

Level of strategy	Some forms of appearance
Production process ■ Divorce of machinery and product ■ Divorce of workplaces and skills ■ Multifunctional tools and work teams	■ Global automation, computer integrated manufacturing ■ Partial automation and workers involvement ■ Artisan production
Product development ■ R&D for new products and processes ■ Innovation versus economies of scale ■ Emphasis on quality and trade marks ■ Renewal of product models ■ Small production runs and short product life cycles	■ Third generation R&D ■ Cooperation of industry and academia ■ Strategic alliances between large and small companies ■ Quality assurance and certification ■ Quality circles
Inter-firm cooperation ■ Vertical disintegration of production ■ Fragmentation of production and near vertical integration systems ■ Network forms of production	■ Top-down business networks ■ Districts of small companies ■ Just-in-time delivery systems
Labour market ■ Flexible labour contracts ■ Cooperative industrial relations ■ Re-skilling and training	■ Fragmentation of the labour market ■ Numerical and functional flexibility ■ Plant versus sector labour unionization

■ There was also a proliferation of small businesses, which proved themselves particularly effective in producing for and operating in market niches. Some firms specialized in market niches in mature industries such as the textile, clothing, and furniture industries where, despite competition from products from low wage countries, they were capable of competing provided that they operated in market segments characterized by higher levels of performance and/or superior design. Other small firms specialized in market niches such as scientific instruments, electrical equipment, industrial machinery and tools where survival depended on the retention of in-house technical skills and the use of technologies developed elsewhere. Furthermore, a good number of technology-based enterprises were created with strong internal scientific teams, innovation capabilities and in-house design and engineering (Britton 1989).

In short, flexible production strategies, developed at the level of production, inter-firm relations, product design and labour organization, demand increased R&D and innovation inputs on one hand, and favour the fragmentation of production and the rise of the small firm sector on the other. This situation is contradictory, due to the difficulties that small firms face in providing high R&D inputs. As early as 1962, K. Arrow argued that firms under-invest in R&D because the social benefits of this type of investment are greater than its private returns. Arrow specified three factors that depress the level of private R&D expenditure: the indivisibility of R&D, its inappropriateness which makes it difficult to establish clear property rights and to control the diffusion and use of R&D, and its uncertainty. In the provision of R&D, markets fail and market mechanisms are imperfect.

Arrow was writing, however, during the mass production era when products' life cycles were long and the large multidivisional corporations realized important scale economies. The existence of R&D market imperfections at that time suggests an increase in their importance in an era of flexible production, vertical disintegration and rapid product changes. The practical consequence is that small flexible firms are unable to provide the required levels of innovation, product design, consultancy, engineering and market information services internally. They have day-to-day needs for applied R&D, but the indivisibility, inappropriateness and uncertainty of R&D do not allow them to provide these services on their own resources. Between the development of R&D and the flexible small firm sector there is a deep economic barrier: small firms have to look to their external environment for R&D and producer services.

This conflict of '*innovation within flexible production*' was quickly recognized as a constraint to knowledge-based development, and different solutions were attempted. In some areas, innovation and R&D needs were covered with the creation of networks and alliances among firms. In other cases, a new round of corporate integration provided the necessary means to technology and innovation. Public support to R&D and the creation of incubator environments was attempted as well.

System-areas and industrial districts are examples of a cooperative solution to innovation within flexible production problems (Sefertzi 1996 and 1998). Clusters of interdependent small firms create systems allowing costs and risks to be spread out and production to be rapidly adjusted to market requirements. The result is a locality composed of small companies having systemic relations, in which the region and not the firm provide the necessary innovation resources (Saxenian 1990).

Global competition and system technologies, which demand a wide range of know-how and advanced technological integration, offer another solution. In particular, integrated Japanese corporations have become main players in world markets, not only for mass-produced high-tech products, but also for the fringes of the markets for customized products. Referring to the case of the USA, Florida and Kenney note that:

The fragmentation and splintering of our high-technology capabilities makes it ever more difficult to build stable companies and industries that can compete over the long haul. Even our stronger, most innovative companies are finding it difficult to grow and prosper in such a highly fragmented environment. The extreme segmentation of high-technology production drastically inhibits technological follow-through and hinders American industry's ability to meet the challenge of emerging global competition.

(Florida and Kenney 1990b)

In these circumstances they point out the need for new corporate integration, which may lead away from the highly competitive, Hobbesian relationships between vertically disintegrated companies.

There was also a wide range of public interventions in the field of innovation, state and local initiatives whose aim was to cover a part of private R&D and transaction costs and to establish networks for technology transfer, engineering and market consultancy. This trend was particularly strong in Europe and was reinforced by the European Commission's technology and innovation policies. Public interventions were based on two simple concepts: on the one hand to give incentives and subsidize private R&D, especially at a pre-competitive stage; and on the other to create technology and consultancy environments so as to provide direct access for small firms to technology transfer and producer services.

The proliferation of science and technology parks presented after the 1980s was part of this third solution.

Technopoles and Science Parks in Europe

Science and technology parks were probably the simplest way to plan and develop new technology districts and industrial spaces. Local authorities, development agencies, European governments, and the European Commission have supported them, with the aim of creating environments favourable to technology transfer and technological development. The main focus of science parks is to boost the creation of technology-based firms. This means a firm whose strength and competitive edge are derived from its knowledge of its field, such as natural science, engineering or medicine, and upon the subsequent transformation of this know-how into products and services for a market (Shearmur and Doloreux 2000). The definition includes not only manufacturing firms but also firms in industry-related services (Lindhom Dalhstrand 1999). To such firms science parks offer a friendly environment to product development, cooperation with R&D organizations, support from technology transfer agencies, brand name and quality premises.

This solution to the 'innovation within flexible production problem' has certain advantages with respect to industrial districts and the search for larger corporate integration. On the one hand, science parks come up from a planning procedure, whereas the district is the result of a long-term social process, which, we may observe, we may hardly imitate through policy and intervention. On the other hand, science parks allow small companies to enter into the new knowledge-based economy and open the field of technological experimentation to all companies, which may contribute to the acceleration of technology and innovation.

A generally accepted understanding of a science/technology park includes the following four components: (1) it is a property-based initiative, which (2) has formal operational links with a university, higher education institution or major centre of research, (3) it is designed to encourage the formation and growth of knowledge-based businesses and other organizations, normally resident on site; and (4) it has a management function that is actively engaged in fostering the transfer of technology and business skills to the organizations on site (Dalton 1987; IASP Directory 1998).

Figure 2.2 illustrates this definition, showing the constituent elements and the relationships of integration, based on technology transfer and cooperation between the R&D institutions and the innovative firms. This definition also provides a set of criteria, which form the basis for eligibility for membership of the UK Science Park Association. The activities are located in a well-designed area to which new or existing research-base

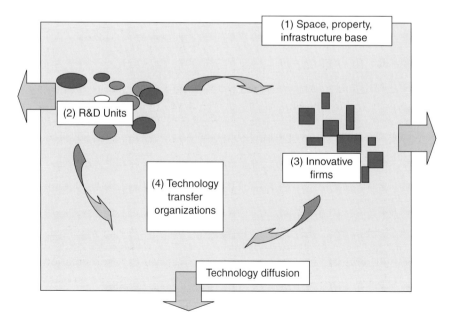

Figure 2.2 Science/technology park: Elements and relationships

businesses or R&D departments of larger companies are attracted by the working conditions, the environment or the physical proximity and connection to a university. The R&D work conducted by companies in science parks is usually limited to the design of prototypes, the production of one-off items, whereas the manufacturing site is located elsewhere.

Several terms, however, are used to describe local initiatives to stimulate investment in high-technology activities, to foster technology transfer between research and industry, and generate employment through spatial concentration of technology-based companies. Apart from science parks, there are research parks, technology parks or technopoles, innovation centres, and business incubators. According to the classification of the Official Journal of the European Communities (C 186/52):

- A *research park* is usually located close to one or more universities or similar academic and research institutions. Its emphasis is on research rather than development and the key is academic/research liaison at the leading edge of science and technology. Normally production plants are precluded.

- A *technology park* is a development to accommodate companies engaged in the commercial application of high technology, with activities including R&D, production, sales and servicing. It is distinguished from science and research parks because of a greater emphasis on production. Academic involvement is also essential. Technology parks meet the specialized location requirements of high-technology companies, but they offer a higher proportion of non-production to production space. The emphasis is on the proximity of high-technology companies engaged in similar operations. There may be restrictions on tenants, and a requirement that they exhibit some high-tech activity.

- An *innovation centre* is a facility catering for the needs of predominantly new businesses engaged in the development and marketing of new technological products and services. The purpose of an innovation centre is to promote the setting up of high-tech businesses with high market risk. The services provided include technical services and advice on finance, marketing, and technology.

- A *business incubator* is a place where newly created firms are located in a rather limited space. Its aim is to increase the chance of growth and rate of survival of these firms by providing them with modular building facilities, common technical facilities, and also managerial support and back-up services. The main emphasis of incubators is job creation and local development, but the technology orientation is often marginal.

The term science park covers most of the above initiatives and projects. Furthermore, technology parks or innovation centres are usually eligible for membership of European science parks associations.

The university or research centre is the basic component of a science park. Around it there are three major groups, which together make up the population of the park: technology transfer agencies, internal companies (relocations, new start-ups, spin-offs) and external companies, which are linked to the park (Felsenstein 1994). The technology transfer agencies may include management services, production information services, market research services, as well as some venture capital fund schemes. The companies located on a science park are usually small, mainly technology-based firms in computing, electrical engineering, chemicals, biotechnology and consultancy, financial and business services. The external group of companies may include small and large firms with some kind of partnering arrangement with the research centres or new ventures in the park. In some cases, supporting activities such as sports facilities, housing, hotels, restaurants and so on are also provided in the park. In its pure form, therefore, a science park is an environment that provides specific resources to technology-based enterprises through technology development and transfer relations.

Science and technology parks stand upon a symbiosis between the universities and the high-technology industry, which in Europe took more than 10 years to be achieved, from the first wave of science parks in the 1970s to the second one at the beginning of the 1980s.

These projects vary significantly from one part of Europe to another. The UK, Germany, Netherlands and Greece follow a model of small parks orientated towards technology transfer and the creation of new technology-based firms, while the parks in France and Spain are larger and seek, at least in their early years, to attract established companies and multinational R&D departments. These differences may be explained with respect to strategy for technology transfer within each country (Sunman 1987).

In the UK there were two distinct periods of science park development. In the early 1970s the Cambridge and Heriot-Watt science parks were set up (Dalton 1985; Segal and Quince 1985). In 1983, after these pilot projects, there was a remarkable wave of establishment of science parks. At the beginning of the 1990s, there were 38 functioning parks and 18 under construction (Worral 1988; Dalton 1992). Most of the UK parks are small. Their surface area ranges from 1 to 5 hectares and only two parks occupy more than 40 hectares. The majority of the companies located in the parks are small, local, single plant, and independent. Average employment is eight persons. The activities of the firms fall under the headings of software (17 per cent), consultancy (19 per cent), product related (22 per cent), contract research (7 per cent), contract design (9 per cent), testing (4 per cent) and training (4 per cent). The industrial sectors to which they belong are computing (34 per cent), electrical engineering (19 per cent), chemicals and biotechnology (12 per cent), mechanical engineering (7 per cent), consultancy and training (19 per cent), and business services (9 per cent) (Monck 1987a; Worral 1988). The main source of funding was the public sector: government development agencies provided 21 per cent of all science park finance, universities 28 per cent and local authorities 11 per cent. The private sector contributed 8 per cent of total investment and tenant companies 32 per cent (Rowe 1988). The development of the parks was very uneven, with those located in the faster growing areas (in South-East England) and those containing computer-related firms growing much faster than the rest.

In Germany, local authorities and universities developed business innovation centres and nurseries rather than science parks. Innovation centres and nurseries are buildings for between 10 and 30 small enterprises, providing services such as management, finance, marketing and technology, as well as conference, common facilities and technical services. Most are part of the European Network of Business Innovation Centres (Allesch 1985). In the 1990s there were 43 operating projects and an equal number under construction. A few of them were later transformed into small science parks (Berliner Innovations und Grunderzentrum, Technologie und Innovationspark) with an emphasis upon technology transfer and support for small innovative firms.

The French case is very different. The term 'technopole' covers both science parks and high-tech industrial zones, and at the beginning of the 1990s, 43 technopoles were functioning or under construction (DATAR 1988). These sites were developed in two phases: three were developed in 1970–1, and the rest were established after 1983 (Club des Technopoles 1988). Technopoles are bigger than UK science parks. The area they cover varies considerably, varying between 8 and 2,800 hectares but with most of them occupying 300 to 400 hectares. They were developed jointly by local authorities, Chambers of Commerce and Industry and universities, either as part of a strategy for the restructuring of declining cities (such as Marseilles, Metz, Nantes) or as strategy for the development of new industrial spaces (Ile de France, Montpellier, Sophia-Antipolis, Cité Descartes) (District de Montpellier 1989; EPAMARNE 1989; Poulit 1989). In their early years there were attempts to attract established companies, R&D departments of multinationals and big public R&D research institutes and to create a local network of alliances, subcontractors and spin-offs. At the maturity stage small firms come and locate in the technopole. In Sophia-Antipolis where this type of strategy was monitored 11,000 direct and much more indirect employment was created in twenty years (Fache 1993; Muller 1985).

In Belgium, science parks started to mushroom in 1971 after a central government decision to support their development. Belgian universities played a dominant role in the development of the parks. There are eight parks with premises, which occupy on average some 50 hectares of land (Mercier 1985; Tomas 1985). The majority of the enterprises located in these areas are small: the average number of employees is 56. The managing authorities have provided investment subsidies and appropriate infrastructures to attract the research centres of multinationals in electronics and pharmaceuticals. Overall, the activities of the firms are diverse and do not always correspond with the expertise of the host university (Van Dierdonck *et al.* 1991).

In the Netherlands, the development of science parks was more recent. The Netherlands is strongly stratified with university graduates starting careers in large organizations, whereas smaller firms draw their employees from middle level technical schools. Among university graduates there is not a strong entrepreneurial culture. At the same time the Dutch government created several regional development agencies to provide firms with consultancy and management services. These two factors limited and delayed science park development (Witholt 1985). Indeed it did not get under way until after 1984 when three parks were created. Of the three, Twente is a business technology centre, established jointly with Control Data. The parks of Zernike and Leiden are proper science parks funded by local authorities, the universities and private industries.

In Spain, a technology park policy was set in motion in 1983. Since then nineteen large and small parks, between 7 and 120 hectares, have been created of which the best known are those in Barcelona, Madrid, the Basque country, Valencia, Asturia and Andalusia. Many elements of their development strategy were borrowed from southern French technopoles with, in particular, the search for joint initiatives with multinationals. What is specific to the Spanish case is the effort to introduce new technologies in existing industries and traditional sectors rather than to promote new industrial sectors (IDEA 1995 and 1997; Gamella 1988; Escorsa 1988).

In Italy, over the past fifteen years there have been numerous schemes to create science parks, eleven of which are located in southern Italy. The objectives of the parks are to develop applied research and to contribute to local development, which explains the involvement of regional authorities in the finance of the projects. Among the most known parks are those of San Raffaele, Bari and Genova Ricerche, Trieste, and Novus Ortus near Bari. The latter is the oldest park in Italy and it is prepared to accept the research activities of national and international enterprises and of small businesses (Romano and Bozzo 1985). In 1994 the Ministry of Universities and Scientific Research decided to create thirteen new parks in central and southern Italy, which should stand on the local research potential and benefit the entire body of regional enterprises.

In Greece, five science parks operate, of which three belong to the General Secretariat for Research and Technology and are located in the cities of Thessaloniki, Heraklion, and Patra, one belongs to the Technical University of Athens, and one to the regional authorities of Thessaly. The parks are rather small in size and orientated towards technology transfer in traditional and new industrial sectors. Most advanced is the Technology Park of Thessaloniki, which was established in 1990 by the Chemical Process Research Institute (CPERI) to meet the need for a greater exchange of ideas, people and facilities between universities and industry. It is located 12 km outside Thessaloniki, in Thermi, with easy access to the local airport and highway system. It is adjacent to the American Farm School, which owns about 150 hectares of land where the TTP could expand its future activities. From the very beginning CPERI created an environment where the physical area, with well-landscaped surroundings provided a good atmosphere. The goal is to promote significant opportunities for interchange with CPERI and local universities. To preserve the nature of the Technology Park, an effort is made to restrict the use of the buildings to: (1) scientific research associated with industrial production, (2) technical and/or management activities linking research to industry, and (3) company supporting activities (accounting, marketing, etc.).

This brief overview of cases shows the diversity of the projects in Europe. Various attempts were made to define the added value of these parks, in terms of the effectiveness of technology transfer, the success of small high-tech firms located in the parks, and the contribution of the parks to the technological restructuring of industries (Phillimore 1999; Luger and Goldstein 1991; Westhead and Bastone 1998).

One of the first assessments was commissioned by the UK Science Park Association (UKSPA), which surveyed 284 high-technology firms on and off science parks (Monck *et al.* 1988). More than 50 per cent of all firms located on UK science parks were interviewed and the findings were compared with those for firms in similar sectors but located off a park, in order to identify the 'added value' of the science parks. The survey considered the characteristics of the individuals who have established high-technology firms; the technological level of the firms; their performance and impact; and their management and financing. To evaluate the impact of the UK science parks, six criteria were assessed: gross job creation; deadweight; displacement; technology diffusion effects; demonstration effects, and multiplier effects. There was evidence that: science parks provided business and financial support services of significant value to tenants; the presence of the parks provided a major stimulus to academics starting their own business; the parks increased informal relationships between the universities and firms; and that they may have considerable long-term effects on changing the attitudes of young scientists towards business. The study concluded:

There are two key conclusions that have emerged from this survey, both of which have crucial implications for government policy. The first is that NTBFs (new technology based firms) stand out as a special group of small firms in terms of performance and their contribution to employment and the economy. The second is that Science Parks are uniquely placed as a local delivery mechanism for a range of technological innovation and entrepreneurship policies directed to NTBFs.

Despite the performance and contribution of NTBFs to the economy, the survey identified several constraints on the ability of NTBFs in general to fulfil their economic potential. These included management capacity, finance and weakness in sales and marketing. The extent to which Science Parks can help firms overcome these constraints depends partly on the quality of the on-site management resources, and partly on access to appropriate sources of equity and loan funds. Already, considerable public funds have been committed to physical developments, but if the wider economic benefits are to be realized, greater attention now needs to be given to the role and resourcing of the on-site management facility in Science Parks. To stimulate the formation and growth of NTBFs effectively, management resources need to be supplemented in four ways:

1 facilitating start-ups via access to small tranches of seedcorn and venture funds;

2 promoting access to top quality, pro-active advice for rapidly growing firms;

3 providing practical assistance to firms on topics such as exports, development, joint ventures and the formation of subsidiary companies, etc. and

4 providing an interface between university research and industry which will actively facilitate knowledge and technology transfer.

(Monck *et al.* 1988: 246–7)

Another assessment examined the total firm population in eight Belgian and three Dutch science parks – 208 firms in total – to see how science parks contribute to the diffusion of technological knowledge (Van Dierdonck *et al.* 1991). The authors claimed that their findings do not provide grounds for much optimism, that the character of the R&D environment in most of the science parks studied is limited and that science parks are not necessarily the most effective path for involvement in industrial science and technology (ibid, pp. 120–2). This assessment is partly due, however, to misplaced comparisons of the Belgian and Dutch science parks with regions like Silicon Valley and Route 128 in the United States (ibid, p. 122). In any case, it identifies some major methodological problems in measuring the performance and added value of science parks.

In France, on the initiative of the association France Technopoles, a survey was conducted with the aid of the University of Lyon among 471 enterprises located in the parks of 26 technopoles belonging to the national association. The study showed that the highest expectation of the companies with respect to a technopole concerns location sites. Support in promoting the company is the second expectation, while networking and contact between companies is the third expectation. In this domain however, there seems to be little satisfaction with the package of services offered by the technopoles (European Commission 1996b).

A comparative survey of science parks in Belgium, Germany, France, Italy, the Netherlands, Spain and the UK, which URENIO realized, brought to the surface some interesting issues concerning science park development, planning and evaluation (Komninos *et al.* 1990).

- The term covers quite different situations: small incubator business centres, technology transfer parks, and high-technology industrial parks. In particular it is important to differentiate parks whose dominant function is to provide a rich technological environment from those that are simple location spaces, even for high-technology firms. At present, a major problem is the tension between the role of science parks as technological environments for technology-based firms and as high-technology industrial areas. The difference between science parks and industrial zones is not always clear, even for science park managers or developers. However, the objective of science parks is not to replace industrial zones, as the aim is to provide an environment with specific resources for high-technology firms (venture capital, production information, and management services) rather than to offer land, infrastructures, and external economies of scale.

- While some parks succeed, others fail. For every science park it is important to examine the extent to which there is or is not an increasing networking activity between research and industry. Calling an area 'science park' does not mean that a technology transfer environment has been automatically created. Science parks fail either because the assessment of the local market potential for the property and non-property services of the park was misguided, or because the conditions for local innovative growth were not appropriate. The rather poor performance, for example, of science parks in northern England has to be attributed to trends in regional development rather than to the character of the parks involved. The study did, however, lead to the identification of two factors that are critical for the development of science parks: the *regional context* and their *technology specialization*. The performance of the parks located in fast-growing areas is better than those located in old industrial areas. The parks specialized in electronics grow faster than those specialized in other industries.

- Every science park must be considered as a specific project and as an output of a planning process. There are analytical guidelines for science park planning, concerning the background analysis, the market analysis, the strategy to follow, the development plan, and the implementation plan (European Commission 1991 and 1994d). Consequently, in any evaluation, account must be taken of: (1) the objectives of the project, (2) the type of park involved, whether there is a technology transfer environment or just promises for high-technology activities, and (3) the regional development context and technology transfer processes. Any appraisal of the 'added value' of science parks must take into account the differences between the projects and the partners involved. The assessment of science parks is at the same time an appraisal of a local strategy for the development of small technology-based firms, spin-offs, and innovative local growth.

Overall, science parks, incubator environments, and links with universities may be good solutions to the difficulties of reconciling R&D with small firms. What they offer is an environment rich in production networks, synergies and linkages with external sources of scientific and technical information and advice. In the long term, the stimulus they give to the development of new companies able to exploit new markets or to introduce new systems and products may help widen the local productive system and improve local innovativeness and adaptability. An appraisal of their long-term impact must be placed, however, in the framework of the fragmentation of the large groups and companies, and the widening of networks of innovators and networking strategies by larger firms (Mansel 1991; Freeman 1990). The critical issue is whether or not they help to consolidate the position of small independent R&D-intensive firms and therefore whether or not technology transfer processes come to count for more than property and real estate exploitation.

Spatial Proximity and Technology Integration

The location of R&D organizations and innovative companies in a rather small area is the starting point for the creation of a nucleus of technology-intensive activities. As Table 2.2 shows, the processes of formation of this technology pole vary considerably between the member states of the European Union, and they reflect the national differences on the levels of technological effort, enterprise support policies, and urban planning.

Germany is the country in which the overall situation seems to best fit the description 'regional strategies', while the United Kingdom is the closest adherent to the 'university strategy'. Between these two poles, we also portray the situation in countries such as Ireland, where central government plays an important role and the French 'technopolis' approach, which combines local policies with emphasis on state scientific and technological resources.

(European Commission 1996b)

European science parks link universities and research centres, technology-based enterprises, and consultancy, training and technology transfer agencies. Between them, different types of technology transfer take place: from universities to companies, from company to company, from the park's occupants to the surrounding environment of the park. These transfers rely on communication practices and partnerships between individual companies, agreements over the links with universities, and the relationships with professional and other agencies (chambers of commerce, venture capital associations providing funds for new start-ups, development banks and local authorities). Four types of relationships sustain technological integration within the parks: (1) the spatial agglomeration of activities, (2) the links with the universities, (3) the venture capital funds for spin-offs and new start-ups, (4) the partnering between firms.

Agglomeration, spatial proximity and technology cooperation: Green field developments, new campuses, new towns, integration of existing communities and villages, renewal and restoration of buildings, a great typology of spaces and localities characterizes the spatial and morphological configuration of the technology poles. The geographical or property dimension, however, is not the most interesting feature of science parks. The contacts established between entrepreneurs and researchers, academic staff and experts from the public and private sectors seem far more important. These relationships serve to identify capabilities, technical expertise, and financial resources that are available locally, and to open these resources to local firms and research organizations (European Commission 1996b). The geographical proximity of enterprises to universities and research institutes cannot guarantee that technology links will be formed between them. The real challenge for science parks is to set in motion technological integration mechanisms, to establish networks between people and activities of different origin and scope, and to create active technology districts.

Links between firms and universities: Universities and research institutes play a fundamental role in the concept of a science park as a major source of innovations and new technologies for existing firms and new technology-based start-ups. The links between individual firms and universities differ from one university and one science park authority to another. In general they involve: (1) the transfer of people and staff from the university to the firm; (2) the access of firms to university facilities such as libraries, conference centres, computer centres and amenities; (3) the opening up of university and laboratory infrastructures and equipment to companies for analysis, testing and evaluation exercises; (4) contracts for or sponsoring of university research by the firms; (5) less formal contacts and the day-to-day interchanges and information flows between academics and managers (Monck *et al.* 1988). In so far as these relationships exist, universities and public research institutes provide external economies of scale for science park firms and can attract small and large companies (Lindhom Dalhstrand 1999; Vedovello 1997). A good example is Toulouse where it was the attractiveness of such infrastructures that led to the location of important high-tech companies (Alcatel-Espace, Matra-Espace, Thomson and Motorola) just after the transfer of the National

Table 2.2 Strategies for setting science and technology parks in Europe

	Number of parks	Type of park
Belgium	8 large and small parks	Science park Incubator
Denmark	5 small parks	Science parks
France	40 large parks	Technology park Technopolis Technopolis networks
Germany	70 small parks	Innovation centre Technology park Business incubator
Greece	5 small parks 5 incubators	Technology park Innovation centre
Ireland	1 large park 1 small	Technology park Incubator
Italy	11 parks	Science park Technopolis
The Netherlands	7 small parks	Science park Business incubator
Portugal	3 large parks	Technology parks
Spain	9 large and 10 small parks	Technology park Business nursery
UK	40 small and large parks	Science park Technology park Innovation centre

Source: European Commission (1996b).

Origin/shareholder	Management	Objectives
Universities Federal ministry Non-profit associations	Administrative council	Technology transfer Housing of large companies
Universities Ministry of research and technology	Business foundation	Technology transfer Housing of large companies
Municipalities Regional government Chambers	Associations of communes Mixed consortia	Development and attraction of high-tech activities Development of networks
Local Lander	Private company	Support start-ups Creation of skilled jobs Translation of R&D into practice
Ministry of research and technology Research institutes	SA	Support start-ups Technology transfer
Regional development agency	National Technological Park Company	Attraction of international investors
Ministry of research Large companies Local authorities Associations	Associations Mixed consortia	Technology transfer Support of SMEs Creation of business clusters
State Local authorities Universities	Consortia of founding institutions	Location of firms near universities Technology transfer Industry–university cooperation
Local government Private companies		Development of local resources Growth of SMEs
Autonomous communities Regional government Universities	Associations Public companies	Attract high-tech companies Industry–university cooperation Development of innovative firms Upgrade regional industry
Universities Local authorities Public agencies Private organizations	Management committee of associated founders	Property development Technology transfer

Centre for Space Studies (CNES) to the city (Hirtzman and Cohen 1988). An equally important but more immaterial factor in the attraction of firms is the prestige of being linked to the university. For many companies, the symbolic value of a relationship with the host university is more important than the direct use of its infrastructures as it enhances the high-tech image of science-park companies and can give a firm a strong marketing advantage.

Spin-off support: In recent science parks more consideration has been given to means of financing companies interested in the commercial exploitation of new ideas, and in many science parks the managing authorities have themselves organized a venture capital fund (Steffensen *et al.* 2000). What, however, is the meaning of this financial backing? A survey of European venture capital indicated that there was no shortage of funds for investment (Hustler 1988). However, only 3 per cent of tenant companies in UK science parks were financed through formal venture capital institutions (Monck 1988). It is clear that venture capitalists were steering away from investments in new start-ups. The problem lay in the size of the firms. The average size of venture capital investments was very large compared with the needs of the companies that were starting up in science parks. Furthermore, an important part of available venture capital funds was going to management buy-outs and later-stage financing. The needs of new tenant companies on science parks were, it seemed, too small to interest venture capitalists.

At the root of this problem was the size of the market in which most science park companies were operating. In Europe, new companies achieving spectacular growth and supplying a large international market within the first five years were few and far between. By contrast, many science park companies showed a predisposition to stay comparatively small, to remain independent of external finance and to avoid the organizational difficulties associated with growth (Dunford 1991). There was, therefore, a problem. On the one hand new start-ups constitute an important channel for technology transfer especially where scientists wish to commercialize their research. On the other it was difficult for them to get venture capital. To solve this, many science park authorities established links with venture capital funds to provide capital for tenant companies. Usually these schemes were associated with the incubator concept and concentrated on high-technology start-ups. What was provided were small sums of money either in the shape of long-term loans or equity participation in the company's assets plus some kind of management guidance and assistance with the development of a business plan (Allen 1988).

Company networks: With the development of science parks it became clear that the tenant companies experience the normal business problems of the small firm sector with particular difficulties in the areas of promotion, marketing, and sales. To overcome such growth barriers, the management authorities of science parks tried to establish partnering agreements between the park's technology-based firms and external companies.

The networking and knowledge transfer between firms is part of the wider increase of business cooperation and the participation of one company in the assets and management of another. Networking takes various forms, such as strategic alliances, corporate partnering, and joint ventures. They concern producer-supplier relations, cooperation on the marketing and distribution of products, joint product development and design, joint commercial exploitation of a patent, joint creation of a new venture. Strategic alliances are a new phenomenon which appeared in the early 1980s, whose roots are at the rise of R&D costs and the reduction of life cycle of high-tech products. Strategic alliances proliferated also because of the innovative performance of small companies, and the investment choices made by venture capital funds (Radke 1987; Freeman 1990). Within the cooperation networks the innovative power of small firms is combined with the management and marketing capabilities of larger firms.

Technology parks take part in this proliferation of strategic alliances. However, most science park managers agree that the problems of inter-firm cooperation and strategic alliances have not been placed at the centre of the management practices. The efforts to attract companies and foster relationships with the universities and research organizations overshad-owed the concern for cooperation and integration between companies. Nowadays, this neglect is recognized as a barrier to the effective function-ing of the parks and a threat to their technology character. Informed man-agement practices pay more attention to the selection of companies to be located in the premises of the parks, to the activity of the industrial liaison service, and to increasing the size of the park, which also raises the possi-bility for spontaneous networks to be formed and cooperation between the tenant companies.

Although not usually a stated objective of technopolitan planning, the real challenge of science parks and planned technopoles is to create self-sustaining communication processes, such as those found in a technology district. To this end, two overlapping processes are contributing: the agglomeration and spatial proximity of R&D and high-tech companies; and the technology transfer and business support.

The agglomeration of activities making the technology pole and the technology transfer practices developed on the site are the main pillars of science and technology parks. The two models of science parks that we usually find in Europe – (1) the attraction-led model focusing on the loca-tion of companies and research organizations on the site, and (2) the technology-led model focusing on the transfer of knowledge and research results to the companies – correspond to cases that prioritize the one or the other pillar. When both pillars are equally developed, a strong integration process is set in motion transforming the park to a quasi-technology district.

The financial circuit linking these two pillars (agglomeration/technology transfer) has strong added value for the viability of a park. The property base of the parks and the exploitation of real estate is the main source of income. Most parks start their operations in remote areas or on the outskirts of cities. If successful, they make their area a brand-name address which brings significant increases in land values and rents. This surplus value is a considerable source of income, at the time of commercialization or rent of land. On the other hand, the income raised from technology transfer activities is rather modest: a few companies are willing to pay for technology brokerage, liaison networks, knowledge dissemination, information retrieval, and other soft actions in the field of technology transfer. However, these activities shape the profile of the park, and make the park a place of distinction in terms of technology and innovation. The indirect effect of technology brokerage and knowledge dissemination on the surplus value of the property is higher than the direct income gained from these activities. The financial circuit is that technology transfer increases the value of the real estate, while the income gained from the real estate finances technology transfer, brokerage, and technology dissemination activities.

Technology integration based on spatial and informal communication interaction developed in science parks is roughly to the coordination mechanisms and industrial organization developed in the districts. The same type of integration processes found in well-known districts – such as the core-ring relationships with coordinating firms in the garment industry of Veneto, the core-ring relationships with a lead firm in aircraft construction in Toulouse, the short-term coalitions in the Hollywood motion picture industry (Enright 2000), and the long-term relationships in the Turin factory automation equipment – can be reproduced within the limited space of a planned technopole or science park. It is a question of good selection of tenant companies, efficient management, and appropriate size of the park allowing the localization of the right mix of companies, intermediaries, and research organizations.

3 Technology Poles in the Less Favoured Regions of Europe

In theory the origin of an industry may be traced back to a key invention, but in practice it is rarely possible to attribute such a decisive role to a single discovery . . . However, there is no doubt that many inventions are a response to problems in existing industries and the individuals responsible for them are often involved with these industries. This type of relationship suggests that the distribution of inventive activity will tend to favour established industrial centres and there is abundant evidence to suggest that this was indeed the case during the nineteenth and early twentieth centuries. On the other hand, established centres may stifle innovation through the adoption of restrictive practices and conservative attitudes and new industries to some extent create their own conditions for growth in new areas as exemplified by the replacement of the former fruit orchards of 'Silicon Valley' in California by electronic plants. In these circumstances, new industries may 'seem to "leapfrog"' in space, establishing growth centres and new growth peripheries that are relatively insulated from existing highly industrialized regions.

(K. Chapman and D. Walker, *Industrial Location*)

The technological development of less developed areas in the European Union is a significant element of the actual regional policy for the convergence and cohesion of the EU. These areas face double competition: on the one hand in traditional sectors from countries with low labour costs outside the EU, and on the other hand, in high-tech sectors from the most developed regions of the EU. This double challenge has made them turn their efforts to the formation of new technology poles and the use of all available sources of technology so as to boost their innovation capability and improve their position in relation to domestic and foreign competition.

This chapter focuses on technopolitan planning in southern Europe. It refers to three Sprint and Innovation projects of the European Commission for the creation of technopoles in Andalusia, Crete, and Sicily. These are Objective 1 regions at the southernmost tip of the European Union, where in collaboration with Andrea Tosi, professor at the Politechnico di Milano and Daniel Mercier, head of technology transfer at the Université Catholique de Louvain-La-Neuve, we examined alternative technological

69

development strategies. These parks follow three quite different trajectories. However, a central problem in all three cases was the creation of
technopoles in an environment lagging behind in technology, and the
special characteristics that technological development takes on in relation
to its reference environment.

Malaga: Technology Attraction in the Andalusia Technology Park

I first became acquainted with the Andalusia Technology Park (Parque
Tecnologico de Andalucia – PTA) in the summer of 1991 when Andrea
Tosi suggested that we collaborate in order to enrich the PTA with a new
Innovation Centre in the environmental sector. This project had been
included in the European Union's (DG XIII) Sprint Programme (Strategic
Programme for Innovation and Technology Transfer), had been approved
and had the unreserved support of the park, the University of Malaga and
the Engineer's Association which considered that just such a centre would
offer much to the environment and to the development of the area (Chef *et
al.* 1995).

At the beginning of the 1990s, Malaga and Andalusia, where efforts to
develop the Technology Park had begun, faced two significant challenges.
The first concerned unemployment. A large percentage of the active population were long-term unemployed, a result of structural changes in the
regional and national economy. Andalusia had been affected more than
other regions in Spain and unemployment was in the order of 30 per cent,
while the national average was 10 per cent lower. Part of the solution to
this problem was the creation of a large Technology Park in the suburbs of
Malaga, which would contribute to the creation of new jobs and the transition of the local economy towards new industrial sectors and activities.
The second challenge related to the structure of the economy in Malaga
and Andalusia, with tourism and the construction sector accounting for
high shares, and the accumulation of environmental management and
housing development problems due to intense tourist activity on the Costa

Table 3.1 Malaga, Andalusia, Spain: GDP and production structure

	Malaga	Andalusia	Spain
Population	1,150,000	6,860,000	39,000,000
GDP (per capita)	9,000	8,500	11,000
Agricultural sector (%)	5.7	10.9	6.2
Industry (%)	11.3	20.6	25.5
Construction (%)	12.3	11.3	8.9
Services (%)	70.7	57.2	59.3

Source: Parque Tecnologico de Andalucia (1994).

del Sol. Part of the solution to this problem was the creation of an Environmental Innovation Centre at the PTA to enable coordinated monitoring and intervention in the environment and housing development sectors.

The Andalusia Technology Park was a catalyst for both challenges. The park continued the efforts in the field of technology and innovation made by the University of Malaga, a new and dynamic university with 23,000 students, and 20 departments in the exact sciences (biology, physics, chemistry, mathematics), engineering sciences (industrial technology, telecommunications, IT, architecture), social sciences (law, economics), and medicine. On the other hand, the park supported the local productive system in terms of future technologies, together with major high-tech firms that were established in the area (Alcatel, Siemens-Matsushita, Fujitsu) and small technological innovation undertakings. The PTA, together with the new airport, were significant interventions in the city of Malaga. It provided a way out of the problems faced by the area, prospects of internationalization of the city and structural change in the local productive system.

Construction work on the Parque Tecnologico de Andalucia commenced in 1989. The project was funded by the regional government of Andalusia (Empressa Publica de Suelo de Andalucia, Instituto de Fomento de Andalucia) and the city of Malaga (Ayuntamiento de Malaga). Ayuntamiento de Malaga participated in the company founded in 1990 to develop the park (PTA SA) by 40 per cent, Empressa Publica de Suelo de Andalucia by 30 per cent and the Instituto de Fomento de Andalucia by 30 per cent. The capital of the company was 6,272 million pta. The initial investment of 6,000 million pta was used for land planning, layout of the area and the construction of infrastructure. The European Regional Development Fund (ERDF) funded 60 per cent of the project cost through the Structural Funds for Objective 1 regions.

The PTA covers an area of 168 hectares and is located 13 km from the centre of the city on the main road network. The park has five main categories of land use:

- An area containing facilities for research and development (26 hectares).

- An area containing facilities for research and production (26 hectares).

- A central area where technology centres and services, the innovation centre, the telecommunications centre, the technological development and technology transfer office, university institutes and public R&D centres, the hotel, conference centre and business and commercial centre are gathered (13 hectares).

- A recreation zone, golf course, sports facilities, club (17 hectares).

- Open areas of which 74 hectares are green areas, gardens, copses and wetlands and of which 12 hectares are roads and service facilities.

The land planning regulation and the morphology of the individual zones change depending on the use of each area. In the research area the minimum surface area of plots is 2,500 m^2, the maximum permissible height of buildings is 10 m, the construction coefficient is 0.6 and maximum coverage is 35 per cent. In the production areas, construction is denser with the minimum surface area of plots being 10,000 m^2, the maximum height 15 m, the construction coefficient 1.0 and the maximum coverage 50 per cent.

The park foresees that enterprises from new technology sectors will establish themselves there: telecommunications, microelectronics, industrial automation, IT, lasers, new materials, renewable energy sources, and biotechnology. In order for enterprises to be accepted they must invest more than 4 per cent of their turnover in R&D and have a staff consisting of between 25 and 40 per cent of university graduates.

During the first five years of operation (1990–5) the number of people employed at the PTA reached 1,450. A total of 40 enterprises established themselves there, the most important of which are Hudges, Telefonica, Alcatel, Air Liquide, Ingenia, and Cetecom. In addition, 14 small enterprises employing 155 people established themselves in the innovation centre (BIC). Moreover, public research institutes such as the Institutes for Standardization, Automation, Image Processing, Quality Software, Computing and Testing established themselves in the park.

In order to attract these organizations, the PTA has developed a strategy which has three main focuses (IDEA 1995):

- The choice of geographical areas of promotion (USA, Canada, Scandinavian countries, European Union, Japan, Korea, Taiwan) and communication with enterprises and organizations in selected high-tech sectors (microelectronics, environmental technology, biotechnology, pharmaceuticals, new materials, telecommunications, software). During the first five years, the PTA approached 15,000 enterprises, 36.2 per cent of which were in Spain, 17 per cent in the EU, 27.7 per cent in America and 19.1 per cent in Asia.

- Promoting the park within Spain and internationally as a place for company location. Central government participated in the promotion via the commercial offices of the Spanish Embassy and the Directorate General for Foreign Investments and the Ministries of Commerce and Tourism. Other participants were the commercial chambers and the Business Association of Andalusia.

- Providing establishment incentives. Regional incentives fund 30 per cent of the cost of investment in the Park. Moreover, enterprises establishing

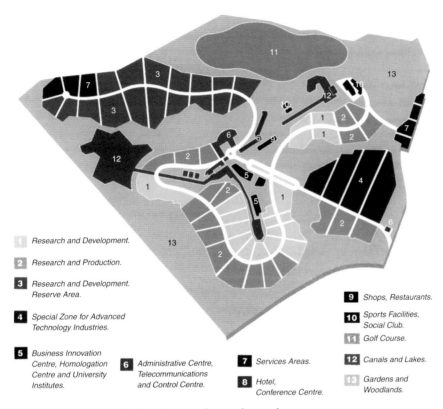

Research and Development.

Research and Production.

Research and Development. Reserve Area.

Special Zone for Advanced Technology Industries.

Business Innovation Centre, Homologation Centre and University Institutes.

Administrative Centre, Telecommunications and Control Centre.

Services Areas.

Hotel, Conference Centre.

Shops, Restaurants.

Sports Facilities, Social Club.

Golf Course.

Canals and Lakes.

Gardens and Woodlands.

Map 3.1 Andalusia Technology Park: Land use plan (key)

	Land Use	Area in hectares
1	Research and Development	9
2	Research and Production	14
3	Research and Development (Stores)	17
4	High-Tech Industries	12
5	Innovation Centre, University Institutes	4
6	Admin. Centre, Telecommunications Centre	2
7	Auxiliary Services Zone	3
8	Hotel and Conference Centre	2
9	Retail Units, Restaurants	2
10	Sports Facilities, Social Clubs	7
11	Golf Course	10
12–13	Green areas, gardens, wetlands, lakes	74
14	Roads	12

themselves in the park enjoy lower lending interest rates, have access to venture capital and support for staff training. The programmed agreement between the PTA and Banco Sabadell provides a preferential line of financing for fixed capital, working capital, and international trading capital. In total, incentives provided to units establishing themselves in

73

the park for the first time come to 47 per cent of the total cost of investment (IDEA 1997).

Parque Tecnologico de Andalucia adopted a classic strategy in order to form a technological district. It started with getting public sector agencies on board, had the area declared a technology park, and then arranged the land use planning and construction of infrastructure necessary for the establishment of enterprises and research organizations. Taking this area, the high quality of the environment, upgraded infrastructure and incentives as a basis, PTA formulated an attraction strategy whose aim was the establishment of multinational high-tech enterprises and large research organizations. These organizations build their own facilities on individual plots in accordance with predetermined building terms and restrictions. Alternatively they can establish themselves in areas using leasing contracts. In parallel, in collaboration with research and technology agencies in the region, PTA created a series of technological centres located in the central area of the park which offer services in the telecommunications, automation, environmental quality, materials sectors and so on. Furthermore by entering into programmed agreements with external organizations, collaboration networks were created, connecting the activities of the park to its integration area. The agreements concern strategic alliances, business collaboration, joint investment programmes, promotion of products on the market, subcontracting, cooperation in the development of products and transfer best production and management practices from the park to its wider environment. The park is transformed into a pole of innovation for the wider local and regional system.

In many technology parks, the company selection criteria, and in particular the emphasis on research, are brushed aside in the initial phases of developing the park when pressure for results in attracting enterprises is great. In Malaga, the fact that the initial investment for the park was public and done using resources from the European Regional Development Fund limits, but does not remove, this parameter.

A crucial point for the effectiveness of the aforementioned strategy and the formation of a technopole capable of transferring innovations to the regional productive system, are the companies/organizations that are attracted to the park and establish themselves there. It is well known that in less developed regions, foreign direct investments in the form of branch plants dominate, with ready technology being taken from the parent enterprise. These branches operate according to principles of self-sufficiency without particular connections with the local productive or research tissue (Giunta and Martinelli 1993). This is particularly negative for technology diffusion and the creation of spillovers and multiplier effects.

However, the question remains: how open are branch plants to the local economy, suppliers, subcontractors, research institutes in the area, and how feasible is it to connect branch plants to more traditional productive activities? Such linkages are essential for the success of a new technopole relying on an attraction strategy. The establishment of a high-tech unit in an environment lagging behind in technology, necessarily leads to an effort to ensure self-sufficiency as the quality of local suppliers, subcontractors and research institutes are under question. Time is needed to restore relations of trust and cooperation. Systematic effort at networking, with which the attraction strategy is completed, is a significant parameter but it cannot always transcend the functional conditions of the high-tech production units in peripheral areas.

Hania: Technology Transfer from the Technical University of Crete

Upon completion of the project in Andalusia, in collaboration as always with Andrea Tosi and Daniel Mercier, we examined the possibility of developing a science park in Hania, seat of the Technical University of Crete. The project had been proposed under the Sprint programme, had been approved and we were assigned the preparation of a strategy and plan of implementation.

When we reached Hania we found that quite a few studies and efforts to create a science park had preceded us. At the beginning of the 1990s a study by the Hellenic Industrial Development Bank had proposed the creation of a large technopole, which included the construction of buildings covering $20,000 \, m^2$ with a budget of 20 million Euro (VIPETVA 1993). Following this, an internal report prepared by the Technical University of Crete had proposed the setting aside of 100 hectares of land within the campus and the construction of building and technology infrastructure. Moreover, D. Fache, from the consultancy firm StraTech, had visited the site to conduct research and proposed a technology park based on the attraction of major public organizations and telecommunications organizations (Fache 1993). In the end, a land use plan for the setting aside of 100 hectares within the campus for use as a science park was drawn up. The central aim of these approaches was that an area would be designated as a science park, basic infrastructure would be constructed and large high-tech enterprises and organizations would be attracted to establish there. In other words a strategy similar to that used by the Parque Tecnologico de Andalusia, which had been successfully implemented in many areas of southern Europe, and particularly so in France, was adopted.

These efforts did not bear fruit. Up to 1995 not even the slightest step had been taken to develop the park. No zone was set aside as a science park, not even a single Euro was made available for investment in infrastructure and the area did not attract a single important technological company or national or international organization. Three reasons contributed to the cancellation of local initiatives to implement an attraction-led strategy for science park development.

- First, was the reserved to negative stance of the government. The then Minister of Industry, Energy and Technology, and now Prime Minister, K. Simitis, had reservations about the need for a second technology park on Crete, after the Heraklion Park. The latter had been founded by the Institute for Technology and Research (FOURTH) and had just started to face many serious difficulties in terms of organization and development. At the end of 1994 the Secretariat General for Research and Technology had assigned the evaluation of Greek science parks to the company Segal Quince Wicksteed. The assessment report pointed out the limited development of the Heraklion Technology Park 'which is as yet far from being a fully fledged science and technology park' and indicated the importance of collaboration with local and international high-tech companies as well as the need to de-couple management of the park from the research orientation of the FOURTH (Segal Quince Wicksteed Limited 1995). These assessments brought to the surface the real problems of technological development in an island and isolated environment with a short tradition in high-tech industry and explained the reservations about financing a second science park in Crete.

- Second, the emphasis on the building programme, on the planning of a large area and on the construction of infrastructure. In the proposal from VIPETVA the cost of the park was estimated at 20 million Euro and in all events the planning and construction of infrastructure for a site covering 100 hectares would have required considerable expenditure. Demand did not justify the large building aspect of the park since there was not stated or documented demand for housing facilities for businesses. On the other hand, a large building programme requires a bulk initial expenditure on infrastructure and landscaping and limits flexibility in terms of financing.

- Third, there was no favourable statutory framework for the construction of science and technology parks; this came later in the form of the law of Industrial and Business Areas (BEPE) including planning regulation on technopoles. Building by way of deviation from the construction regulations or according to a local town plan, was not allowed since a technology park has a business rather than a welfare character.

Taking these difficulties together: lack of political support, barriers to financing, inappropriate legal framework, it is easy to comprehend why there was failure in making progress. The science park of the Technical University of Crete, as a real estate project based on the attraction of enterprises and high-tech organizations to the island, was not a feasible programme. The starting point and support for a science park needed to be sought elsewhere.

Hania is a prefecture with 135,000 residents and continuous demographic increases over the past two decades in the order of 5 per cent each decade. The area is among the most dynamic in all of Greece with a 3.5 per cent increase in GDP per year between 1980–90, a figure higher than that for all of Crete and for Greece as a whole. Demographic and economic robustness are due to services and tourism and the construction activity related to these sectors. By contrast, the primary sector is stagnant. Manufacturing, in which sectors connected to agriculture and raw materials predominate (foodstuffs, clothing, furniture, building materials), with low-tech production processes and products in the late stages of their life cycle, is shrinking both in terms of employment and products. The dualism of the productive system expresses the main weakness of the area. High-entrepreneurial and high-profit activities in the tourism and service sector which exploit the advantages of climate, environment and history on the one hand, coexist with low-intensity, low-effectiveness agricultural and processing activities on the other hand. The lack in terms of specialized work and technical staff is great, as is the lack in business services for the promotion of new products, collaboration networks, information and the dissemination of new technologies.

The establishment of the Technical University of Crete at Hania, with its clear production and technological orientation, was the most significant step in upgrading the weak aspects of the local productive system. The Technical University includes five departments: production and management engineering, electronic and computer engineering, mineral resource engineering, environmental engineering, and sciences, as well as around 30 research labs for applied research, undergraduate and postgraduate studies. The impression received from the research activity and technological environment of the Technical University was exceptionally positive. What is impressive is the interest shown in research, state-of-the-art technology, and the effort put in and the climate created, all of which bode particularly well for a new academic institute. However, with a few exceptions, the size of the research units and labs is small. The same holds true for the number and size of research projects being carried out. The Technical University of Crete, with its upgraded research and technological environment and the architectural quality of the new campus had clear modernizing repercussions on the area. The science park could have been a supplementary step in the same direction transferring, in the most integrated manner, technology to the productive system of the area and promoting technological innovations in agriculture and manufacturing.

These observations led the park's development strategy in a direction that would make best use of the existing technological resources in the area, place emphasis on institutions and in particular on technology transfer. Important choices we made were for: (1) the character of the science park to mainly be 'intangible', to be based on institutions and organizational mechanisms rather than on land, infrastructure and property development, (2) the park to be based on the Technical University's and two agricultural research and training institute's existing technological capacity rather than on attracting technology, enterprises and organizations, which without underestimating this, did not prove to be the central strength in its development, (3) the park to focus on supporting small enterprises in the manufacturing and agricultural sectors and to meet demands for industrial technologies, the development of new products and improvements in quality, and (4) the management of the park to be assigned to a new company in which the Technical University, the Olive Oil and the Mediterranean Agronomic Institutes, and agencies representing production and local government would participate.[1]

Corresponding to these guidelines, the development plan for the Technical University of Crete Science Park starts with the Park Management Company (SA and scientific committees) and focuses on the creation of four centres for technology transfer, provision of technological services, financing innovation and housing newly established enterprises. These centres operate in collaboration with the university laboratories and research institutes, exploit their research and infrastructure and offer services for the development of new products and production processes, improvements in quality and the dissemination of new IT, telecommunications and automation technologies.

The *Technology Transfer Centre* is the park's basic point of reference and organization. It includes: (1) the industrial liaison unit, (2) the innovation and technological development observatory, and (3) the career office. Inside the park the Centre ensures cohesion and coordination of research lab technology transfer activities. In relation to the park's external environment, the Centre operates as a node for disseminating technological knowledge, techniques and methods for innovation, information on new technology applications and contributes to the development of technology cooperation networks both at the level of local clusters and at the level of international technological cooperation.

The *Technological Services Centre* is the core of the science park. It is based on the technological skills of the Technical University's labs and those of the research institutes in the area. The mission of the Centre is to provide product development services, lab analyses, quality services (destructive and non-destructive control), applications and demonstrations of IT to agricultural and processing enterprises. The Centre has formed clusters of labs in the following sectors: (1) product quality, (2) business administration, (3) IT, (4) telecommunications, and (5) automation, and in this sense offers a structure promoting technological integration and advanced business services. It complements the research labs on the basis of interdisciplinary approaches, synthesizing technological skills scattered among smaller units. Its intervention is expected to expand the local market for the use of new technologies and the pace of technological innovation.

The creation of a *Centre for the Financing of Innovation* springs from the need for financing connected with innovations, new or improved products, and the creation of new high-tech businesses (spin-offs) that is usually provided by venture capital, start-up capital, equity participations in high-tech companies, acquisitions and so on. The Centre has been designed so as to offer: (1) financing for the start-up of new enterprises created by the university graduates, and (2) venture capital for the development of new products and production processes. These services, aimed at different target groups, are provided in collaboration with established banks and financial institutions of the region.

Finally, the *Centre for Housing Newly Established Enterprises* is a classic incubator that has been designed as a high-quality building infrastructure for housing small high-tech enterprises and in particular for supporting the Technical University's spin-offs. Two alternative locations for the Centre with various advantages and disadvantages are the restoration of a listed building in the centre of the city or the construction of a new building on campus. By housing high-tech enterprises, assisting spin-offs and attracting enterprises, the Centre aims to create a small pole for innovative enterprises.

The initial investment for the development of the Science Park with the four centres described above has been estimated at 7 million Euro. The overall development programme for the park consists of 12 projects, which are independent of each other and can all be financed separately. This offers flexibility in financing since the total amount is not needed up front and the park can be developed in stages. The most likely sources of financing are the Community Support Framework, the operational programmes of the Ministry of Development, the Regional Programme for Crete, related community initiatives, and financing under pilot projects of the ERDF.

The environment of innovation in the Science Park of the Technical University of Crete is based on the know-how of the Technical University's labs and the agricultural research institutes in Hania. It is an environment that operates as a catalyst and intermediary. It does not repeat the functions, equipment, staffing and mission of the labs, but synthesizes their capabilities with declared or latent technological needs in the region. For enterprises in the area the park is a turning point, a starting point where they can seek solutions to problems of technological development and product innovation. For the research labs, the park is an environment for turning their know-how into products, processes, and innovative applications. In this environment, human skills and technological know-how play a leading role, while real estate, land, buildings, landscaped areas and large material infrastructures take a back seat.

Belice: Innovation in a Wine District of South Italy

The idea for a science park or innovation centre in the Belice valley 100 km south of Palermo, Sicily, was accompanied by a sense of unease. We had worked together with Andrea Tosi and Daniel Mercier to enrich the Parque Tecnologico de Andalucia in Malaga, but there the presence of a large technology park and the character of the Costa del Sol provided an extremely favourable environment. The same is true of Hania where the organization of a science park followed the successful development of the Technical University of Crete. However, on Sicily, and especially in the valley of Belice, it was only reasonable for us to be concerned about the character of a technopole in that location.

What could an environment of innovation synthesize in such a traditional area? Is there ground for innovation and internationalization in a landscape which over a long period has retained a tradition of closed local relations? Could methods for organizing an environment of innovation, which were tried and tested successfully, be used here? As is usually the case, expectations fall short of reality. What we encountered was much simpler, with the frugality and purity of what is real.

From the Straits of Messina, the road and railway line on a narrow strip of land beside the sea lead to Palermo; a Mediterranean, a Greek landscape. Palermo, princedom of the Italian south, is buzzing with life and dynamism, a continuation of the autonomous life of Italian cities. As Rafaelidis pointed out, following the death of Charlemagne three centres of power developed in Italy and formed pockets of German, French and Papal power, which left their mark on modern day Italy. These three powers through their many-sided forms of competition initially favoured multiple noblemen's estates, followed by principalities and then city-states which developed during the late Middle Ages and the Renaissance. The city-states escaped from the power of the German, Holy Roman emperors, the French kings and the leaders of the Church and developed into closed democracies, or rather, oligarchies. In response to the three powers spreading their influence across the peninsula, the city-states organized themselves along the lines of closed principalities, as closed associations of local interests. It was here that the idea of the 'closed community' first appeared as a political concept, a concept later promoted by Nicolo Machiavelli as a theory for political administration in order for a small, closed group headed by an intelligent and cunning leader to defend its interests (Rafaelidis 1996).

The town hall of Santa Margeritta is host to the first meeting and discussion on innovation and development of the area. The town hall is the restored summer palace of Giuseppe Tomasi di Lampedusa, prince of Sicily and author of The Leopard (*Il Gattopardo*), a personality famed for his critical stance to the up and coming bourgeoisie and from the film by Lucino Visconti bearing the same name and awarded the Golden Palm at Cannes.

From a methodological viewpoint, the terms in which the challenges and problems of the area are described are clear. On the one hand is the character and course of development in the region: the demography, structure of the gross regional product, composition of production, the character of farming, small industry, services, the quality characteristics of local development, the type of needs in terms of technology and innovation created. On the other hand are the available technological infrastructure, research and technology institutes installed here, technologies available, technology transfer and collaboration between bodies involved in research and production. In relation to these terms and the lag in technological development both in terms of use and the supply of technology, the issue of technopole arises, a technopole that would make best use of available resources and introduce innovation into basic sectors of production, organizations and enterprises in the area.

The Belice valley unites a series of small towns and communities; Santa Margeritta, Menfi, Montevago, and Sumbuca di Sicilia, with a population of 60,000 people who live off farming, small industry, and tourism. The most important activity is farming; the cultivation of cereals, olives, vines, prickly pears, an activity which involves one-third of the population. Small industry has grown up alongside farming together with an industry for processing agricultural produce, which employs 8 per cent of the population. The largest processing complexes are cooperatives and they process and promote agricultural produce from the area on the market. There are large cooperatives in the wine, oil and fruit processing and packaging sectors. In relation to services, the reference point is tourism. Tourist infrastructure (hotels, guest houses, apartments, restaurants, etc.) is concentrated in the area's urban centres and a few large units have been built outside the towns along the southern coastline of the island.

Thus, the two sectors that are at the core of the local productive system, are the production and processing of agricultural produce, and tourism. Both sectors are organized along very traditional lines. Wine, for example, is produced and packaged in large barrels, exported to northern Italy and then the same wine is imported in well-designed packaging with attractive names. However, a significant difference is that agricultural processing activities, due to the cooperative structures, are more well-knit and organized, compared with tourism where activities are scattered among many small units.

Technological infrastructure is almost non-existent. The University of Palermo has not developed activities connected with the development of

Belice. No agricultural or other research institutes have established themselves in the area. Just recently, a small IT training centre began operations with European funding. Cooperatives cover the gap in the provision of technology to the extent that they can. For example, the mushroom cooperative is attempting to introduce new cultivation methods in a controlled, rapid growth environment. And the wine cooperative provides technical support to growers, information, methods for combating diseases caused by parasites, production planning, promotion and marketing of products, training on how to use toxic chemicals, agricultural processing and environmental management.

In this environment the creation of a technopole is an exceptionally difficult exercise (Cappellin and Tosi 1993). We examined a series of alternative scenarios for forming the technopole which could not be adopted for three reasons: (1) there were no available sources of technology for endogenous formation of a technology cluster, (2) the creation of a technopole using exogenous procedures to attract technology had little likelihood of succeeding. Any high-tech organizations with a reason to establish themselves in the area would choose the metropolitan area of Palermo which has better access, infrastructure and a range of services, and (3) obtaining funding from European programmes was difficult since Sicily is marked by a large number of failed projects that were started but never finished.

Analysis of local potential and prospects showed that the most realistic scenario for the creation of a technopole was connected to the upgrading of existing agricultural produce processing activities. In this case technological innovation would focus on activities that already exist, regardless of their technological level, and does not foresee the creation of new high-tech sectors from businesses located in or attracted to the area.

We selected the Wine District formed by the respective cooperative and all interconnected activities involved in the primary sector, processing and trade in wine in the Belice valley, as the field for pilot implementation of this strategy (Tosi *et al.* 1998). The wine cooperative was selected as reference point and catalyser of the district since it is a dynamic organization with high active social participation.

The creation of a technopole with respect to the latent wine district was based on setting up three interconnected centres: a wine centre, an agricultural engineering centre, and a networking and technology transfer centre. These centres supplement and extend the technological presence of the cooperative, introduce new varieties for cultivation, transfer technological innovation in the making of wine, and develop and introduce new end products to the marketplace.

- The Wine Centre transfers the most up-to-date information on varieties, cultivation, winemaking, quality and consumer standards with the aim of moving the local wine production towards flexible and quality production. Best practice from the development of similar activities in Alsace and southern Europe provides models for the formation of such a centre.

- The Agricultural Engineering Centre aims to improve the equipment used in cultivating vines, and the making and bottling of wine. The centre will ensure a common infrastructure in tools and machinery not usually owned by small producers necessary for the transition to the production of many different small quantities.

- The Networking Centre aims to enrich productive cooperation relations. These collaborations may be local, directly with growers and winemakers. They may be at a regional level between growers, winemakers, university agricultural and wine analysis research labs. There may even be cooperative relations between producers and wine merchants at a national or international level.

This programme of three supplementary technology centres around the cooperative and its wine activities clearly makes reference to strategies used in industrial districts and for flexible specialization. The issue is the transition from a model where large quantities of wine at a standardized quality are made, to a model where small quantities of high-quality wine are made, which can be better incorporated into the marketplace and which can guarantee high prices for winemakers. For Italy, this route is the most common one for creating new technology-based clusters, particularly in the central regions of so-called Third Italy. In the Belice valley, the tradition of productive collaboration between vine growers, the cohesion of the Sezione Operativa di Menfi, and the wider tradition of a closed local community are parameters that may allow the model of variable and flexible collaborative relations between producers to take root.

Technology Poles in the Less Favoured Regions of Europe

The planning approach adopted in the technology park at Malaga, the science park at Hania and the wine district at Belice correspond to three distinct theories and strategies for technological development.

- In the first case, the formation of a technopole was based on attracting high-tech enterprises and organizations to a defined and planned area. Critical parameters are the general accessibility of the area, the level of response to criteria determining the mobility of foreign direct investments and the adequacy of the attraction policy (Ifo Institut 1989; European Commission 1994e; Giunta and Martinelli 1993).

- In the second case, the formation of a technopole is based on the activation of technology transfer mechanisms. In large part these mechanisms are intangible. They concern technological brokerage, demonstration of technology, the introduction of new products and production methods, dissemination of information and training in new technologies, and the financing of technological innovation (Komninos 1992b; Monck *et al.* 1988). Despite the small area of land taken up by a technopole of this nature, its sphere of influence may be extremely large and transcend local and regional boundaries.

- In the case of Belice, the technopole overlaps with a flexible specialization industrial district. In the district, dynamism arises from the ability of small producers to produce high-quality products, which are produced via variable (flexible) collaborative relations and joint production agreements (Amin 1989a; Mintzberg 1990; Pyke *et al.* 1990).

These three forms of technology park creation correspond to three major theories and practices for technological development, with respect to attraction procedures, technological diffusion procedures, and flexible specialization relations. It is important, however, to try to explain the factors behind this diversification of the procedures adopted for the formation of technopoles, in other words why it is that in Malaga an attraction strategy is prioritized, in Hania a strategy based on technology transfer and in Belice an approach based on flexible specialization principles.

This radical diversification of the procedures for establishing three technopoles has occurred in areas that share many common features. Andalusia, Crete, and Sicily are Objective 1 areas with GDP per head less than 75 per cent that of the European average. They are marked by traditional productive systems, industry concentrated in the foodstuffs, textiles and clothing sectors, with significant agricultural sectors and an expanding tourism sector.

Despite the similarities in terms of the level of development, productive structure and sectoral dualism, the three regions differ significantly in terms of available local technological supply. Table 3.2 codifies and ranks these resources into three categories: technological skills in high-tech enterprises, technological skills in universities and those in technology transfer centres.

The three regions are extremely unequal in terms of locally available technological resources. In Malaga, before the creation of the technology

Table 3.2 Malaga, Hania and Belice: Local technology resources

	Malaga	Hania	Belice
High-tech sector	+		
Universities and research institutes	+	+	
Technology transfer centres	+	+	+

park, there were already quite a few multinational firms (Fujitsu, Alcatel, etc.), some of which later relocated to the park. This demonstrates the ability of the area to attract branch plants of multinational companies, a fact on which the PTA strategy was based. By contrast, in the two other areas, either due to their island character or to their small local market, this ability was lacking. When a similar strategy was attempted at Hania, nothing was found to demonstrate that it was feasible, and it didn't work out. The presence of university and research facilities varies significantly from region to region. Both in Malaga and at Hania there are two new universities with engineering and exact science schools and labs with significant know-how. To this should be added the know-how of the sectoral research centres in operation in both areas. By contrast, in Belice the research infrastructure and the resultant local supply of technology is lacking.

The inequality in local sources of technology significantly influences the strategy selected for technological development. Both at Hania and in Belice a strategy of attracting high-tech enterprises and the creation of a new, exogenously led high-tech cluster had little likelihood of succeeding.

A second parameter, which is definitive in the choice of technological strategy, is the existing technology transfer structures. Table 3.3 codifies and ranks these structures into four categories: technology transfer via education and training, technology transfer via research consortia, via programmes and public policies on technology transfer, and via clusters and industrial districts.

The diversification of these structures increases or limits the feasibility of certain technological strategies. A development plan based on spin-offs, for example, cannot be implemented in an area where research relations do not breed business activities. Likewise, it is exceptionally difficult to activate technological integration relations outside industrial clusters and flexible specialization districts.

The parameters concerning local supply of technology and technology transfer capabilities are built into the productive history of each region. They operate restrictively, reject models and scenarios for technology formation, and orient planning choices. Their significance has been

Table 3.3 Malaga, Hania and Belice: Technology transfer structures

	Malaga	Hania	Belice
Technological education and training	+	+	
Research consortia	+	+	
Technology transfer programmes	+	+	+
Clusters and industrial districts			+

assessed in all methodologies for planning for technological development, such as economic background analysis, SWOT analysis, local supply and technology transfer analysis. As mentioned in the previous chapter, in a statistical analysis of the development of European technology parks, two basic factors influencing success were noted: the character of the region into which the park is to be integrated; and the technological/industrial orientation of the park (Komninos and Hatzipandelis 1992).

The conclusion we should stress is that the formation of technopoles in less-developed regions is highly determined by the existing technological environment and the local technology supply structure. The less technologically developed an area is, the more constraints there are and the fewer choices (Arufe and Prieto 1988; O'Farrel and Oakey 1993). The availability of local resources of technology development and technology transfer institutions strongly restricts the development of the technology poles, and this is little influenced by the funds available for the creation of the technopole. Regardless of how much money is dedicated to supporting a technopole, the conditions for the geographical mobility of technological investments, local technological integration relations, and the interface between research and production cannot be radically transformed. This does not seem feasible, at least in the medium term.

If these limitations are understood, the turn in technology development strategies observed today from focalized, as is the case of technopoles, to more integrated strategies of intervention, which deal with the overall local conditions for the supply and demand for technology, can be accounted for.

4 The Weak Link

Technology innovation is the process that leads from the idea of new products or processes to its successful commercialization. It is not the same, and should not be confused with Research and Development (R&D). Both concepts complement each other, but there is a great deal of innovation without R&D, and research is far from systematically leading to innovations. Innovation is often the result of combining existing technologies in a new product or process.

(European Commission, *Good Practice in Technology Transfer*)

Science and technology parks are recognized as important institutions and infrastructures for industrial innovation and technology transfer because of the interface they create between universities, R&D, and production activities. However, after two waves of technopolitan development in Europe (1969–73 and 1983–93) some major disadvantages in this technology transfer mechanism have become apparent.

This chapter starts with a critique of the innovation and technology transfer concepts that are associated with technopoles and science parks, characterized by highly localized and low institutionalized technology transfer practices. We discuss the lessons learnt from the technology transfer policy of the European Commission, in particular from the Strategic Programme for Innovation and Technology Transfer (SPRINT) and the technology transfer activities included in the R&D Framework Programmes. These experiences point towards new tools for research–industry communication and cooperation, which add to the spatial cluster of the technopole innovation diffusion mechanisms based on network structures and learning-led institutions. The recognition of the effectiveness of these tools for innovation support is gradually changing the nature and direction of technopolitan development. The emerging orientation is characterized by a change of focus from real estate and clustering priorities to institutional settings and soft actions with emphasis on business intelligence, technology skills, the financing of innovation, and the provision of advanced technology services.

Weaknesses of the Innovation Environment of Technopoles

More than 25 years of technopolitan development in Europe have contributed to the creation of a phenomenon with substantial dimensions and expectations. The first wave of science and technology park development occurred at the beginning of the 1970s (1969–73), and it was rather experimental. It concerned a small number of cases, the science parks of Cambridge and Heriot-Watt in Britain, Haasrode in Belgium and Sophia-Antipolis in France. These pilot projects appeared as spontaneous initiatives of the universities and private economic groups and searched for focal links between the universities and industries (Komninos and Sefertzi 1992; Muller 1985). A second wave started at the beginning of the 1980s, during which the phenomenon achieved importance with the creation of more than 100 science parks and technopoles in all the member states of the European Union. These parks were connected to the wider political and economic framework of restructuring towards flexible accumulation, the disintegration of productive activities, the rise of small businesses, and the new demands for R&D, innovation and producer services. Since then, the coordinated efforts of the public and private sectors in favour of an economic activity based on technology and learning, sustain science parks as serious instruments of innovation and industrial competitiveness.

In most of the technopoles created during the two waves above, the same components are more or less present. A number of innovative firms create an innovation pole capable of diffusing technology and know-how to the wider productive system around the park; research organizations establish an environment that is friendly to technology and innovation, and open to firms; consulting companies and technology intermediary organizations transfer technology and business services to both the small and the larger firm (Dalton 1992; Dunford 1992).

Science and technology parks vary significantly from one part of Europe to another. In the UK, Germany, the Netherlands, Belgium, and Greece a model of small 'incubator-led' parks predominates. These parks support new technology-based firms, on the levels of production, product development, and finance. By contrast, in France and Spain technology parks (technopoles) are larger and clearly declare their mission to change the entire productive system of that area, through the attraction of large high-tech companies and multinational R&D departments. This 'attraction-led' model acts as a catalyst and influences the location and housing of innovative firms in particular regions. In both models, science and technology parks appear as clusters of innovation and cooperation among R&D, industry and higher education, including networks and technology exchange practices that link research institutions, innovative companies, start-up firms, and suppliers.

Innovation and technology transfer activities constitute the essential part of science parks. Around these practices are set the population of the parks, consisting of R&D institutions, small and larger firms, infrastructure and supporting services. Technology transfer is realized through different forms of cooperation agreements and management practices, including:

- Agreements between firms and the universities, which assure: (1) the opening up of university infrastructures and research facilities to companies, (2) the flow of information and R&D results through common projects, personnel transfer, and day-to-day contacts, and (3) the support of spin-offs and the new ventures of scientists who wish to commercially exploit their research.

- Agreements between firms in the form of strategic alliances, producer–supplier relationships, marketing relationships, common R&D or product design projects, and new joint ventures, which resolve the usual difficulties that small firms face in production and marketing.

- Support for the creation and finance for technology-based start-ups. In the absence of affluent seed capital financing, many parks have organized seed and venture capital funds where the purpose is to support new start-ups that constitute an important channel for technology transfer and innovation.

Various claims were made for the benefits and positive effects of science parks in terms of new firm formation, encouraging university–industry links, and high-technology enterprise. In many cases, however, the technological dimension and the technology transfer mechanisms of the parks were proven to be inefficient (Massey *et al.* 1992; Massey and Wield 1992). Left to the vagaries of spatial proximity and the play of market forces, technology cooperation in planned technopoles had rather marginal effects, and technology transfer was neglected while other types of entrepreneurial activity were favoured. Three situations, inherent to the constituting concepts of science parks, contributed to the weakness of the technology character of science parks.

First is the emphasis on property and real estate management. An important part of the park's activity is to provide new high-quality and flexible buildings and spaces. This quality space attracts companies looking for brand name locations and premises, as well as the qualified employees of high-tech firms, and promotes the parks as centres of innovative activity and business excellence. Much of the park's management is related to property, to buy land and sell lots, to build and fill-up incubators, to manage the location of large companies, and to invest the profits from the increase in land value. In larger parks, the stake of property is more important and property management usually causes a neglect of technology resources and technology dissemination. In these parks, one might be tempted to evaluate their impact in narrow cost-per-job terms by comparing the scale of public investment with the number of jobs created in 'academic' businesses (Hennebery 1992).

The second reason is the emphasis on marketing and image strategies developed by the management in order to attract tenants. It was observed that a major motif for the location of firms was the high-tech image of the parks which attracts tenants independently of their real technological potential (Monck *et al.* 1988). In many cases, marketing and promotion strategies prevailed, although the local business environment was very poor in innovative activities, and the technology potential offered by the park very low (Technopolis International 1992; Komninos 1993).

The third reason for the neglect of technology transfer is the low institutional links between the parks and the higher education and research institutions. Universities have developed relatively few science parks, and many parks have been developed without a functional relationship to academic and research institutions. This considerably restrained the supply of technologies and innovation services that the parks were supposed to provide. As mentioned, the assessment of science parks in the diffusion of technological knowledge pointed out the moderate technological environment that many parks offer (Van Dierdonck *et al.* 1991; Van Dierdonck and Huysman 1992).

The orientations of science parks towards the physical accommodation and the attraction of innovative companies have diverted their function, and tend to transform them from technology-supporting mechanisms to property-intensive developments. The spatial and marketing issues prevailed, while technology transfer and the improvement of corporate practices were frequently neglected. The emphasis on space and physical infrastructures created a disproportion between the investments needed for the development of the parks and their real added value in the innovation and modernization processes.

A renewed focus on the technology and innovation issues is needed if science and technology parks wish to achieve their policy objectives and remain key elements in the regional technology infrastructure. Some new directions and solutions to this problem have been elaborated through the European Commission's innovation and technology transfer policies.

Good Practice in Science Park Planning

Since the 1980s and the early 1990s, the European Commission's technology transfer policy has opened new ways in the planning of innovation support infrastructures and services (European Commission 1995c). The major contribution came from the Strategic Programme for Innovation and Technology Transfer (SPRINT), while later technology transfer activities were clearly introduced into the 4th Framework Programme for Research and Technological Development. These programmes allowed for the accumulation of important experiences in technological cooperation and created generic tools for technology transfer and innovation diffusion.

SPRINT was the main European Community programme for technology transfer between 1984 and 1993. A first programme covered the period 1984–8, and a second the period 1989–93. SPRINT had three objectives:

- To facilitate the diffusion of new technologies to firms with the financing of specific projects for technology transfer, support for innovation financing by smaller firms, and inter-firm cooperation.

- To strengthen the European innovation and technology support services, including support for science park planning, innovation services, networks of technology and innovation specialists.

- To improve the awareness and understanding of innovation with the creation of the European Innovation Monitoring System, support for the exchange of knowledge and experiences between the member states.

The major achievement of the projects supported from SPRINT was the identification and opening of technology transfer routes to small businesses. Three basic technology transfer routes were identified: (1) the research to industry route, which can provide sophisticated new knowledge, (2) the inter-firm technology transfer route, based on sub- and co-contracting relationships, and (3) the technology licensing and related contractual forms of technology transfer. A second important achievement was the building of trans-European networks for cooperation and application of new technologies in sectors and regions where they are yet to be utilized. These networks aimed at promoting inter-firm cooperation and helping small businesses from different countries to trade technology, carry out joint R&D, to market complementary innovative products or to engage in cooperation in the fields of technology and innovation (European Commission 1994a). Since January 1995, SPRINT was included into the 4th Framework Programme for R&D, as part of the Third Activity devoted to the dissemination and exploitation of research results, technological development and demonstration.

In the field of technopoles, SPRINT introduced the Science Park Consultancy Scheme and the Science Park Evaluation Scheme. The first provided assistance towards the establishment of new science parks or the development of existing ones. The second helped the park promoters and managers to develop an evaluation methodology that they will implement as a guideline for the parks' development. Both schemes have contributed to the definition of best practices in science park management, in the sense

---

The 4th R&D Framework Programme
The programme was divided into four activities, which concern specific RTD projects, international cooperation, dissemination of RTD results, and training and mobility of researchers. The First Activity of the programme, which covered 87.3 per cent of the budget, was concerned with the development of generic technologies. Major projects funded were about information and communications technologies (28.2 per cent of the activity's budget), energy technologies (18.5 per cent), industrial technologies (16 per cent), biomedicine and biotechnologies (13.1 per cent), and environmental protection technologies (9 per cent). These choices reflected the technological needs of the European industries and services and linked directly the 4th Framework Programme to the European policy for industrial competitiveness. The Second Activity was concerned with international cooperation, having 4 per cent of the programme's budget. The Third Activity continued the VALUE and SPRINT experiences for the dissemination and exploitation of research results, with 2.5 per cent of the budget. Finally the Fourth Activity concerned the stimulation of training and mobility of researchers, with 6.2 per cent of the programme's budget (European Commission 1993a).

---

that they introduced credible evidence from independent experts, transferability of practices between regions and countries, feedback with users, and continuous improvement of the guidelines through successive funding cycles.

Table 4.1 describes the modules and topics of the planning approach. Background analysis is about the definition of weaknesses in the regional economy that the park should seek to address, and investigation of some of the key factors that will shape the project. The aim of the market analysis is to assess whether there is sufficient demand to justify the initiative in the specific locality and to define the scale of buildings and services for a short-term period. The strategy and the detailed development plan are to provide a blueprint for the launch and operation of the project, defining the role of each party involved in the process.

The Science Park Consultancy Scheme financed a large number of feasibility studies for the planning and development of science parks, research parks, technology parks, and business innovation centres, including multisite and non site-specific initiatives. Each planning approach was divided into two stages. The first stage involved a strategic analysis and was concerned with demonstrating that the park was needed and had a good chance of proceeding to successful implementation. The second stage was more operational and focused on the preparation of a detailed development plan.

The Science Park Evaluation Scheme was introduced later and was applied through the Innovation Programme that succeeded SPRINT. The

Table 4.1 Science park planning modules

BACKGROUND ANALYSIS
- Economic background
- Key organizations involved or competing with the initiative
- Available technology resources
- Local/regional property market
- Assessment of prospective sites for the initiative

MARKET ANALYSIS
- Assessment of market potential
- Definition of target market
- Market testing

OUTLINE STRATEGY
- Potential roles of the initiative
- Main strategic options
- Main elements of strategy
- Broad assessment of financial viability
- Organizations involved in strategy

DETAILED DEVELOPMENT PLAN
- Strategic focus
- Organization and management
- Property provision
- Services provision
- Networking provision
- Promotional plan
- Budget and funding plan
- Implementation plan

Source: European Commission (1991).

objective of the Commission was not to pass a value judgement on the parks, but provide the promoters with evaluation tools and help to review their initiatives after some years of development and refine the strategic objectives. The evaluation should take into account the viewpoints of the various stakeholders (promoters, companies, research centres, local and regional authorities), who might have different expectations from the growth and maturing of the parks.

The evaluation exercise was divided into two stages. The first stage was concerned with the definition of the objectives of the evaluation in close cooperation with the promoters or the management team, as well as the definition of the methodology to follow. The second stage was about the fieldwork needed to collect the data and the use of the results of the evaluation in order to define new objectives for the park or to correct invalid ones. Table 4.2 outlines the main modules of the evaluation methodology. These themes allow the understanding of interests of the various shareholders, as well as the factors that influence the fulfilment of the objectives of the parks.

Table 4.2 Science park evaluation modules

RELATIONSHIPS BETWEEN ACTORS
- The links between tenant companies
- The interactions between tenant companies and their environment (local, national and international). In particular, has the park facilitated the development of international links?
- The links between tenant companies and the local scientific and technological environment
- The motivation of local actors (existing, new or intensified cooperation, between universities and economic development agencies, local research and companies, etc.)

BUSINESS AND JOB CREATION
- Nature and number of businesses created on the park
- Nature and number of jobs created on the park
- Analysis of job qualifications compared with the local situation
- Nature and number of jobs created in relationship with the park

TECHNOLOGY TRANSFER
- Businesses created on the basis of technology transfer
- Number of research contracts in tenant companies
- Technology transfer between firms
- Attraction of technological resources on the park

SERVICES PROPOSED BY THE PARK TO TENANT COMPANIES
- Information
- Promotion
- Managerial support
- Business development
- Partner search
- Assistance in networking
- Technical support or facilities

IMAGE OF THE PARK AS RECEIVED BY
- Tenant companies
- Companies located in its catchment area
- Researchers and scientists
- Local government
- Bodies and companies located out of its catchment area

EXPECTATIONS OF THE STAKEHOLDERS IN THE DEVELOPMENT OF THE PARK
- Quality of the environment
- Existence of services
- Financial expectations
- Facilitation of networking
- Facilitation of business

Source: European Commission (1994d).

Looking at the guidelines and modules of science park planning and evaluation we realize the importance given to technology transfer and innovation support. It is upon these issues that the wider developmental role of the parks is constructed. For instance, in the description of the potential roles of science parks, the only alternative options mentioned are: (1) increasing the pace of innovation, (2) improving technology transfer, (3) improving technology diffusion, and (4) upgrading innovation, technology transfer and diffusion infrastructure. These roles are directly related to technology transfer and innovation diffusion (European Commission 1991). No other role is considered. The same concern is also reflected in the module of analysis of technological resources (assessment of the scope and quality of local technological sources, assessment of technology transfer infrastructure, specification of potential roles of key sources of technological expertise, investigation of spin-out activity), as well as in the evaluation modules concerning the relationships between the actors, technology transfer, and business services offered by the park (Table 4.2).

Though important and necessary, technology transfer and innovation support services cannot easily be customized and offered. Technology dissemination should not be confused with R&D, which is present in the parks with the R&D institutes, university research centres, and private company R&D departments. On the other hand, technology transfer is much more than helping companies to find licensed technology. It is a broad portfolio of services supporting all the stages of the technology acquisition process: strategic audit, technology evaluation, partner research, contract negotiation, and implementation consulting. The difficulty providing these services is about marketing. Have no illusions: commercial technology transfer services are hard to sell. Operating on a totally commercial basis requires a sophisticated approach. Public support is available in many circumstances, but it only covers part of the costs involved. In simple words, it seems much more difficult to develop commercially valid technology transfer and innovation services than pure R&D. There are, however, some tools and practices developed in the framework of the Science Park Consultancy Scheme that might contribute to this end.

Strengthening the Technology Dimension of Planned Technopoles

The experiences gained and the concepts developed by the SPRINT and INNOVATION programmes allow the improving of tools for technology transfer, research and industry cooperation, and innovation support. Among the technology and innovation dissemination tools that were tested, the most appropriate ones for strengthening the technology profile of planned technopoles seem to be innovation observatories, technology cooperation networks, centres for the provision of advanced technological services, and schemes for spin-off financing. The main shared feature of these tools is that they combine a market and an institutional dimension. They are market-led in the sense that they take into consideration the business needs and market trends in products, technologies, processes, and quality assurance topics: but in parallel they are institutionally sensitive as they take advantage of the opportunities of public support for business purposes (Komninos *et al.* 1996). The key issue for success is also the direct connection of innovation support instruments to corporate strategies and the technology needs of businesses.

Observatories for Innovation

A solid base for sound technological development is to raise the awareness of the organizations constituting a technology pole about the new economy, and to inform them about advanced production practices, R&D results, new products, technological capabilities, and policy frameworks. Various structures may be useful to this purpose, among others, innovation observatories, information centres, telematics networks, and online databases.

Such information mechanisms rely on a double interface. On the one hand, a unit for the selection of information on technology issues that interest companies and producers. It may cover both the supply of technological services by institutions of research and brokerage agencies, as well as the demand side for specific technologies, solutions, and technology providers. On the other hand, a unit for the dissemination of information to producers, the public administration, and the research community. This would cover a wide range of issues related to specific problems of companies, and the opportunities given by the policies and programmes for technological development, or the venture capital funds. It may include formal and informal procedures of communication, meetings, and other forms of information exchange. Additionally, the use of multimedia technologies and powerful bases for data storage and processing, permit the formation of user-friendly interfaces for online communication and information.

Two good examples of innovation-related observatories are the European Innovation Monitoring System (EIMS) and the patent information provided by the Organizations of Industrial Property. EIMS seeks to establish a knowledge base and to develop research capabilities on innovation. It encourages the exchange of knowledge and experience between the member states and the European Commission concerning innovation policies and innovation support measures, through: (1) the development of a network linking experts and research teams performing applied innovation research and surveys at a European level, (2) the systematic diffusion of results, studies, and surveys performed in the EU, and (3) the establishment of a permanent Community-wide data collection network for monitoring the innovation capabilities and performance of industries and regions.

Patent information is complementary. About a million patent documents are published every year in the 100 nations that have signed the 1883 Paris Convention for the Protection of Intellectual Property, which is the cornerstone of the modern patent system. Patent information may have a double role. It may provide inside information on existing competition, markets that might be exploited, starting points for R&D, and informed reviews to the state of the art in specific technologies. But it may also inform on solutions to specific problems and enable savings to be made on development costs by preventing duplication of existing research. No need to reinvent the wheel because of inefficient or a lack of targeted information (Derwent 1986).

Technology Transfer Networks

Technology transfer networks are another major instrument for effective technology transfer in science parks. Technology networks are built upon supplier–producer relations, regional agglomerations of firms, international strategic alliances in new technologies, consortia for technological cooperation, and specialists for long-term cooperation. The concept refers to a decomposable system in which the system is more than the sum of its interacting components, which means that there is synergy and multiplication effect from the interaction of the networks' members (Autio and Laamanen 1995; Cooke and Morgan 1991; Freeman 1990). Major issues for the technology networks concern the focus, the membership, and the services (Bianchi and Bellini 1991; Debresson and Amesse 1991).

Technology networks can be built on three different bases: to be focused on a sector-focus, on a technology, or on a combination.

- Sector-focused networks are very common and the narrow specialization of industrial sectors makes cooperation easier across a wide geographic area. Such networks may include companies, sectoral technical organizations, and specialized research institutions.

- Technology-focused networks tend to be closer to the state of the art in the area of expertise, but the lack of natural affiliation to particular industries makes the partnership more difficult. A usual base for technology-focused networks are the Community R&D Framework Programmes since they offer a breakdown of technologies and links to working groups, experts, research teams, and industrial applications.

- Mixed-focus networks combine the benefits of the previous types, the facility for industrial application and awareness of the state of the art of specific technologies.

For the membership, two different forms of technology cooperation may be distinguished: (1) technology exchange, where technologies pass from one member of the network to another, and (2) technology exploitation, where technological knowledge developed by research teams of the network is transferred to firms. So, networks may include firms, private consultants (including technology brokers, management consultants, consulting engineers, industrial property consultants, patent attorneys), research and technical organizations (contract research organizations and sectoral technical centres), and public and non-profit organizations, such as regional development organizations, chambers of commerce and industry.

Technology transfer networks may offer a wide portfolio of services. Apart from information transfer, broad service categories include technology transfer, skills transfer, and specialist support (Table 4.3).

The choices made on the focus, the membership, and the services of the network set the initial framework for its management: the internal cooperation and alliance, the leadership, the procedures and rules of management, the conflict and under-performance resolve, the creation of new markets based on synergy, and the long-term perspectives.

Centres of Advanced Technological Services

A wide range of specialized technology applications and services are increasingly demanded by companies that cannot provide them internally; but often the local market does not contain specialized companies offering such services (Britton 1989). This is a gap to be filled by the technology park. These services primarily concern production and research services, like new product development, multimedia for product promotion, CAD-CAM, modelling and rapid prototyping, software and computational tools, and various types of laboratory analysis, including destructive and non-destructive analysis, chemical analysis, laser and opto-electronics analysis, and other measurements for quality testing and certification.

Table 4.3 Services provided by technology transfer networks

Technology transfer	Skills transfer	Specialist support
■ Technology brokerage	■ Training and education	■ Financial advice, market research
■ Licensing in, licensing out	■ Recruitment	■ Technology application and management
■ R&D and technology audits	■ Skill search	■ Demonstration
■ Research for products and processes	■ University–industry liaison	■ Product evaluation, patent
	■ Location of R&D resources	■ Intellectual property advice

Source: European Commission (1994a).

Fieldwork data from technology surveys and audits in different EU regions show that most demanded services fall into three categories. In order of importance, first is the demand for services related to quality and certification, which is increasingly important for the competitive presence of products on the European and international markets. Following this, is a demand for specialized business services such as the technological evaluation of new products (analyses of technology-based inventions, technical feasibility, market research), the protection of intellectual property (patents, model protection, registration of trademark, licensing, royalties), the design of development plans (business plan preparation, building and testing of prototypes, user questionnaires and product improvement), and marketing (choice of marketing route, establish a new venture/find a partner, licensing, design of marketing strategy). Third, there is an increasing demand for information technology applications in the area of marketing, e-commerce, product promotion, web design and other related information technology applications and platforms. These services are linked to technologies that have become very important in contemporary production and management practices, such as automation, quality marks and certification, energy saving, environmental protection, and information technologies for business purposes. They have a direct impact on upgrading the technological level of companies and the improvement of competitiveness.

In many regions, consulting companies do not have the technological expertise and infrastructure to cover this demand. However, if the market fails to offer advances in technology services for business purposes, then various organizations and centres may fill the gap, belonging mainly to the public and semi-public sector. This is good for the region, but also good for the science parks, which may recognize this opportunity to develop a portfolio of services, targeted upon emerging company technology needs.

Innovation Financing

In science and technology parks, innovation financing stems from the need to encourage spin-offs and new business start-ups. It is true that bankers and financiers have misunderstood the logic of technology-based and innovative companies. Their characteristics differ markedly from those of more traditional businesses and this has led to a serious gap between businesses and financing institutions (European Commission 1995a). When it comes to providing start-up and initial expansion financing for small-scale projects, the more conventional financing tools are ill-suited to companies' needs or only partially able to satisfy them. There are, however, some tools specifically designed to provide equity capital, which increases the chance of long-term survival. The European Seed Capital Fund Network (ESCFN), for instance, is a source of experience and good practice on the functioning of funds appropriate to technology-based, small companies. This is a pilot scheme of the European Commission, having an overall objective to foster enterprise creation (and employment) in the Community by strengthening the financing opportunities available to new businesses. ESCFN supports a number of newly created funds, provided that they agree to make their investment in start-up or early stage businesses. Some funds, if located in specific areas, may also benefit from a contribution to the funds available for investment (European Commission 1993b).

Typical components of a fund targeted on spin-offs and new high-tech companies include the fund itself, and accompanying measures for technology assessment and promotion. The making of such a funding scheme includes:

- To create the fund on an equity basis, probably in cooperation with existing financial institutions or banks. Alternatively, it is possible to create a separate finance line into an established venture capital fund.

- To set an appraisal unit for innovative projects. What is needed is a methodology for evaluating the risks and the technical feasibility of proposals with respect to the market environment in which the new products will operate. Such appraisals may also consider the management, marketing, and technical skills of the business, and make use of external technology and marketing experts.

- To inform small companies and spin-off potential creators on the financial capabilities of the scheme, and the comparative advantages vis-à-vis traditional financing tools.

- To design exit routes, always in cooperation with the financial institution or bank involved, for withdrawal from the individual project via the financial route, the industrial route, the selling of the stake to the investee company, and other.

Science and technology parks have been started by universities wishing to exploit commercially their research through the proximity and provision of physical accommodation to technology-based firms. The activity of high-tech firms, as well as start-ups in new industrial activities, have produced needs for new types of spaces, the chief characteristics of which are flexibility, quality, and information technology infrastructure. In turn, the agglomeration of high-tech companies in science parks created poles of technological capability and diffused innovation around their location (Miège 1992).

However, the spread of new effective tools for technology transfer, based on networks, institutions, and services, questions the established character of technopolitan development. The novel feature of these tools is that they operate without property or spatially polarized dimensions, based mainly on institutions, networks, and information technology infrastructure. A new post-technopolitan profile is emerging, in which the functions of science and technology parks may be decentralized in many parts of a local productive system and the spatial aspects of technopoles may become less important.

Indicative of such trends is that more and more technology transfer initiatives, based on technology networks, observatories, and centres for advanced technological services, are developed out of science and technology parks. This multiplication of technology transfer initiatives involves a great number of social actors at the local, regional, national, sectoral, and associative levels. The consciousness of the role of innovation in the defence of jobs and income has increased the demand for technology intermediaries to be included in local and regional development programmes. On the other hand, many universities created new tools for technology transfer and information diffusion (industrial liaison offices, career advisory units, technology information centres) without any formal reference to technopolitan structures. They take the form of networks and institutions supporting the university–industry cooperation and are placed under the usual university administration and decision-making structure.

From the multiplication and spread of non-spatial tools for university–industry cooperation, new technopolitan designs are emerging. The technology transfer environment has deepened, leaving behind the isolated technology park, at the outskirts of the city, as the unique technology intermediary. In the new innovation environment, composed of many players and multiple initiatives, the real issue is the establishment of networks and 'command centres' that assure coordination of the various technology initiatives and avoid duplication and waste of effort.

Property and marketing-led technopoles enter into a process of transformation, as they are incorporated into a multi-centre and multi-level research–production interface. The strengths of this post-technopolitan interface rest in the multiplicity of the tools for technology transfer that it contains, which do not rely on heavy and costly infrastructure, nor on the size of the cluster of innovative firms. Networks and information channels do not presuppose the spatial proximity of the participating members, but open their linking capacity over larger geographical scales. It seems that these solutions to technology transfer may give convincing answers to the technology inefficiency of established technopolitan agglomerations and the constraints of technology transfer based exclusively on spatial proximity.

Part II

Innovating Regions

Innovation as an Institution

5 Regional Innovation Strategies in Europe

Then there is the term 'system'. Although to some the word connotes something that is consciously designed and built, this is far from the orientation here. Rather, the concept is of a set of institutions whose interactions determine the innovative performance of national firms. There is no presumption that the system was, in some sense, consciously designed, or even that the set of institutions involved works together smoothly and coherently. Rather, the 'systems' concept is that of a set of institutional actors that, together, play the major role in influencing innovative performance. The broad concept of innovation that we have adopted has forced us to consider much more than simply the actors doing research and development.

(R. Nelson, *National Innovation Systems*)

Innovating Regions: A Radiant European Strategy

The *Green Paper on Innovation* points out that over the past ten years Europe has devoted most of its efforts to increases in productivity. However, these increases can be negated if they are used in conjunction with a technology that is obsolete or obsolescent. Innovation must be the driving force behind the entire business policy, both downstream and upstream of the actual production of goods and services. European firms and governments should therefore re-deploy their efforts, improve their capability to translate into commercial successes and better fund intangible investments, which are a deciding factor for the future of competitiveness, growth and employment (European Commission 1996a).

Innovation is a key issue for the real convergence and cohesion of the European regions. To bridge the development gap, the less favoured regions (LFRs) should intensify their efforts in technological development and the creation of new knowledge, and enrich their production tissue with capabilities found in universities and research centres. The challenge is not to imitate what the most advanced regions have achieved, but to invent new trajectories for a creative integration into a knowledge-driven economy of global dimensions.

Against this background, at the beginning of the 1990s, the European

Commission introduced a new family of policy schemes with a strategic view over technology and innovation at the regional level. Regional Innovation and Technology Transfer Strategies and Infrastructures (RITTS), Regional Technology Plans (RTP), and Regional Innovation Strategies (RIS) provide co-finance and guidance to regional governments to undertake an assessment of their regional innovation potential, and define strategies that promote the cooperation and capabilities of the small firm sector, the research and technology community, and the public authorities. A comprehensive appraisal of these policies to European regional cohesion is yet to come, but we argue that their success is depending on the institutional thickness of the regions in the field of technology and innovation, and the capability to match regional technology supply and demand. Given that in many LFRs, technology and innovation supply and demand are extremely latent, one of the main challenges of regional innovation strategies is to transform the latent demand into an active demand. This objective is, however, linked to a radical change of the respective regional systems of innovation.

A major contribution to innovation and technological development at the regional level came from the European regional policy and the Innovative Actions of the European Regional Development Fund. Regional Technology Plans, later renamed Regional Innovation Strategies, are initiatives aiming to enhance the synergy between technological development and cohesion policy. The Directorate General responsible for the regional policy (REGIO) manages them, and Mikel Landabaso and Guy Durand had leading roles in the formulation of this policy. In 1994, eight RTP were launched in Objective 1 and 2 regions, in 1997, 19 new RIS were started, and in 1999 about 20 more (European Commission 1994b). Overall, DG REGIO introduced more than 60 initiatives related to regional innovation strategies, including the continuation of some regional projects with RIS+ exercises.

The first pilot projects, which forged the profile of the policy, have been launched in four regions of northern Europe, Leipzig-Halle-Dessau (Germany), Limburg (The Netherlands), Lorraine (France), and Wales (the UK), and one year later four less favoured regions joined the programme, Abruzzo (Italy), Castilla y Leon (Spain), Central Macedonia (Greece), and Norte (Portugal). Typical deliverables of the RTPs/RIS were: (1) the description of strengths and weaknesses of the regional innovation system, both on the supply and demand sides, (2) the definition of a plan for regional technological development based on the consensus of the main actors in the public and private sector, to be implemented through the Community Support Framework, Community initiatives, and other investments from the public and the private sector, (3) the organization of a system for continuous monitoring and evaluation of innovation and the new economy at the regional level, and (4) the exchange of experience and best practices with the regions participating in the EU RIS network. The management of an RIS is based upon two local bodies: a Steering Committee and a Management Unit supported by a process consultant. The Steering Committee, composed of representatives from the public and private sectors, the universities and other research institutions, has the political leadership of the whole operation and guarantees a regional consensus among the actors involved. The Management Unit assures the day-to-day work of the project, launches the necessary studies, and supports scientifically and technically the orientations from the Steering Committee (European Commission 1994a; Landabaso 1995). After the period of preparation, which lasts about 18 to 24 months, the strategy is implemented with the contribution and support of the mainstream structural funds. The link between the RTP/RIS and the structural funds is crucial since it actualizes a large-scale implementation and the mobilization of financial, administrative, and human resources for the application of the RIS action plans.

In parallel, support to innovation and technology diffusion at the regional level was given by the actions of the R&D Framework Programmes, the specific programmes targeting on technology dissemination (SPRINT, VALUE), the Community Support Frameworks, and the Community Initiatives designed to encourage R&D in peripheral regions (STRIDE, SME). A major step was made under the SPRINT Programme with the Consultancy Scheme for Regional Innovation and Technology Transfer Strategies and Infrastructures (RITTS), managed by DG XIII, which was later included into the Innovation Programme of the 4th R&D Framework Programme. The scheme was aimed at regional governments and associated regional development organizations wishing to improve or change the focus of infrastructures and services for innovation and technology transfer. It covered a wide part of the Community, not just Objective 1 or 2 regions, and it had a trans-national dimension in order to encourage the spread of best practices. On the methodological level, each assignment was divided into three stages. The first stage was concerned with the strategy's organizational structure, and the creation of the managing and guidance bodies: the Steering Committee, the management unit, the advisory/expert teams, and the participation of end-users. The second stage was concerned with the strengths and weaknesses of the regional economy, drawing up an inventory to define infrastructure support elements, business needs for R&D, and types of possible public intervention. The third stage was concerned with the elaboration of a strategy for regional innovation, the implementation of the action plan, and follow-up mechanisms (European Commission 1994a).

At the first two calls of the RITTS, 42 EU regions were supported, and the call in 2001 allowed for the participation of regions from the Newly Associated Countries. Achievements of the RITTS schemes were at various levels. There was creation of new knowledge on the functioning of regional innovation systems with reference to the needs of small businesses; there was a re-organization of the innovation and technology transfer infrastructure, with the design and implementation of new projects; there was an enhancement of the institutional capacity to build consensus and raising of innovation awareness; finally the RITTS contributed to monitoring and evaluation with instruments, and the dissemination of best practice through benchmarking and inter-regional learning (CURDS and MERIT 2000).

RTP/RIS/RITTS are constructed upon a number of specifications to assure their distinctive regional and technological character (European Commission 1994b). They are built upon:

- A *bottom-up approach*, giving emphasis on the regional technology demand.

- A *regional approach*, focusing on the development of a territorial entity on the basis of a consensus between the government, the private sector, the universities, and the research centres.

- A *strategic approach*, combining the analysis of the regional technological development and the definition of long-term priorities and short-term actions.

- An *integrated approach*, linking the efforts of the public and private sectors towards the common goal of increasing regional productivity and competitiveness.

- An *international approach*, considering the global market trends and enhancing international technology and economic cooperation.

The rationale behind the RIS movement (RTP, RITTS, RIS, RIS+) is about regional technological cohesion and closing the technology gap between the EU regions. In fact, both RIS and RITTS seek to sustain the endogenous technological development of the European regions: to improve the capability of regional actors to design policies that correspond to the real needs of the productive sector and the strengths of the local scientific community, and to support local consensus among the public authorities, the private sector, and the universities about the character of technological development of the region.

This is clearly acknowledged in the *Fifth Periodic Report on the Social and Economic Situation of the Regions in the European Community*, which was published a few months after the introduction of the first Regional Technology Plans. One of the new elements of this report was the view that many of the causes of EU regional disparities in economic development may be traced to disparities in productivity and competitiveness. In turn, regional productivity and competitiveness were considered as

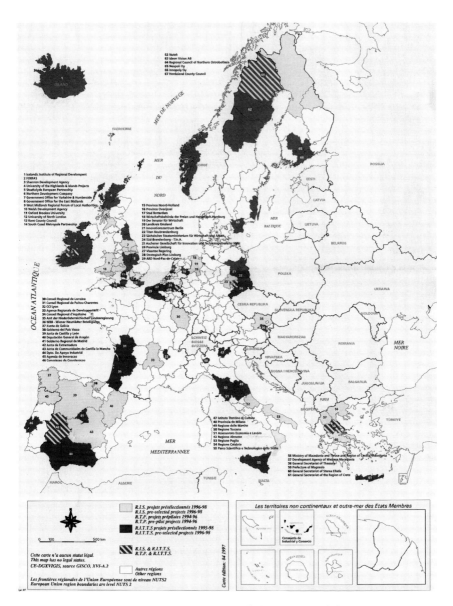

Map 5.1 Regional innovation strategies of the ERDF and the Innovation Programme

dependent variables of the capacity of regional firms to innovate the production process, to introduce new products in the early stages of their cycle, to lower costs through innovations in logistics, and to increase market adaptability.[1] Innovation and intellectual property were defined as the strongest drivers of competitive achievement. The report insists on the statistical links between, on the one hand, R&D, technology capability, intellectual property, and innovation, and on the other hand, a rising market share, growing added value and jobs creation.

Although innovation has become a key issue for the wealth and prosperity of the regions, analytical quantitative data have established that the geographical distribution of technological and innovative effort in the European Union is extremely unequal. Many of the factors sustaining innovation, such as research and technological development (RTD), availability of scientific personnel, and technology infrastructure, are unevenly distributed between EU regions. Table 5.1 indicates that regional disparities in factors of innovation (RTD, BERD, R&D scientists, patents) are far more important than disparities in development, GDP, and unemployment.

- The Community's four weakest members (Greece, Portugal, Spain, and Ireland) have R&D expenditure levels that are two to three times lower than the Community average. The gap in terms of regional product per head is 1 to 2.5, while in terms of R&D expenditure it is much higher at 1 to 6.

- Business expenditure for R&D in Greece and Portugal is one-tenth of the Community average, and 15 to 20 times lower than that of France and Germany. State expenditure for R&D in the same southern countries is one-quarter of the Community average.

- R&D personnel in Greece, Portugal, and Spain number only one-quarter to one-tenth of the same personnel in the more advanced states, and one-third of the Community's average.

The above disparities are accentuated by the fact that inside the member states, R&D activities are concentrated in just a few areas around capital cities and metropolitan areas. Resources for research and development, the large research institutes, the engineers and scientists that work in research are located in a small number of regions, the so-called *Islands of Innovation*, such as London, Paris, Stuttgart, Munich, Lyon, Grenoble, Toulouse, Turin, and Milan. On Europe's fringes, the scant technology resources are found mainly in the national capitals and the large metropolitan centres. In Spain, Greece, and Portugal, 60–90 per cent of all public and private spending on R&D occurs in Madrid, Athens, and Lisbon respectively (European Commission 1999b).

The regional technology and innovation gap, measured by regional disparities in R&D, innovation financing, scientific personnel, and technology infrastructure, is far more important than the 'cohesion gap' between core and less developed regions of the Union. The technology gap is important both in quantitative terms, and in terms of effects on regional convergence because it has a catalytic role to feed and enlarge the development gap. This becomes critical given the existing arrangements for public assistance

Table 5.1 Regional technology gap in the European Union

	LOW				HIGH				EUR (15)
	GR	P	ES	IRL	DK	NL	FR	D	
GDP per head (1995)	66	67	77	93	116	107	108	111	100
Unemployment % (1997)	9.6	4.4	21.1	10.1	5.7	5.2	12	9.8	10.7
GERD as % of GDP (1995)	25	31	42	73	93	106	122	119	100
BERD as % of GDP (1995)	11	10	30	81	90	89	118	124	100
Government RTD as % of budget (1994)	0.57	1.76	1.90	0.86	1.58	2.65	4.61	3.71	2.88
RTD personnel as % of the labour force (1995)	15	27	35	88	153	98	133	137	100
Patent applications per million of population (1995)	4	2	12	37	120	117	96	120	93

GDP: Gross Domestic Product.
GERD: Gross Expenditure in Research and Development.
BERD: Business Expenditure in Research and Development.
Source: European Commission (1999a and b).

that are tending to increase rather than reduce the technology gap between more advanced and less favoured regions (Landabaso 1995).

A Pilot Project: The Regional Technology Plan of Central Macedonia

The Central Macedonia Regional Technology Plan was a pilot project undertaken as a precursor to RIS exercises. From this point of view, its objective was twofold: on the one hand to enhance innovation and regional competitiveness and to enable the industry of Central Macedonia to work at the best practice level and, on the other hand, to elaborate methodologies and planning tools appropriate for the wider movement of EU regional innovation strategies. These objectives have focused the RTP, both in terms of analysis and actions, on the regional innovation system of Central Macedonia, composed of institutions that drive technological development in the region and linking R&D, education and training with the technology and innovation needs of enterprises.

The regional innovation strategy in Central Macedonia was developed in five stages, as illustrated in Table 5.2. *Setting up the Plan* included the methodological, institutional, and organizational structure of the RTP.

Table 5.2 Stages and tasks of the Central Macedonia RTP

	II. REGIONAL INNOVATION SYSTEM IN CENTRAL MACEDONIA ■ Productive system and competitiveness in Central Macedonia ■ Application of horizontal technologies in the region ■ Analysis of regional technology demand ■ Analysis of regional technology supply ■ Analysis of regional technology transfer
I. SETTING-UP THE PLAN ■ RTP concept ■ Objectives ■ Method and working programme ■ Steering Committee ■ Management Unit	III. ELABORATION OF REGIONAL INNOVATION STRATEGY ■ Strategic orientations and priorities ■ Investigation on projects ■ Technology demand and selection of projects
	IV. ACTION PLAN ■ RTP strategy ■ RTP projects
	V. IMPLEMENTATION ■ Implementation framework ■ Feasibility studies and project's implementation ■ Monitoring and evaluation: the RTP Observatory

The *Regional Innovation System* analysis focused on the productive system of Central Macedonia and the technology demand, technology supply, and technology transfer in the region. The *Elaboration of Regional Innovation Strategy* dealt with the formulation of a strategy, which exploited the conclusions of the analytical approaches in order to identify and formulate problems and deficiencies, and to define an intervention on the level of the regional innovation system. The *Action Plan* codified the conclusions drawn from the strategy and attempted to create an innovation-friendly environment supporting all innovation-related organizations in the region. Finally, *Implementation* examined the ways the regional innovation strategy could be interwoven with the Community Support Framework and some relevant Community Initiatives that constitute principal financial sources for implementation of the RTP (Kafkalas and Komninos 1999; Komninos 1998).

The RTP corresponded to a collective effort to support technological innovation in this region. It started from the Aristotle University of Thessaloniki and united all the regional bodies that promote applied research, cooperation between research and industry, technology transfer, human technology skills and entrepreneurial capabilities. The plan opened a window on to intra-regional cooperation. Reaching consensus was an ongoing concern and implied a participatory planning process, from setting up the work programme to the definition of strategy, priorities and the selection of projects. Preparation of the plan lasted for two years and more than 200 scientists, public officials and businessmen participated in the drafting.

Setting Up the Regional Technology Plan

The RTP was built upon previous experiences of the R&D Framework Programmes targeting on technology dissemination, and the Community Initiatives designed to encourage R&D and innovation in peripheral regions. The starting point was a set of objectives found in most technology planning approaches: (1) the understanding of the technological trajectory of the region and the outline of strengths and weaknesses of the regional innovation system, (2) the agreement between the principal regional actors in the government, the company system, the workers' organizations, and the universities, on the priorities for regional technological development, (3) the selection of actions sustaining technology and innovation in the region, (4) the design of an effective implementation framework, and (5) the setting up of a monitoring system to evaluate the effects of the plan on regional innovation and competitiveness.

The first pillar of the RTP was to target the plan on the Community's regional policy, and the Structural Funds in particular. This concern was not a rigid constraint of the RTP/RIS concept, but came out of the development situation in Greece and Central Macedonia. At that time, the process of Economic and Monetary Union and the intense effort of the country to meet the targets of the Maastricht Treaty channelled most public and private investments into the Structural Funds and the Community Support Framework. The principal concern was to make correct use of these resources, to sustain projects with major multiplication impact, and to coordinate the public and private initiatives for modernization and convergence. Targeting on the structural funds and the EU's regional policy was a major political choice of the Central Macedonia RTP.

The second pillar and major working assumption was to trigger a process of company improvement and to enable regional industry to work at best practice level with respect to technologies relevant to it, to enhance the emergence and growth of new industrial branches, and to promote international technology cooperation and competitiveness to international markets (Figure 5.1). A logical consequence, from the learning region theory point of view, was to focus the exercise on the regional innovation system. This system makes up part of the productive tissue of the region and the established mix of activities, inter-firm linkages, and institutional regulation. Driving technology to companies and intermediary organizations in the region, the regional innovation system creates the friendly environment and necessary conditions for innovation.

Focusing the plan on the regional innovation system was the principal methodological choice. The rest of the method was based on usual plan-

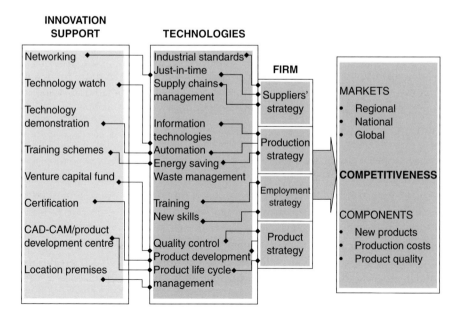

Figure 5.1 RTP-induced improvement process

ning approaches, such as the articulation of analysis and strategy, the specification of strategy into projects, the investigation of the implementation framework, and the organization of monitoring and evaluation.

A third pillar in the overall decision-making process was the effort to create a broad base of regional support for the RTP. Coordination and consensus activities included meetings of the Steering Committee, and workshops organized at the prefectures of the region, and in the industries of food and beverage, textile and clothing, chemicals, and intermediary products. To increase the motivation of the parties involved in the planning process, the RTP tried to assure their participation in the implementation and evaluation. After the period of preparation, a promotion committee was established to assure a permanent link with the regional operational programme and the structural funds. The general support expressed for the RTP justified these orientations and indicated a growing interest in its promotion and implementation. As the evaluation report points out:

The whole planning process of the Central Macedonian RTP can be considered as a success story, though a very peculiar one. The merit of the project is that it introduced a voluntary planning process in a region where there was neither the culture, nor the will to do so and where the national approach to regional coordination was not mature. Through a rather 'unorthodox' alliance of a university and a ministry that exceeded (if strictly defined) its task assignment, a gap could be filled. 'Unorthodox' in this context denotes two issues: (1) The Regional Authority considered the ministry as taking responsibilities that actually belonged to the Regional Authority, (2) The university took a much more pro-active role than what is usually the case in the RTP/RIS/RITTS process. But as the outcome was positive and (one may observe the establishment of a culture of regional planning and consensus building – reinforced by the RTP/IRIS cooperation – in a previously completely virgin ground) the lack of 'orthodoxy' only demonstrates again that diversity in Europe requires different practices for good solutions and it is beyond any doubt that in Central Macedonia there would have been no RTP, if the orthodox model was pursued.

(Technopolis 1998)

In practical terms, two bodies, the Steering Committee and the Management Unit, managed the RTP. The Steering Committee was composed of 16 representatives from the public sector (five members), the private sector (six members) and the scientific institutions (five members), and was responsible for the political orientation of the plan, ensuring an agreement on the major decisions. The Management Unit provided scientific expertise and support for the policy guidelines of the plan and introduced proposals to the Steering Committee. It was composed of four persons from the Department of Urban and Regional Planning, the Aristotle University of Thessaloniki, and the Department of European Programmes of the Ministry of Macedonia-Thrace. The work of the Management Unit was

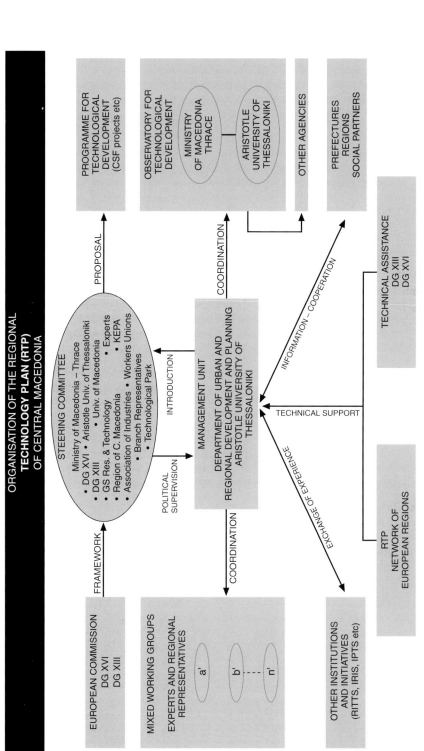

Figure 5.2 RTP decision-making structure

supported by a large number of external working groups, which provided scientific expertise and analysis on issues related to regional development, technology demand and supply, technology transfer, and planning for innovation infrastructure.

The Innovation System in Central Macedonia, Greece

Central Macedonia, the major industrial centre of northern Greece, is a prosperous region with a dynamic and specialist workforce. It has quality transport and communication networks, and occupies a strategic position within the European Union as it is bordered to the north by the Balkan States and is in close proximity to Eastern Europe. Thessaloniki is the second largest city in Greece and home to numerous national and international organizations. The region, which is divided into seven prefectures – Halkidiki, Imathia, Kilkis, Pella, Pieria, Serres and Thessaloniki – has a total population of approximately 1.7 million, and represents a good opportunity for investors.

This region boasts over 27,000 manufacturing companies, most of which are small, working in a wide range of industries including food and drink, clothing and footwear, and furniture. Larger companies are involved in textiles, metal production, chemicals, and plastics. Agriculture provides the largest job market for all the prefectures with the exception of Thessaloniki, which is dominated by the service sector. Emerging industries throughout the area are also service-related, and include medicine and health services, software, international retail chains, business services, and tourism. Central Macedonia has a strong, higher-education and research base and includes the Aristotle University of Thessaloniki, which is the largest university in Greece, the University of Macedonia, two technical educational institutes and the Thessaloniki Technology Park.

Table 5.3 tabulates some comparative figures for population, employment, and GDP. The region is compared with the whole country, and

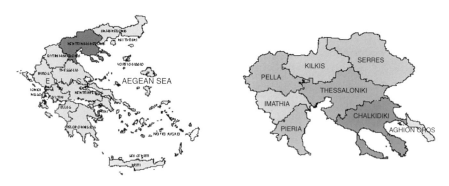

Map 5.2 The region of Central Macedonia, Greece

Table 5.3 The region of Central Macedonia in figures

	Greece	Central Macedonia	% in Greece
Surface area (hectares)*	13,195,743	1,914,616	14.5
Population*	10,259,900	1,710,513	16.7
Total	*100*	*100*	
Active population	3,886,157	675,288	17.4
	37.9	*39.5*	
Employment†	3,853,000	623,909	17.5
Total	*100*	*100*	
Primary sector	765,000	136,000	18.0
	19.8	*19.5*	
Secondary sector	866,000	178,000	21.0
	22.5	*25.6*	
Tertiary sector	2,223,000	381,000	17.0
	57.7	*54.8*	
GDP (million GDR)‡	14,422,533	2,326,649	16.1
Total	(68% EU, 1996)	(67% EU, 1996)	
	100	*100*	
Primary sector	1,982,789	393,747	19.9
	13.7	*16.9*	
Secondary sector	3,714,774	640,966	17.3
	25.8	*27.5*	
Tertiary sector	8,724,970	1,291,936	14.8
	60.5	*55.5*	

* National Statistical Service of Greece (NSSG), Population Census 1991.
† EC, 6th periodic report for the European regions (1996).
‡ NSSG, National Accounts, current prices, million GRDs, estimations 1993.

certain basic figures are also given for the Prefecture of Thessaloniki, the second most important urban centre in Greece after Athens. Its importance is due to the fact that it is a transport hub, that most of the region's industrial activity is concentrated there, and that its port and airport handle a substantial percentage of the country's imports and exports. The area immediately surrounding the city contains most of the region's manufacturing and processing industry, whereas banking, commerce and services are concentrated in the city centre.

Understanding the innovation system in Central Macedonia was a central issue at this stage of the RTP process. In contrast to a long-standing tradition of technology planning emphasizing the supply side, in the assumption that industry would adapt to improved technology supply, the RTP was highly determined by a demand-led perspective, which defined both the strategic priorities and the selection of projects. The regional innovation system was analysed from four different angles, concerning the spread and application of generic technologies, the regional technology demand, the endogenous regional technology development, and the transfer of technology. Understanding the regional innovation system is not just to present a series of indicators on R&D and technology performance,[2] but also to go deeper into the structure and processes of technology offer, exchange, and use.

Regional technology demand was examined through a multilevel survey based on questionnaires, audits, and experts' reports, which outlined the technology needs of firms. Technology objectives and requirements of the surveyed firms clearly state the needs for product improvement (through the purchase of new equipment, implementation of new technologies, installation of automation systems, better materials), development of new products (via new technologies in accordance with market requirements), and improved quality control procedures by the addition of supplementary equipment and trained personnel. The high cost and the limited innovation funding available to companies hinder modernization and innovation in these fields.

Most companies surveyed placed great weight on producing quality products to meet market demands. Suggested ways of improving quality include automation and certification of production processes. A certain number of companies have already been awarded certification (mainly under ISO 9002), or are in the process of doing so. In fact, certification is one of the major company trends for the future. Most large companies already apply or are prepared to apply Total Quality Management procedures, which reflect the industry's realization of the importance of the human factor in the production of quality products.

The audits show also a clear need for qualified middle management, especially in the prefectures other than Thessaloniki. In certain sectors (textiles, non-metallic minerals) there is a tremendous need for middle-level and qualified staff, such as foremen and qualified technicians, who are usually trained on the job rather than in technical schools.

Supplementary information on the regional technology needs was made available from an extended survey through a questionnaire. This survey was based on a directory of 1,900 businesses, which is 92 per cent of the total number of businesses having more than 10 employees in Central Macedonia. The data gathered includes information on the location of the firm, number of employees, turnover, and industrial sector, as well as figures from the annual accounts and other quantitative indicators (current assets, net worth, gross income, investments, etc.). This survey allowed the description of the use and need for more specific technologies and innovation services, such as: (1) industrial information technologies, (2) automation, (3) quality control, (4) anti-pollution technologies, (5) agro-technologies, (6) funding for modernization, (7) funding for research, technology and innovation, (8) participation in the European R&D Framework Programme, (9) participation in business technology cooperation networks, (10) improvement of human resource technology skills,

(11) cooperation with technology transfer organizations, (12) technology cooperation with the universities, and (13) new infrastructure for telematics, quality premises for company location.

The main conclusion of the technology demand analysis was the latent character of this demand. Latent technology demand means a lack of active technology demand and low awareness in industry about the capabilities of new technologies to deal with production, competition, and marketing problems. Latent technology demand is documented either by the stratification of firms and the small proportion of firms that express clear views on technology and innovation, or by the comparison between in-depth technology audits and technology market research in the same population of firms.

Lack of awareness and low information limit the ability of firms to understand their real needs and to develop adequate solutions to fulfil these needs. This concerns both the spheres of marketing and production. Market variability and the globalization of competition make information on market requirements extremely complex. Barriers to relevant and up-to-date market information are sharper in firms that usually operate on regional markets. It is well documented that with the current industrial setting, technology and innovation are market driven, as markets set productivity and product quality standards. However, there is a serious gap between markets and the changing needs for product quality and specifications, as well as for flexible solutions to adapt to the production processes. Peripheral firms have an additional difficulty in following and filling this gap. On the other hand, a constant trend appears in firms to seek competitiveness through defence strategies such as de-skilling, low use of human resources, and exceeding investments in equipment and automation. Innovation needs are concealed both in the production process, where automation problems prevail, and in product development where dominant problems are those of quality, rather than new product design and development.

Latent technology demand, with respect to market globalization and defence production strategies of de-skilling, tend to undermine innovation initiatives. Technology audits have also documented that many consulting companies developing R&D, technology, and innovation services have underestimated the effort needed to open the market and the difficulty to develop the SME's appetite for technology and innovation-related services.

On the other hand, *regional technology development* in Central Macedonia is fragmented into a large number of small labs and research units. A total of 277 research units for applied R&D were identified and listed, of which 138 are university laboratories (130 in the Aristotle University of Thessaloniki and eight in the University of Macedonia), 110 belong to Technical Education Institutes in Thessaloniki and Serres, five are associated with the laboratories of the Foundation for Research and Technology

(FOURTH), 19 belong to the National Agricultural Research Institute, two to the Institute for the Control of Cultivated Plant Species, and one each to the Geology and Mining Research Institute, the National Tobacco Board and the National Cotton Board. The main technology areas, in which most of the above units are concentrated, are related to agro-technologies, biology and biotechnology, and the technologies for materials. The concentration is lower around automation technologies, energy, and communications.

Despite the significant number of research labs capable of providing technology services, the degree of collaboration between research and enterprise does not appear to be satisfactory. Only one-third of the units polled feel that they provide substantial support services, replacing company R&D departments with their own R&D services. The main source of their inability to develop strong bonds with companies is considered to be the companies themselves. About half the research units attributed the low levels of collaboration to a lack of interest on the part of the companies concerned. A significant number attributed the difficulty of collaborating to the lack of infrastructure, personnel, equipment and space. Another restrictive factor was the institutional framework within which the public entities function, especially with regard to billing for services rendered.

The main conclusion drawn from the technology supply analysis was the non-correspondence between the scope of technology suppliers and the needs of regional companies:

- There are no large research poles, especially in emerging technologies with a broad range of applications.

- The provision of technology is mainly focused on the Aristotle University of Thessaloniki, but fragmented into a large number of research laboratories.

- The overall organization of technology development is not clear, and many entrepreneurs think that information about and access to such services is extremely difficult.

- Interest expressed by enterprises in the research activities carried out by the laboratories and their possible applications is limited.

- A few laboratories are active in the transfer of technology to enterprises.

For the companies that were surveyed, the main source of technology is the purchase of equipment. The development of internal R&D departments is generally low, and exists only in large companies. Very few companies have dedicated R&D departments, while in some companies either the production department or the quality control department carries out

R&D. Low research and development activity is due on the one hand, to the funding for R&D, which in many industrial sectors is fairly low, and on the other hand to the information flow and dissemination of research results which are insufficient.

Technology transfer was the third important field of investigation in the regional innovation system. Technology transfer was analysed from the point of view of the related public support, the university–industry cooperation, and inter-firm technology cooperation in Central Macedonia. For the latter, a small survey was carried out covering the technology collaboration between companies (subcontracting, networks, licensing), as well as the foreign direct investment in the region and the technology cooperation between local and foreign firms.

Here, the principal conclusion is about the informal operation of technology supply and transfer, in which in-flows of technology and innovation in the company sector are not recognized as distinct issues. Field research reveals that this event is associated with three causes:

- The main route by which businesses acquire new technology is through the purchase of mechanical equipment. In-house R&D departments are rare, although internal research activity affects seriously the capability for technology transfer.

- Inter-firm collaboration, which is a major source of technology know-how, is primarily in the form of subcontracting. The subcontractor works according to the plans, production methods and product specifications provided by the principal: this dependence seriously restricts motivation as well as the incentives for innovation.

- Technology dissemination and collaboration between industry and research are both limited. Research activity is primarily concentrated in university laboratories, where it is fragmented among numerous small units without any specific clear industrial goal or connection. This structure does not allow for the development of complementary, inter-disciplinary activity, and the institution of large-scale poles of technology competence.

Thus, technology supply, including both technology development and technology transfer, also appears latent, because all three routes for technology supply in industry and in companies in particular (technology purchase and licensing, technology exchange, technology dissemination) are covered by broader activities and relationships. The purchase of technology is integrated into the purchase of equipment and machinery, the exchange of technology is covered by subcontract relationships between firms, and technology dissemination is lost in a loose relationship between industry and the academia.

These findings led to the conclusion that technology transfer constitutes the number one problem in Central Macedonia's technology and innovation capacity. On the one hand, companies cover their technology requirements by turning to external sources and, on the other hand, the external sources that are active in the region cannot take into account the needs and demands of local businesses.

A more recent study on motor regions in the European Union, codifies as following the strengths and weaknesses of innovation capability in Central Macedonia:

Strengths

Central Macedonia can build on a number of major strengths that assist in making full use of the local RTDI system. The research infrastructure is well developed and equipped. In several areas, the local knowledge production is of high economic relevance and world-leading.

A number of valuable activities have been launched in frame of the RTP and the RIS+ follow-up that aim to create critical masses in several industrial sectors to absorb and apply (locally produced) knowledge, linking public RTD actions better with the regional economic fabric. The regions can rely on a comparably well developed industrial basis, though R&D performance at the business enterprise level is in general low.

However, some encouraging progress especially in certification and quality assurance (ISO 9000/9002) can be seen and (though starting from a very low level) R&D related expenditures in the private company sector is estimated to get boosted by factor eight.

Weaknesses

Major weakness in the regional RTDI panorama constitute the still limited level of in-house R&D activities in firms which operate in majority in traditional, non-high-tech sectors. One key constraint in this context forms the limited access to legislative, market- and product-related information, and particularly what technological implications this bears for the individual companies.

Main source of innovation is still the purchase of equipment, around 5–7 per cent more budget is spent on external purchase than on in-house research activities. This has to be seen in association with a weak interaction with the local knowledge supply fabric as well as a low level of interfirm collaboration and limited creation of clusters/networks among SMEs.

In order to respond to this diagnosed deficits, the new national/horizontal R&D programme (EPAN) as well as the regional operational programme (ROP) for Central Macedonia has reserved substantial budget volume to support the continuation of the already started technological upgrade of production and services (e.g. the persuasive use of ICT in all sectors) in the local economic fabric.

The introduction of the new spin-off legislation introduced in time-frame of CSF III (adopted end of March 2001) is certainly a valuable step heading in the right direction to strengthen innovative capabilities in the region.

Above mentioned issues imply as well an intensification of efforts to expand the already existing strong poles of excellence in concentrating on a few selected technology areas of strategic interest. Regarding the proposed new FP6 structure, Central Macedonia appears qualified to drive networks of excellence and to conduct large integrated projects e.g. in the priority thematic areas of fuel cells, polymer production processing catalyst testing and pilot planting as well as renewable and efficient use of energy. Further areas of potential competence are the development of health-promoting food and sustainable transport/higher safety of transport systems.

(Tsagaris 2001)

Regional Innovation Strategy

To be effective, a regional innovation strategy should constitute a programmatic action organized into the necessary stages of application (analysis of the regional innovation system, use of good practice, formulation of priorities, definition of action plan, definition of implementation procedures, monitoring, and evaluation). Furthermore, it should improve the existing and create new mechanisms for technology supply and transfer matching the technology and innovation needs of businesses, and integrate the regional innovation system through dense networks/institutions for information, technology dissemination, and cooperation between the businesses, research, and the public administration.

A SWOT[3] analysis of Central Macedonia's regional innovation system revealed that the main weakness in the region's technology performance is due to the latent character of both technology supply and demand.

On the supply side, the neglect of local research resources deprives regional firms of technology inputs based on local scientific skills and expertise. Low inter-firm technology cooperation weakens technology input from an important technology transfer route, as well as local technological consolidation between producers and suppliers. Rationalization of technology supply is poor, as competition between technology suppliers remains low. Regional companies lack both in-house technology capacity and external input from their immediate environment. On the demand side, low active demand for technology and innovation services does not allow a regional technology market to prosper, nor does the clustering of innovative firms and the positive multiplication effects of a vivid regional technology pole. The private sector remains out of the R&D and innovation dynamics, and the innovation support system and services are placed exclusively under the public initiative.

At the centre of these weaknesses are the region's *industrial firms* and the difficulties faced in following advanced strategies based on business excellence and world-class manufacturing concepts. For the average European industrial firm, innovation is not an abstract concept, but is bound up with the firm's ability to apply new methods and technologies to production (automated machinery, flexible workshops, horizontal shop-floor structures), to the product (new products, small batches, small production runs, quality circles, total quality control), to inter-firm relationships (just-in-time delivery systems, production networking, externalization of services, steady producer/supplier relationships) and to the workforce (flexibility, upgrading of skills, multifunctional work culture). The gap between firms in Central Macedonia and their counterparts in Europe's more advanced regions reflects in miniature the true technology gap, which covers the fields of commercial strategy, technology in-flow and individual ingenuity in adapting to an ever-changing international environment.

The strategy of the RTP therefore focuses on Central Macedonia's industrial firms, and especially on their latent research and technology integration. This is the plan's basic orientation for action. In this context, the priorities established for the Central Macedonia RTP are grouped into six different areas, each with a distinct thematic objective and goal. Five priorities pertain to Central Macedonia's businesses and the factors affecting their ability to innovate, while the sixth covers monitoring, evaluation and adjustment of the RTP actions.

Increase funding for research, technological development and innovation promotes both the modernization of existing businesses, as well as encouraging the creation of new high-tech companies. In numerous dynamic areas in Europe and the United States, risk capital funds have greatly contributed to the development of high-tech industries. However, the actions recommended by the RTP have less to do with the creation of new institutions, like the venture capital institutions included in the national Operational Programme for Industry, rather than addressed to the direct utilization of existing funding mechanisms. More specifically,

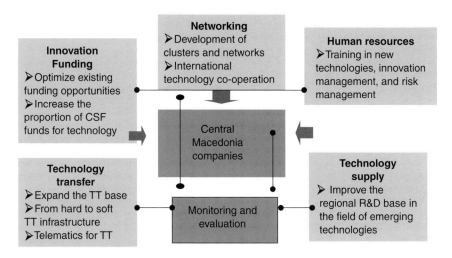

Figure 5.3 RTP strategy

actions were designed to utilize funds available under the Community Support Framework and the R&D Framework Programmes of the European Commission.

Support for technological cooperation among businesses constitutes a central priority for the expansion of innovative production technologies and products. It is claimed that 'businesses learn better from other businesses', and on this basis inter-firm relationships, supplier-producer relations and networks are all crucial factors in innovation. In this area, RTP focuses on the development of collaboration networks within specific industrial sectors and the making of technology clusters, and also on attracting technology-intensive foreign investments which would then act as poles for the rise of new industrial sectors. The actions in this area are designed to complement the actions for business networks and clusters included in the national programme for industry, 'The future of Greek industry'.

Increase of human resource technology skills is designed to promote new business strategies that depend on the active participation and technology capability of the firm's executives and employees. The RTP emphasizes in-house personnel training, and stresses the link between training and finding (or keeping) a job. Particular weight is given to training for entrepreneurs and senior executives on matters relating to innovation management, export promotion, and risk management associated with investment in south-eastern European countries.

Support technology transfer and businesses access to external sources of technology deals with the external technology and innovation environment of firms. The complexity and rapidity of technological change have shown that external sources and technology transfer are important factors in the technological performance of any business, be it large or small. Especially in Central Macedonia, the limited development of in-house R&D departments makes turning to external sources of technology even more important. RTP actions in this area focus on two principal orientations: on the one hand, they aim at the development of horizontal technology transfer mechanisms, in which all those involved in research, technology and business would cooperate in order to cover broad technological sectors and, on the other, they seek to develop sector-specific mechanisms for technology transfer, thus ensuring coverage of the technology requirements of the region's principal industries.

Supplementing these orientations is the *support of endogenous technology supply and demand*, which is concerned with the development of know-how within specific technology sectors (information technology, quality, environmental technologies, agro-technologies). As mentioned, a major problem to deal with is the latent technology demand. The RTP actions are designed to broaden the local market for a number of important technologies. However, these are actions that cannot be undertaken by the businesses themselves exclusively, since they require significant effort with no guarantee that they will pay off in the long run. Their effects are diffused, making them collective actions from which all the businesses in the area will benefit, either as users or as providers of these technologies.

The five areas of priorities just mentioned focus on Central Macedonia's businesses and technology development/transfer organizations. They promote innovation in all areas of business strategies: production methods, products, supplier–producer relationships, and personnel and executive training. At the same time, they facilitate access to various kinds of technology: horizontal technologies, sectorial technologies, and specific technologies as well.

The sixth priority area is different: it is associated with the application and effectiveness of the regional technology strategy promoted by the RTP. This includes monitoring the RTP actions, developing criteria and evaluation indicators and fine-tuning the plan while it is being implemented. In this case, the sole action is the expansion of the RTP Observatory and Innovation Portal, as a mechanism for the monitoring, evaluation, and adjustment of all actions pertaining to the upgrade of the innovation system in Central Macedonia.

These priorities of the RTP provide a general strategic framework for orientation. However, the decisive factor is the manner in which those priorities are specified and translated into particular actions and projects. In this sense, the transition from priorities to projects and the action plan is a process of evaluation by which specific projects are accepted or rejected. A system of evaluation, according to which a project may or may not become accepted within a priority, is thus required.

The Action Plan

Following the strategy guidelines, the formulation of an action plan demands three main components: (1) thematic priorities, (2) projects to specify the priorities, and (3) an assessment method to select the projects that best fit the priorities. In the case of the Central Macedonia RTP, the priorities came from the analysis of the regional innovation system, the projects emerged 'from below' (in the form of proposals submitted by political and economic agencies in the region), and the evaluation of the projects was based on a survey dealing with the investigation of the technological demand related to them.

The procedure for assembling the projects that specified the priorities was relatively simple. The political and economic agencies of the region had been informed about the Regional Technological Plan, on its objectives and priorities, and they were asked to submit appropriate projects. Each project was supposed to determine a set of services to support the technological and innovation capacity of the region (e.g. funding of innovation, technology transfer, dissemination of research) and an implementing agency as well.

Using this method, a large number of proposals were assembled. They were then systematically discussed at successive meetings of the Steering Committee and evaluated on the criterion of their feasibility and the interest that the businesses in Central Macedonia might display in the services

Table 5.4 RTP action plan

Priority 1. INCREASE FUNDING FOR TECHNOLOGY AND INNOVATION
Projects
  1 Funding Businesses for Technological Modernization.
  2 Funding Businesses for Research and Technological Development.
  3 Funding Businesses from European R&D Programmes.

Priority 2. SUPPORT TECHNOLOGICAL COOPERATION AMONG BUSINESSES
Projects
  4 Foreign Direct Investment and International Technology Cooperation.
  5 Networking in the Food Industry.
  6 Networking in the Textile Industry.

Priority 3. INCREASE OF HUMAN RESOURCE TECHNOLOGY SKILLS
Projects
  7 Employee Technology Training.
  8 Training in Innovation Management.
  9 Training in Risk Management for Investment in South-Eastern Europe.
10 Training in Quality and Exports.

Priority 4. SUPPORT TECHNOLOGY TRANSFER AND BUSINESS ACCESS TO EXTERNAL SOURCES OF TECHNOLOGY
Projects
11 Technology Transfer Department at the Thessaloniki Technology Park.
12 Textile Institute of Northern Greece.
13 Centre for Research Dissemination at the Aristotle University of Thessaloniki.
14 Food Institute of Northern Greece.
15 Local Centres and Network for Technology Services.
16 Centre for Industrial and Developmental Studies of Northern Greece.

Priority 5. SUPPORT ENDOGENOUS TECHNOLOGY SUPPLY
Projects
17 Association for Industrial Information Technologies.
18 Association for Anti-Pollution Technologies.
19 Association for Automation Systems.
20 Association for Quality Control.
21 Association for Agro-technologies.

Priority 6. MONITORING AND EVALUATION
Project
22 Expansion of the RTP Observatory.

each project was offering. From a large number of projects submitted, 22 projects were selected.

With respect to this procedure, the Action Plan of Central Macedonia RTP was composed of six priorities and 22 projects. Each priority covers projects falling into two groups: lead projects marking the character of the priority, and projects that fulfil the conditions for immediate implementation. Most projects are fairly elastic with respect to size. In other words, they can be implemented on different scales, from experimental through small to large. The extent of the implementation will be finalized at a later stage, with respect to the funding opportunities and inclusion in the structural funds.

RTP Implementation

The particularity of any RTP is that its implementation is expected via separate operational programmes within the Community Support Framework and some relevant community initiatives (SME, INTERREG, ADAPT, etc.). This decentralized implementation structure requires, on the one hand the trimming of the RTP Action Plan to the procedures of the Structural Funds, and on the other, the organization of a central hub to record, monitor, and assess the progress and the results of the various actions on the regional innovation system and the innovation capacity of the region.

An effort was made to identify and list all the actions of the Operational Programmes within the Community Support Framework and the Community Initiatives that could support the implementation of the Action Plan. This survey led to a selection of the sub-programmes, measures and actions from varied Operational Programmes, such as the Central Macedonia Regional Operational Programme, the Operational Programme on Industry, the Operational Programme on Research and Technology, on Energy, and the Environment, as well as the Operational Programme of the Community Initiatives for SMEs, RETEX, INTERREG II, and ADAPT. All these Framework Programmes may sustain the projects described in the Action Plan and show that there is substantial potential for linkage with the RTP, and fund the designed actions. It should also be noted that many of the above programmes contained measures that at the time of the RTP preparation have not yet progressed to the final implementation stage, and in this sense their shopping list was 'open' for the introduction of new projects and actions.

Analytical feasibility studies were conducted for every project included in the RTP Action Plan. The studies were compiled using set specifications and a common thematic structure consisting of ten sections: (1) objectives of the project, (2) description, (3) services offered by the project, (4) demand in Central Macedonia for the technological services offered,

(5) phases in the implementation of the project, (6) time schedule, (7) budget, (8) implementation agency, (9) evaluation indicators, and (10) viability. Feasibility studies were an important step in the application of the Regional Technology Plan since they provided a detailed description of every project and made it possible to decide whether or not to include it in a funding and implementation framework.

For the monitoring of the plan, a Regional Innovation Observatory was developed as a local hub for the collection, evaluation, and dissemination of information relating to the RTP and its results. This information system was composed of an experimental infrastructure functioning at the Aristotle University of Thessaloniki and the Ministry of Macedonia-Thrace. It permitted the storage of large quantities of information, accessible via the Internet, at the address, http://rtp.rc.auth.gr. The web supported the dissemination of information relating to the RTP, the innovation system in Central Macedonia, and the full presentation of the objectives, method, work packages, strategy and projects prepared within the framework of the plan.

A good record of visitors was registered from the countries of Europe, the USA, Canada, and Australia. The thematic structure of the Observatory, at its first stage, included three main sections dealing with:

- The regional technology plan (objectives, administration, deliverables, working programme, work packages, action plan, interim and final reports).

- The economic and technological development in Central Macedonia (geographical units, population, employment, industrial structure, GDP, technology demand and supply, etc.).

- The innovation support infrastructure in the European Union, Greece, and Central Macedonia (innovation infrastructures, innovative urban and regional development projects, support for innovation and technology from the R&D Framework Programme, etc.).

Later, the website was reorganized to present the results and services developed by other innovation projects, the RIS+, InnoRegio, Innovation-on-Line, and others.

The implementation of the RTP Action Plan is expected to be a long-term process. In effect, it will be an open-ended procedure leading to the formation of the mechanisms of a *Regional Innovation Support System*, having an institutional capacity and organizational form. It is the ambition of the Regional Technological Plan in Central Macedonia that it should serve as the starting point for the formation of that mechanism.

According to the independent evaluator commissioned by the European Commission, regional technology policy was almost non-existent before the development of the RTP in Central Macedonia. There were no bridges between research institutions and firms – with few individually promoted exceptions – and virtually no contacts between the research community and institutional actors (Technopolis 1998).

The most important impact of the RTP was its influence on a new working practice and the fact that it brought together people that would normally not sit at the same table. Before the RTP exercise, it was common for regional authorities to ignore researchers in their planning process and to therefore push the latter to establish alliances outside the region and even outside the country. Companies also needed the regional authorities (mainly for financial incentives), but these needs could not be fulfilled because of the lack of credibility of the regional authority when it came to implementing a consistent planning process. Thanks to the RTP, innovation has become more prominent in the regional agenda, although in higher political circles, it is still believed that tangible physical infrastructure always represents a better investment opportunity than funding 'software' (innovation support actions). However, this attitude is slowly disappearing in the middle layers of the regional authorities.

In 1999, the Directorate General for Regional Policy, in the form of a RIS+ project, approved a continuation and extension of the RTP. The main thrust of the RIS+ is the funding of the experimental phase of nine projects selected from the RTP action plan. These projects concern regional firms, especially their latent research and technology needs. Eight projects pertain to the factors affecting the ability of firms to innovate, whereas the remaining project builds a portal to the regional innovation system, and covers monitoring indicators, and evaluation reports (Table 5.5). RIS+ includes three groups of activities related to the management structure, the implementation of pilot projects, and the promotion of activities and international networking. All work packages are implemented on the basis of intra-regional cooperation and working teams. A Steering Committee and Management Unit provide guidance, monitoring and on-going evaluation for the project as a whole. The implementing authorities of each pilot project provide their own evaluation of their respective pilot action.

The RIS+ also focuses on: (1) elaborating a revised innovation action plan for Central Macedonia, and (2) maintaining and expanding the particular social network (web of socio-professional relations) that has been created in the region around issues of technology development and regional innovation.

The revised strategy and innovation action plan are focusing on the making of an environment of innovation to accelerate the introduction of the region's businesses, research centres, and technology intermediary

Table 5.5 RIS+ pilot projects and implementing agents

Pilot project	Implementing agent
1 Funding Businesses through European R&D Programmes	▪ Thessaloniki Technology Park
2 Attracting technology-intensive foreign investments	▪ Region of Central Macedonia ▪ Regional Development Fund
3 Virtual wine cluster	▪ Association of wine producers 'Roads of Wine'
4 Technological cooperation and modernization of industrial estates	▪ Association of Industries of the Industrial Estate of Kilkis
5 Risk management for investments in South-Eastern Europe	▪ Confederation of Industries of Northern Greece
6 Establishment of a Business Innovation Centre (BIC) in Thessaloniki	▪ Region of Central Macedonia ▪ Regional Development Fund
7 Promotion of agro-technologies	▪ National Centre for Research and Technological Development
8 New premises for R&D university institutes	▪ Research Committee of Aristotle University of Thessaloniki
9 Innovation Observatory of Central Macedonia	▪ URENIO Research Unit, Aristotle University of Thessaloniki
10 Update of the RTP Action Plan	▪ ADE consultants ▪ BCS consultants

organizations to the world of business intelligence, smart products, technology watch, and foresight, and promote a knowledge-based regional development.

At the heart of the revised strategy/action plan are a number of selected clusters representing important and emerging industries in the region (i.e. agriculture, food and beverages, textiles and clothing, chemicals and pharmaceuticals, electrical machinery, telecommunications, software, medical services). For each cluster, a detailed development plan introduces 'business excellence' and 'world class manufacturing' principles and working methods in order to strengthen its outward orientation and competitiveness on a global scale.

Beforehand, the drafting of development plans for the selected clusters is facilitated by a regional technology foresight exercise to identify promising technologies for the coming decade at the industry level, and a digital research centre to inform on existing regional capabilities in terms of R&D and technology supply, research results, and scientific human resources.

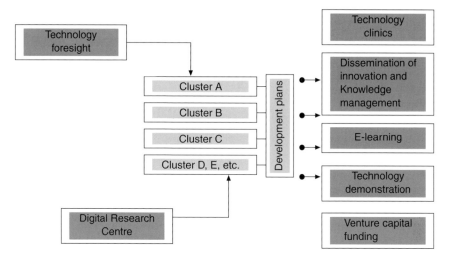

Figure 5.4 RIS+: RTP revised strategy and action plan

Afterwards, a series of pilot practices (including technology clinics, training, e-learning, technology demonstration, risk capital funding, etc.) support the endorsement and implementation of the development plans and disseminate the principles of 'excellence' to regional organizations and companies. The Regional Innovation Observatory monitors and evaluates these pilot projects, and transfers the most promising actions and results to the Regional Operational Programme 2000–6 and other mainstream structural funds for large-scale implementation.

Foundations of Regional Innovation Strategies

The transition from flexible specialization theories and technopolitan practices to regional innovation strategies mark a break in the continuity of mainstream views issued from the discussion on post-Fordism. The conception of regional innovation strategies was made possible because of the rise of a different set of ideas emphasizing networks, institutions, learning, and a systemic understanding of innovation (Cooke 1988; Cooke and Morgan 1991; Camagni 1991; Debresson and Amesse 1991; Ribeiro 1998).

At the beginning of the 1990s, the pioneering work of Lundvall on systems of innovation suddenly widened the debate on districts, flexible specialization, new industrial spaces, and technopoles, introducing a clear interest for learning and R&D issues in the analysis of product and process innovation. Lundvall put forward two propositions: (1) that innovation is an interactive learning process between firms and the basic science and technology infrastructure, and (2) interactive learning between firms is supported by a wide range of institutional mechanisms. These include habits,

133

routines of everyday life and social conventions, which are rather 'intangible' and 'invisible', embodying knowledge that is often tacit (held in the human brain but not in any recorded form), and skill-like (Lundvall 1992).

A number of attempts have been made to link the literature on networks, institutions, learning, and innovation on the one hand, and urban and regional development on the other. Cooke and Morgan (1997) developed the concept of the learning region to connect networks, innovation, and regional development. However, Morgan (1997) refers to Storper's *Regional Worlds* as the fullest and more sophisticated attempt to marry innovation dynamics and the regions. Storper (1997) looks at what he considers to be the principal trend of contemporary spatial economies: the rise of the local at the time when the forces of globalization appear to reduce the world to a 'placeless' mass. A key part of the explanation, he argues, is the association between innovation and technological learning with the agglomeration. This association has two roots: the first concerns localized input-output relations in the agglomeration, which are essential to information exchange and the user-producer coordination. The second concerns the role of untraded interdependencies (like labour markets, local conventions, norms, values, public or semi-public institutions), which coordinate the process of organizational and interactive learning. Both localized input-output and untraded interdependencies make interactive learning place specific, and the agglomeration, *par excellence*, the site for innovation (see also Storper 1993 and 1994; Salais and Storper 1993).

The Innovating Regions Strategy and the RIS movement are part of this theoretical construction and evolution of the debate on 'learning regions'. It focuses on the regional innovation system rather than the cluster, and seeks to upgrade this system with actions promoting the institutional practices for production adaptation, learning, technology transfer, and endogenous technological development.

Regional innovation strategies are based on interactive and institutional theories of innovation, emphasizing the non-linear relationships between R&D and innovation, the user contribution on the pace of technology and innovation, and the institutional capacity to manage technological innovation (Hassink 1993; Isarken 1999). The key concept, in this perspective, is the Regional System of Innovation.

Figure 5.5 shows some major components of a regional system of innovation that drive technology and innovation from R&D and intermediary organizations to companies and other users, and includes parts of the financial and knowledge institutions facilitating this transfer. The regional system of innovation is part of the regional productive system, the established mix of activities, the interactivity linkages, and the institutional regulations. It might be considered as the intelligent component of the production system, since it has the responsibility for the adaptation of production to changing external conditions, markets, and technologies.

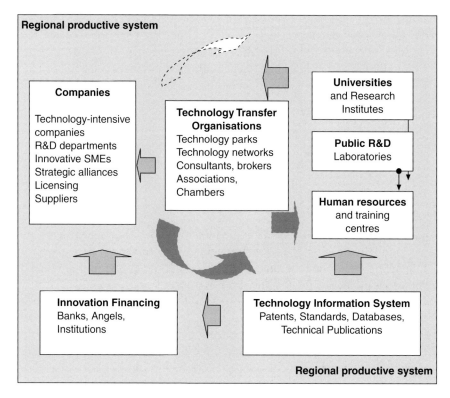

Figure 5.5 Regional system of innovation

An attentive reader should already realize that regional systems of innovation are not built upon technological assets exclusively. The change of denomination from RTPs to RIS suggests this view. In the recent theoretical discussion, innovation is strongly related to learning processes and explained by the capacity of regions to create institutions that adapt to changing markets and competition environments. Maskell and Malmberg for instance, have examined a growing literature on localized learning, innovation, and industrial and regional competitiveness, and argue that:

It is the ability of regions and countries to learn, change, and adapt rather than their allocative efficiency which determines their long-run performance.

and

As knowledge becomes a crucial asset in modern production systems, the ongoing creation of new knowledge has become a key process when trying to increase/sustain competitiveness. The competitiveness of an increasing number of firms is no longer primarily obtained by cost-reduction, for instance in labour wages, but mainly by generating entrepreneurial rents through innovations in the production process, by accessing new, distinctive markets in new and unconventional ways or by producing new, improved or redesigned commodities or services with a significant contribution to the perceived customer benefit of the end product.

(Maskell and Malmberg 1995)

There is no doubt that innovation has become a key factor for regional competitiveness (Howells 1996; Patchell 1993; Simmie 1997a; Storper 1993). Less dependable, however, are the notions of production and product innovation as mainly learning processes, and the equation of innovation to knowledge capacity (Autio 1996). Information and knowledge are important innovation factors, but in the absence of a comprehensive theory of innovation they cannot be considered either exclusive or the more important ones. Other factors may be equally important in the innovation process, such as adaptability, intelligence, strength, long-term pursuit of objectives, etc. Innovation may be defined as an equation of research, invention, and commercial exploitation (Innovation = research + invention + exploitation). Research and commercial exploitation are normative, and established rules and models command their practices. By contrast, invention is a black box consisting of a variety of factors such as information, knowledge, culture, intelligence, cooperation etc., and is assumed to be rather unpredictable (Drejer 1996).

We should stress also that a major problem and challenge for RISs in the less favoured regions is to confront effectively the tendency towards neo-Taylorist corporate strategies in production, product, supplier–producer relations, and employment. Neo-Taylorism is an option of the current productive restructuring and re-engineering, which is deepening the Taylorist production divide between skilled and unskilled labour with the use of new technologies, and deploys a corporate strategy along four main features: (1) restructuring of production with respect to exceed automation and process machinery, (2) export-oriented product design and specifications, (3) further functional and spatial separation of specialized and routine activities through the externalization of tertiary activities, subcontracting, and international integration of firms, and (4) labour market flexibility based on de-skilling, low wages and on-off mechanisms adjusting the labour mass to market fluctuations (Komninos and Sefertzi 1998). Neo-Taylorist strategies have become a dominant solution in peripheral productive restructuring because of the specific characteristics established in the less favoured regions: precarious industrial base, skill shortages, traditional local technical culture, and lack of innovation support services and infrastructure. High use of automation, and the integration of firms into wider production networks minimize local technology input and conceal the real need for technology and innovation.

In these conditions, regional innovation strategies have to deal with the causes sustaining neo-Taylorist trajectories. Knowledge is power, but solutions should not be sought in training schemes and information exchange exclusively, as a 'knowledge shortage' explanation of the innovation gap may suggest. More appropriate solutions may be those motivating companies to introduce knowledge management and learning processes into their corporate strategy. Emphasis on learning and systemic relationships is opening a route towards new technology supply, the use of regional research resources, and the development of networks of cooperation and genuine technology alliances.

A prime problem, however, remains out of the equation between innovation, technological development, and growth. Conventional economic growth cannot offer a solution to the problem of employment. In the everyday life of the EU inhabitant, the difference between a growth rate of 2 per cent and a growth rate of 5 per cent is meaningless. By contrast, the difference between having a job or not, at any level of growth, is of primary importance. Employment, however, may become part of the overall innovation strategy. In any region or country there are three employment trends: (1) creation of high-wage, high-skill jobs in sectors of intense intellectual labour in new industrial branches and in producer and financial services, (2) creation of low-wage jobs usually in consumer and retail service sectors, and (3) job losses in manufacturing, producing standardized products, and in agriculture due to either the automation or the relocation of routine production activities to low-wage countries (Storper 1997). Location is a key factor in this process since the mix of the above processes differs from region to region. Standardization of productive activities, the new Taylorism shaped at the end of the twentieth century, is a major threat to employment. Standardization, however, is the opposite of innovation. Once the activities of a production system are standardized they may be easily imitated, and downward pressures appear in employment and wages. This is a threat for backward regions, but is equally important for core regions, which are not immune from the danger of standardization and relocation of high-tech activities. The successive restructuring waves in advanced regions show that the search for innovation should never stop, and regions need to constantly renew this propulsive dynamic for growth and employment.

6 Regional versus National Innovation Strategies

Urban areas can compete for those key control and command functions in high finance and government that tend, by their very nature, to be highly centralized while embodying immense power over all manner of activities and spaces. Cities can compete to become centres of finance capital, of information gathering and control, of government decision-making. Competition of this sort calls for a certain strategy of infrastructural provision. Efficiency and centrality within a worldwide network of transport and communications is vital, and that means heavy public investment in airports, rapid transit, communication systems, and the like. The provision of adequate office space and linkages depends upon a public–private coalition of property developers, financiers, and public interests capable of responding to and anticipating needs. Assembling a wide range of supporting services, particularly those that gather and process information rapidly, calls for other kinds of investments, while the specific skills requirements of such activities put a premium on urban centres with certain kinds of educational provision (business and law schools, computer training facilities, and so forth).

(D. Harvey, *The Urban Experience*)

Regional and National Dimensions of Innovation Strategies

Regional innovation strategies are addressed to European regions wishing to improve their environment supporting R&D, technological innovation, and technology transfer. Each RTP-RIS-RITTS project focuses on a particular region with the scope to strengthen the respective regional innovation system and support the organizations that use technologies or are involved in technology transfer, technology supply, and innovation finance. As mentioned, the decision-making during an RIS is determined by a Steering Committee composed mainly of regional actors representing regional political concerns and interests. Both national and interests external to the region's innovation capabilities are often neglected.

However, regions are open spaces and the components of a regional innovation system interact dynamically and compete with innovation

factors located outside the region. Research and development organizations, for example, cooperate with similar organizations located in other
regions in order to deliver scientific and technological services; firms
acquire technology from R&D and technology transfer organizations both
internal and external to the region; innovation finance is provided by local,
national or international organizations; regional technology infrastructure
is linked to national and international infrastructure and innovation services. The functioning of a regional system of innovation is linked to an
intense inter-regional exchange of competences and know-how, which is
illustrated in Figure 6.1.

Since regional innovation systems are open to external influences, the
application of regional innovation strategies in neighbouring regions or the
coverage of a national space by a juxtaposition of regional innovation
strategies has important inter-regional consequences. The RIS model,
which is widely used, is based on the demand and supply analysis of rather
'autonomous' regional systems of innovation, and underestimates inter-
regional issues and innovation factors located in other regions. Further-

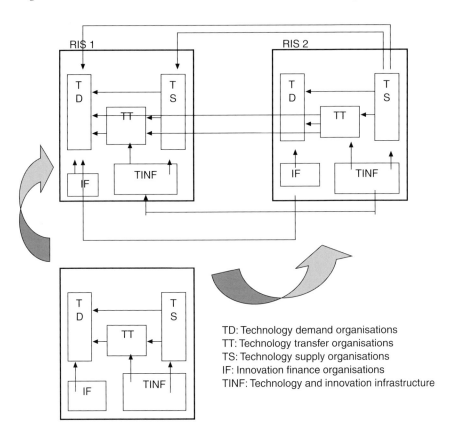

Figure 6.1 Interaction between regional systems of innovation

more, neighbouring regions usually compete for the development of a similar innovation support infrastructure, and the difficulty in coordination leads, in many cases, to duplication of efforts and infrastructures. The fact that companies acquire technology and innovation services from sources internal and external to the region, increases the range of technology providers, but it also sustains inter-regional competition between R&D and technology transfer organizations offering the same or similar services.

In the seven years from the launch of RTPs in 1994 to the last call for RITTS in 2001, more than a hundred RIS exercises have been implemented throughout Europe. In some member states, with the multiplication of regional strategies, all the national territory is more or less covered. As the RIS movement goes on, bottom-up initiatives fill the national space, and regional strategies interweave more and more to national innovation and technology policies.

Between the regional and the national innovation strategies there exists, however, a significant discontinuity due to conceptual and institutional differences between them:

- RIS is a bottom-up regional strategy based on a consensus of regional actors belonging to the private, university, and technology sectors. It is a demand-driven strategy giving emphasis to local clustering and networking, spin-offs of innovative companies, local matching of technology demand and supply, the local innovation environment. Their implementation is primarily based on regional programmes, incentives, and funds.

- On the other side, the national innovation strategy is a top-down governmental policy focusing on the big technology and innovation infrastructure, the state R&D institutes, the policy for the universities, the national schemes for technology finance. Main structuring concepts are those of authority and power in the distribution of public R&D and education funds and opportunities. Technology push is the dominant view.

These differences are particularly evident in the measurement of the innovative performance. In most OECD countries, the analysis of innovation and technology performance has focused on input (expenditure on R&D and number of research personnel) and output (patents) indicators (OECD 1997). Gross Expenditure for R&D (GERD), Business Expenditure for R&D (BERD), State Expenditure for R&D, expenditure for higher education, R&D personnel per 1,000 inhabitants, and numbers of patents, which usually measure the intensity of the national innovation capability, are meaningful in a linear and technology-push conception of innovation. This implies that size matters more than quality, relationships of cooperation, and technology interdependences. By contrast, RIS seem to have embraced the newest advances in innovation theory stemming from the flexible specialization theory, the national innovation systems theory, and institutional and evolutionary economics. Local untraded interdependencies, localized input-output relationships, matching of technology demand and supply, are all vital relationships and indicators of a smooth and efficient regional innovation system.

Differences in concepts, operation practices, and assessment indicators between the regional and the national innovation strategies, at the time of their factual overlapping, is a source of conflicting behaviour and practice, particularly negative for the promotion and implementation of innovation policy. Regional innovation strategies deconstruct and reconstruct the national space for innovation, and need better coordination and convergence to the national innovation framework. Two promising points for bridging the gap are the widespread use of non-linear and interactive models for understanding the innovation process at the national and regional levels, and the adoption of similar planning procedures from the regional and national responsible authorities.

Theoretical Convergence

National innovation systems theory is a key element in bringing together the understanding of innovation at the national and regional levels. This conceptual convergence is, however, a major step towards the adoption of common support practices and innovation policies at these two levels also.

The national innovation systems (NIS) literature reflects the rise of systemic approaches to the study of the knowledge and technology-based development. Institutions and economic structures affecting the rate and direction of technological change in society constitute a system of innovation that is larger than the R&D system. Not only does it include the R&D system and the system of technological diffusion, but also institutions and factors determining how new technology affects productivity and economic growth (Edquist and Lundvall 1993; Blind and Grupp 1999; Chiesa 1996).

NIS literature is poles apart from a 'linear' understanding of the innovation process, in which knowledge flows from science and assumes that an increase in scientific input will directly increase the available new technological products and processes emerging from the downstream end. In fact, ideas and inspirations for innovation may come from a variety of sources, not just from research institutions, but also from technology transfer organizations, innovation finance, business services, suppliers, competitors, and customers as well. This is all about the environment of innovation we described in Chapter 1. Innovation is the result of a complex interaction between various social actors and institutions, and proceeds through feedback loops within the system. At the centre of national innovation systems are companies that have an internal organization to develop technology and innovation, and external channels to acquire technology from outside sources of knowledge. The innovating firm operates within a complex web and interactive environment linking firms, universities, suppliers, and customers.

National innovation systems have been defined in a variety of ways, but the definitions always emphasize the institutional and network characteristics. The OECD study on NIS provides a good sample of definitions (OECD 1997). An NIS is:

The network of institutions in the public and private sectors whose activities and interactions initiate, import, modify, and diffuse new technologies.

(Freeman 1987)

The elements and relationships which interact in the production, diffusion of new, and economically useful knowledge . . . and are either located within or rooted inside the borders of a nation state.

(Lundvall 1992)

A set of institutions whose interactions determine the innovative performance . . . of national firms.

(Nelson 1993)

The national institutions, their incentive structures and their competencies that determine the rate and direction of technological learning in a country.

(Patel and Pavitt 1994)

That set of distinct institutions which jointly and individually contribute to the development and diffusion of new technologies and which provides the framework which governments form and implement policies to influence the innovation process.

(Metcalfe 1995)

The impact of the NIS literature on the national innovation policies and the regional innovation strategies has been diverse.

At the *national level*, NIS literature provides the conceptual framework to redirect national innovation strategies towards more pragmatic goals. It is believed that countries tend to develop certain technological paths or 'trajectories' determined by past and present patterns of knowledge accumulation. The specific path a country takes is determined largely by institutional factors including a broad range of interactions between the components of the national innovation system (OECD 1997; Padrmore and Gibson 1998). The immediate consequence of this conceptualization was to broaden the scope of national innovation strategies beyond the technology supply system, and to embrace technology users (mainly companies), patents and intellectual property, spin-off support, and innovation finance mechanisms. Enhancing the innovative capacity of firms became a primary objective, associated with goals to improve the ability of companies to identify relevant technologies, to have access to technology networks and information, and to adapt knowledge to their own needs.

A second, but equally important contribution is the reorientation of national technology policy towards systemic relationships and networking. In the interest of maximizing returns to the general public, technology policies have focused on stimulating R&D spending through direct support and incentives. The theory of national innovation systems re-channels this attention towards the interaction of actors, the mismatches between the basic research and the more applied research to industry, the collaborative relationships between companies, the interface between companies and universities, and the technology diffusion (and informal networking) processes.

At the *regional level*, the influence of the NIS literature is clearer. This is largely due to the fact that NIS discussion matured in parallel to regional innovation strategies. At the time of the RIS-RITTS launch in the EU, it represented the emerging debate and predominant theory of innovation. Nowhere else is this impact better acknowledged than in the work of Cooke, Uranga-Gomez and Extebarria on regional innovation systems.

In 1993, Richard Nelson published an influential book on *National Innovation Systems*. The book was the outcome of a comparative research project on the technological innovation systems in three groups of countries: large high-income countries like the US, Japan, Britain, France and Germany, smaller high-income countries like Denmark and Sweden, and lower-income countries like Korea, Taiwan, and Israel. The studies illuminate the institutions and mechanisms supporting technical innovation in 15 countries, the similarities and differences between them. At the heart of the discussion is the concept of the national innovation system itself, which combines three dimensions (Nelson and Rosenberg 1993). First, the term innovation is interpreted rather broadly, to encompass the introduction of new product designs and manufacturing processes into firms; this interpretation is not limited to the behaviour of leader firms at the forefront of technology or to institutions involved in the most advanced scientific research, but to any firm introducing a product or process new to the specific firm. Second, the systemic dimension is associated with a set of institutions and institutional actors whose interactions determine the innovation performance of national firms. Third, the national dimension refers to the fragmentation of the innovation systems in different fields (i.e. pharmaceuticals and aircraft) that operate with little overlap, and stressed the role of governments in shaping the institutional setting of innovation.

Cooke *et al.* (1997 and 1998) directly transfer this thinking to the regional level. Taking an evolutionary economics standpoint, they specify the concepts of 'region', 'innovation', and 'system' as a prelude to an extended discussion on the importance of financial capacity, institutionalized learning and productive culture to systemic innovation. The conclusion is that the concept of National Innovation System retains its validity at the sub-national level, and a new concept, that of Regional Innovation System, may be useful in explaining the locational distribution and policy impact of regional high-tech industry, technology parks, innovation networks, and innovation support programmes. Accordingly, regional innovation systems can be evaluated from a dual perspective. First, from a regionalization point of view, relating to the regional jurisdiction to develop policies and manage the constituting elements of the innovation system, as well as the financing capacity for strategic investments in infrastructures. Second, from a regionalism approach, related to the region's cultural base, which strengthens its systemic dimension.

National innovation systems theory acts like a hook for bringing two policy levels of different origin closer: on the one hand, the national innovation and technology policy, whose background is the R&D state policy and the idea of a linear continuity between research and innovation; and on the other hand, the regional innovation policy, whose starting point is the districts and institutional theories, as well as the innovative actions of the European Regional Development Fund. Due to the diffusion of the NIS literature, regional and national innovation initiatives may communicate more easily and share more common objectives than in earlier days when national innovation policy was just R&D policy, and the regional technology policy equalled technology poles and clusters.

Planning Convergence

Planning convergence means the adoption of similar planning procedures and methods to deal with innovation at the national and regional levels. The pressure towards this kind of convergence comes from the multiplication and the coverage of national spaces by regional innovation strategies. In countries where most regions have implemented an RTP-RIS-RITTS project, there is *de facto* overlapping of regional and national innovation policies since they manage innovation over the same geographical space. In southern European countries, for example, Spain, Portugal, and Greece, RIS initiatives tend to cover the entire national space. Furthermore, in Greece, Spain, Portugal, and the UK, national innovation associations have been created to coordinate better the regional initiatives and their role in the national innovation policy.

We may follow these developments in Greece, where from 1995 to 2000 twelve regional strategies (RTP, RITTS, RIS, and RIS+) and a number of trans-regional innovation projects have widely introduced the agenda of innovation into regional planning and development. These initiatives involve most of the Greek regions and establish a new understanding of regional development in which the driving forces are innovation, learning, clustering, technology transfer, demand-driven technological development, international technology cooperation, and systemic interaction.

Regional innovation strategies in Greece started in 1995 with the Regional Technology Plan of Central Macedonia. The initiative for launching the RTP was taken by the Aristotle University of Thessaloniki and the Department of Urban and Regional Planning. Before the RTP, this department had prepared a research proposal on regional innovative development in the EU, together with five other European universities, which was submitted to the European Commission, DG XVI. By pure coincidence, at that time, DG XVI had envisaged the extension of the RTP exercise to Objective 1 regions, and discussed with the university the conditions for setting up a project in Central Macedonia. The regional authority responsible for the management of the mainstream structural funds in Central Macedonia was not interested in such an initiative, and the priority given to technology and innovation within the Regional Operational Programme was rather low. At this time the Ministry of Macedonia and Thrace gave the necessary support through the intervention of the minister himself. While the intervention of the ministry opened an opportunity to start a successful project in the region, it also triggered a long-standing confrontation with the regional authority, which considered that the ministry had gone beyond its legal competence (Technopolis 1998). It took about five years to overcome this hostility, and the continuation of the RTP in the form of an RIS+ project started under quite different and positive conditions in 1999.

In the following years, the successful project in Central Macedonia and the promotion of RIS at the European level stimulated 11 more projects in Greece:

- 1997–9: Three RIS in Western Macedonia, Thessaly, Sterea Ellada, and the RITTS of Crete.

- 1998–2000: Two RIS in Epirus and Northern Aegean, and the RITTS of Eastern Macedonia and Thrace.

- 2000–: Four RIS+ in Central Macedonia, Western Macedonia, Thessaly, and Sterea Ellada.

Today, bottom-up RIS initiatives in Greece have created a critical mass allowing a visible role in the national innovation strategy. The actual challenge is the institutional link of RIS to the national innovation strategy, meaning on the one hand, to influence the regional and sectoral operational programmes of the 3rd Community Support Framework covering the period 2000–6, and on the other hand, to diffuse the culture of innovation leading to a substantial increase of the national private and public spending for innovation and technology.

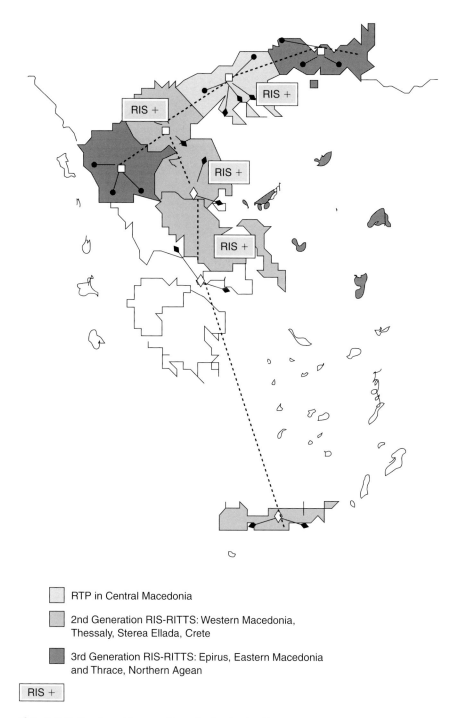

Figure 6.2 Regional innovation strategies in Greece

In support of the RIS projects, a national network has been created, namely, the Hellenic RIS Association. It is a non-profit association, created in July 1997, on the occasion of a 'Forum on Innovation Strategies in Greece', which gathered together the Greek RIS regions and 70 other organizations involved in innovation and technology transfer. Members of the association may be any participant in the Steering Committee and the Management Unit of αRITTS-RIS project, or a scientist or expert involved in regional innovation, or a representative of a local/regional authority interested in the network objectives and policies. The core of the association consists of RTP-RIS-RITTS regions, but technology parks, business innovation centres, branch technology companies, university liaison offices, university laboratories, businessmen and public officials involved in innovation development, planning, and management are also represented.

The association is a valuable tool for dealing with the problems emerging from the maturing of RIS and the synthesis of regional initiatives with the national innovation strategy. Major objectives are to assist the implementation of RIS, and to ameliorate the positioning of RIS into the national schemes for technology and innovation. However, these are not easy tasks because of the differences discussed in the previous section. RIS assumes a bottom-up approach, with emphasis on regional consensus, regional needs and demand, and innovative companies, and the implementation is based on regional programmes and initiatives. On the contrary, the national technology strategy is a top-down government policy, prioritizing technology push, R&D, and state R&D institutes, and its implementation is based on national support programmes for R&D, industry, and education.

The activities of the RIS association focus on issues of inter-regional coordination, the diffusion of best practice on innovation management techniques, joint projects for the development of services helpful to the exchange of information and technology, and the promotion of RIS.

Coordination of RIS aims to resolve problems of inter-regional competition and duplication in the creation of innovation infrastructure and services. The implementation of innovation strategies in neighbouring regions, for example, in Central Macedonia RTP, Western Macedonia RIS, and Thessaly RIS, has shown that inter-regional coordination is necessary for many reasons. Not only are the regional boundaries meaningless in the everyday operation of companies and organizations, but also the technology and innovation needs of small companies are extremely similar across neighbouring regions, and regional actors usually demand the same kinds of support infrastructure. In many cases, the decisions for the geographical location of higher education, R&D, and technology transfer facilities have raised severe conflicts, as recently happened with the creation of the National Centre for Technological Development in Thessaloniki.

Exchange of information between RIS initiatives, cooperation during the design and implementation of regional action plans seems effective for finding solutions acceptable to regional authorities and influential actors, smoothing inter-regional competition for R&D, technology transfer, and higher education institutions.

Exchange of best practice on innovation management is another key area for inter-regional cooperation. Planning practices related to innovation projects are more or less relevant for any geographical scale of a nation. Furthermore, the RIS projects have shown that small companies have important needs for information and learning on new production and marketing technologies. It is estimated that best practice in many fields of innovation planning and management (intellectual property, product cycle management, total quality control, zero defects, supply chains management, outsourcing, electronic commerce, etc.) can be promoted more effectively on an inter-regional basis, because the needs and the technological solutions are very similar across a nation's regions, while the regions usually lack expertise and skills needed for the implementation and dissemination of such techniques and technologies.

Joint projects are to promote innovation services needed for companies in the field of technology supply, technology transfer, innovation finance, business intelligence, inter-firm networking, etc. Among the immediate objectives of the Hellenic RIS Association is to develop further telematic applications and to integrate the information technology tools sustaining innovation already developed by various initiatives. It is estimated that such services may reduce the demand for the same innovation infrastructure, and introduce the innovation services into a more global and efficient supply architecture.

Most important, however, is the *positioning of RIS* in the national innovation framework and the efforts to assure the compatibility of the regional with the national innovation strategy, to remove the obstacles due to the different departures, actors, implementation procedures, and to promote the RIS achievements at the national level. The activities of the RIS association focus on the promotion of innovation at any scale and authority. The network has organized a number of major conferences and meetings to discuss innovation at the regional, national and company levels; there was coordination and design of joint pilot actions to diffuse and measure innovation at the regional level; there is a constant communication to resolve the day-to-day RIS management problems. But mainly, the association has opened a dialogue with the concerned regional and national authorities in order to convince them that innovation and technology should be at the centre of the regional and national development efforts, and that RIS initiatives may provide elaborated solutions, practical guidance and operational support towards a knowledge-based economy and society. Funding for these activities comes from the contribution of the members of the association, the contribution of RIS projects, and other national sources. Indirect funding, i.e. funding of specific activities, is provided from the budget of the RIS-RITTS projects that undertake the costs of the activities. Some specific actions are co-financed by more RIS-RITTS.

Taken together, such objectives and activities mobilize inter-regional capabilities to deal with innovation at any geographical scale. By theoretical concept and practice, RIS remain tied to bottom-up/regional procedures, but inter-regional coordination and the actions of national RIS associations may contribute to enlarging their regional horizon and have some bearing on the corresponding national effort.

Coherence of Innovation Strategies

We will repeat the rather obvious statement that in designing innovation strategies we need to recognize the limits of unilateral action on any single spatial scale, be it regional, national, or supranational. Each level has its virtues for certain factors affecting innovation, but successful strategies depend on the combination of all three levels. But what is the connecting line for a coherent strategy involving actors from all three levels and how can one avoid authorities of a given level contesting the role of others in the promotion of innovation? We argue that a coherent innovation strategy involving EU, member state, and regional actions should rely on a clear understanding of the different, but complementary roles of each contribution, and their integration into a unified framework for action.

At the *level of the European Union*, the actual orientation for a multi-level coordination in the area of innovation is defined in the strategy of the structural funds for the period 2000–6. The overall strategy approved at the Lisbon European Council in March 2000, prepares for the transition of the Union to a knowledge-based economy and society by creating better policies for the information society and R&D, as well as by reinforcing the process for competitiveness and innovation. More than the increase in the available funding, the intervention of the structural funds is opening new thematic fields and actions that will equip the regions with the means to confront the challenges of globalization, competition on international markets, and technological excellence.

It is, however, in the innovative measures under the ERDF for the period 2000–6 that this new orientation is more clearly reflected. The prime objective of innovative measures is to influence the quality of the assistance co-financed by the ERDF under Objective 1 and 2 operational programmes. Links between innovative measures and operational programmes require the introduction of incentives to experiment with innovative regional policy methods and practices. In the past (1994–9), the Commission distributed the ERDF resources available for innovative measures among eight themes: new sources of employment, culture and heritage, spatial planning (Terra), urban pilot projects (UPPs), internal inter-regional cooperation (Recite II), external inter-regional cooperation (Ecos-Ouverture), promotion of technological innovation (RIS and RTTs), and the information society (RISI I and II). These resulted in some 350 innovative projects and made it possible to experiment with new practices that promote public–private partnership and stimulate cooperation between different regions within the European Union. The experience gained from innovative inter-regional cooperation measures such as Terra, Recite II and Ecos-Ouverture prompted the preparation of the Interreg III Community Initiative. While this gained from the urban pilot projects it also inspired the new Urban II Community Initiative (European Commission 2000).

For the period 2000–6, the above eight thematic fields are reduced to only three, with the aim of exploring the future orientation of the regional policy in areas of strategic importance for the regions of the Union. These fields are:

Regional economy based on knowledge and technological innovation. Innovative measures under this field should focus on the cooperation between the public sector and the bodies responsible for RTDI and businesses, with a view to creating efficient regional innovation systems. The aim is to encourage links not only between enterprises, but also with the universities, advisory services and financial markets and other technology partners. The content of regional programmes of innovative measures in this area could cover the main aspects of a regional innovation system, including: innovation financing and contribution to the development of new financial instruments (risk capital) for business start-ups; dissemination of research results and technological adaptation within SMEs; technology transfer with the support for incubators for new enterprises which have links with universities and research centres; encouragement for spin-offs from university centres or large companies oriented towards innovation and technology, as well as schemes for assisting science and technology projects carried out jointly by small companies, universities and research centres; and networking, with the creation or reinforcement of cooperation networks between firms, research centres and universities, organizations responsible for improving the quality of human resources, financial institutions, and specialist consultants.

e-EuropeRegio: the information society serving regional development aims to bring all citizens, households, businesses, schools and administrations into the digital era by giving them online access. It intends to diffuse a digital culture underpinned by a spirit of enterprise that encourages the development of new ideas, and to ensure the compatibility with social integration and cohesion. Innovative regional measures may investigate methods: to improve digital and mobile services for young people, the elderly and the disabled; for healthcare purposes; to encourage companies to include electronic commerce in their development strategies; to provide collective access to the Internet, digital applications and multimedia resources; and to use and experiment with advanced digital technology for the benefit of rural, isolated, or landlocked areas.

Regional identity and sustainable development concerns the development of an integrated approach to economic, environmental, and social activities, and the improvement of the living and working environment of the Europeans. Innovative regional measures may explore the contribution of micro-enterprises in the craft or traditional production sectors aimed at improving their technological level and thereby achieving greater market integration, the development of culture- and nature-based tourism, the establishment of better relations between the public and private sectors in order to optimize the use of existing resources and infrastructures, and the development of schemes targeted at environmental management, adoption of clean technology, recycling of waste, and rational energy use.

The meaning of the above guidelines is to prevent the innovation and technology gap among the EU regions from widening and, at the same time, to take advantage of the opportunities offered by the new economy to less favoured regions for catching up. These guidelines inspire the actual negotiation between the Commission and the member states for the content of the new structural intervention. The Commission is clearly pushing towards innovative actions and information society projects, although some member states seem reluctant to move that way, insisting on more traditional infrastructure and hard actions.

A level below, *at the national level*, the main challenge concerns the creation of institutions and conventions that permit innovative systems and learning economies to take shape and operate. This is a critical issue, and nation states have a long tradition of setting up such institutional frameworks.

In 1992 Lundvall and Johnson advanced the notion of contemporary capitalism as the 'learning economy'. Those firms, industries, and regions that can learn faster or better become competitive because their knowledge is scarce and cannot be imitated or transferred to competitors. In fact, this learning is about new knowledge, which firms, industries, and regions have to produce. It is innovation. And what makes innovation and learning possible is a set of institutions with many different conventions and types of relations, gearing the collective action to this objective. Rules, institutions, and frameworks for action have always been important, but they were regarded principally as imperfections of the economy. They were viewed as extra-economic forces that prevent the autonomous market regulations from functioning and creating equilibrium. The irony is that the contemporary triumph of capitalism on a global scale, coincides with more intervention of non-market forces seeking to establish new mechanisms for learning, innovation, and growth.

The role of the state, in building the institutional base of the national/regional innovation systems should not be limited to the creation of conventional research institutes and state technology centres. It should involve state and non-governmental organizations, universities, business associations, financing institutions, etc., which together build the institutional framework and regulations of the learning region. The overall institutional edifice may be characterized by institutional thickness, meaning overlapping, and why not involve redundant institutions, offering multiple itineraries for innovation and learning.

Two issues that should be stressed are the differences in the organization of innovation systems in different countries, and the difficulty (or rather impossibility) of defining universal models. The institutional framework for innovation appropriate for a nation is shaped by complex political, economic, and cultural factors forged over a long period of time. On the other hand, in many countries a major restructuring in the state research, technology, education, vocational training, and finance institutions is necessary. This involves both organizational and cultural changes, and the building of institutions capable to substitute rules with conventions of trust and cooperation.

Whether one questions the notion of a national innovation system or not, there is no doubt that the state policy for innovation is a key factor (European Commission 1999a; Landabaso *et al.* 1999; Nelson 1993). Firms, as major organizations involved in the process of innovation, are increasingly forced towards sub-national and supranational relations with suppliers and technology providers. This should not be interpreted as a weakening of the state and national role, since this role is primarily institutional. It seems easier to create the norms and conventions of trust and association on a national scale, taking advantage of the cultural and political consistency of the nation, and use them for action on the global and local scales.

Finally, *the region* is the level of concrete action, which is inspired by the thematic orientations defined by the structural funds and the institutional framework formed by the national state. At this level, the elaboration of the innovation strategy involves real actors and takes into account the strengths and weaknesses of specific productive systems and the real capabilities of the research and academic community. This is the level of detailed and informed action, and cannot be replaced by national or supranational programmes (Morgan 1996).

The ingenuity of an RIS lies in the capacity to translate the concrete innovation demands and needs expressed by the regional actors into action lines appropriate for institutions of the learning economy. The simplest way to do this is to start from a simplified institutional model of a regional innovation system and integrate the conclusions and actions determined by the demand and supply analysis. The outcome of RIS should not only be projects, but also institutions that guarantee the continuity of action beyond the first preparatory stage (Table 6.1).

Table 6.1 Twenty-one key institutions for an 'innovating region'*

In the field of R&D	• Universities
	• University labs
	• Public research centres
	• Private R&D centres
	• Patent offices
In the field of innovation finance	• Venture capital funds
	• Business angels
	• Regional incentives for technology-based companies
In the field of technology transfer	• Science or technology parks
	• Business innovation centres
	• Technology networks
	• Industrial/university liaison offices
	• Technology brokers
	• Best practice clubs/associations
In the field of new product development	• Specialized consulting companies
	• Graphic design companies/centres
	• Marketing companies
In the field of business networks	• Industrial districts
	• Knowledge-intensive tertiary clusters
	• Suppliers' associations
	• Distribution networks

*Defined with respect to the components of the environment of innovation discussed in Chapter 1 (see Figure 1.3).

This is, however, only one side of the problem. The other is implementation of the regional strategies. RIS is potentially the most important regional planning scheme for technological development and innovation on a global scale. However, the critical issue in transforming this planning and strategic approach into concrete action, at least for the less developed regions of the European Community, is to tie the strategy to mechanisms, national or European, for project selection, funding, and implementation. There is no panacea on how to achieve this, but this is part of the innovativeness of each regional innovation initiative.

7 Technology Intelligence in Innovating Regions

Theoretical discussion on regional technological development gives no satisfactory answer to the question of the technologies that should be prioritized at the regional level. There are many references to 'new technologies', but this is not an adequate definition of the best thematic areas for regional technological development. The same applies to the technology-driven regional development strategy of the European Commission, the 'Innovating Regions Strategy' designed to promote technology and innovation in the less favoured regions of the Union. Regional authorities are not adequately informed which technologies they should promote through regional incentives, which technologies accelerate more regional development, and which are the critical technologies for the coming years. This is the question on which we focus. We discuss technology-based regional development, and the procedures which allow the creation of technology intelligence guiding the decisions of the regions in technology investments, technology attraction, technology training, and learning. We start with a review of the technological priorities found in the European R&D programmes. Then we examine some major technology foresight studies, their conclusions concerning emerging technologies, and the technology priorities suitable for the less favoured regions. In the last two sections we describe some tools for regional technology intelligence, and the institutional procedures needed in order to develop the capacity to manage complex innovation environments.

Technology Intelligence and Regional Innovation Strategies

Since the 1980s, the literature on urban and regional development has shown an increasing interest in technology and innovation. The globalization of the economy and the rise of technology-based cities and regions have created a new context for regional development in which vital factors are R&D, technology-intensive products and processes, and the innovation environment. There are, however, very limited indications of the content of technologies that should be prioritized to sustain technology-based regional development. The discussion frequently refers to electronics, information technology, and 'new technologies' (Glasmeier 1987;

155

Grasland 1992; Masser 1990), but obviously this is not an adequate definition of the thematic areas for regional technological development. From another point of view, the analysis of territorial concentrations of science and technology mainly utilizes indicators such as R&D spending, R&D personnel, publications, and patents, which leads to a rather 'horizontal' understanding of technology, as if the particular technology sectors and thematic areas that are cultivated in the islands of innovation have no particular significance.

In 1994 the European Commission, Directorate General for Regional Policy, introduced a high added-value policy to sustain the technology and innovation capability of the less favoured regions of the Union. Regional Technology Plans and Regional Innovation Strategies are central planning instruments for Innovating Regions, and support social engineering practices which reorient the interventions of the Structural Funds towards endogenous technological development, technology transfer, and international technology cooperation. In these initiatives, the interest seems to be in generic technologies and innovation services; no technological areas are predetermined as priority areas, and the technology targets and thematic technologies are specified with respect to the needs, the objectives, and the development trajectories of the regions. RTP-RIS-RITTS projects applied during the past five years in more than 100 European regions gave two answers to the question of technology orientation and priority.

- On the one hand, there was observed an interest in horizontal technologies such as information technologies, technologies for the environment, technologies promoting quality, and technologies for the sustainable development of rural areas.

- On the other hand, in many RIS regions, technology priorities were defined with respect to the needs of the leading industrial sectors and clusters in the regions concerned (i.e. agriculture, textiles, food, metal products, electronics, etc.). Again, because of the interdisciplinarity that governs the industrial problems and needs, this approach has not led to the definition of good practice on technology thematic fields and topics.

We feel that both sides, the theoretical thinking and the policy making, have failed to provide a sufficient answer to the question of technological priority at the regional level. Regional authorities are not well informed on which technologies they should promote when applying regional incentives, nor on the strategies needed to develop capability in emerging or critical technologies, nor on the barriers found to entering these areas.

Technological Priorities in the European R&D Programmes

An important development in the Community research policy was the adoption of the 5th Framework Programme (FP5) by the European Parliament and the Council in December 1998 that sets out the priorities for the European Union's research for the period 1999–2002. A budget of 13,700 million Euros has been agreed for the implementation of the programme, which combined with 1,260 million Euros allocated to the Euratom programme brings the overall budget to 14,960 million Euros. This represents an increase of 4.61 per cent in comparison with the FP4.

FP5 is divided into four thematic and three horizontal programmes (Table 7.1). The thematic programmes, covering the targeted R&D activity, are composed of 22 'key actions'. These are problem-oriented science and technology areas including small and large, applied, generic and basic research projects directed towards a common European or global challenge. The horizontal themes link key actions to the wider Community policies for external relations, innovation, SMEs, and human resources (CORDIS 1999).

The research priorities of FP5 were defined with respect to: (1) the principles of subsidiarity, aiming to establish a 'critical mass' of researchers at the European level, to enhance the Community policies and the development of Europe, (2) the concerns of employment, quality of life, and preservation of the environment, and (3) the harmonious development of the European Community in terms of science, technology, and business effectiveness. The programme has been conceived to solve problems and to respond to the major socio-economic challenges facing Europe. A crucial question was that of the benefit to the citizens of Europe from the 15 million Euros to be spent in FP5.

FP5 differs considerably from its predecessors. A comparison with FP4 reveals the integrated and problem-solving approach, targeted on social and economic issues (Table 7.2). The streamlined structure brings together

Table 7.1 Fifth EU R&D Framework Programme

Thematic programmes	Horizontal programmes
1 Quality of life and living resources	5 Confirming the international role of the Community research
2 User-friendly information society	
3 Competitive and sustainable growth	6 Promotion of innovation and encouragement of participation of SMEs
4 Energy, environment and sustainable development	7 Improving human research potential and the socio-economic knowledge base

Source: http://www.cordis.lu/fp5

Table 7.2 FP4 and FP5: A comparison of thematic areas

Technology areas in the 4th EU Framework Programme

A 1	**Information technologies:** (1) Software technologies, (2) Technologies for IT components, (3) Multimedia systems, (4) Focused clusters
A 2	**Telematics applications:** (1) Telematics-services of public interest, (2) Telematics for knowledge, (3) Telematics for the quality of life, (4) Telematics engineering/information
A 3	**Advanced communications technologies and services:** (1) Interactive digital multimedia, (2) Photonic technologies, (3) High-speed networking, (4) Personal communication networks, (5) Intelligence in networks, (6) Quality/safety of communications
A 4	**Industrial and materials technologies:** (1) Manufacturing technologies, (2) Materials/technologies for product innovation, (3) Technologies for means of transport
A 5	**Standards, measurement and testing:** (1) For quality European products, (2) Standards and technical support to trade, (3) For the needs of society
A 14	**Transport:** (1) Trans-European multimodal network, (2) Network optimization
A 6	**Environment and climate:** (1) Natural environment, environmental quality and global change, (2) Environmental technologies, (3) Space techniques applied to environmental monitoring, (4) Human dimensions of environmental change
A 7	**Marine science and technology:** (1) Marine science, (2) Strategic marine research, (3) Marine technologies
A 11	**Non-nuclear energy:** (1) Energy models and methods, (2) Rational use of energy Renewable energies, (3) Fossil fuels
A 12	**Nuclear fusion:** (1) Exploring innovative aspects, (2) Reactor safety, (3) Radioactive waste management, (4) Radiological impact on man and the environment, (5) Mastering events of the past
A 13	**Controlled thermonuclear fusion:** (1) Design and methods in plasma and superconducting, (2) Concept improvements, (3) Tritium breeding blankets, radiation resistant materials, safety
A 8	**Biotechnology:** (1) Cell factories, genome analysis, plant and animal biotechnology, (2) Immunology, transdisease vaccinology, structural biology, (3) Demonstration, ethical aspects, public perception
A 9	**Biomedicine and health:** (1) Pharmaceutical research, (2) Biomedical technology and engineering, (3) Brain research, (4) Diseases with major socio-economic impact, (5) Human genome research, (6) Public health, (7) Biomedical ethics

Technology areas in the 5th EU Framework Programme

A2 **User-friendly information society**
(1) Systems and services for the citizen
(2) New methods of work and electronic commerce
(3) Multimedia content and tools
(4) Essential technologies and infrastructure

A3 **Competitive and sustainable growth**
(1) Innovative products, processes, organization
(2) Sustainable mobility and intermodality
(3) Land transport and marine technologies
(4) New perspectives for aeronautics

A4 **Energy, environment and sustainable development**
(1) Sustainable management and quality of water
(2) Global change, climate and biodiversity
(3) Sustainable marine ecosystems
(4) The city of tomorrow
(5) Cleaner energy, systems and renewable
(6) Economic and efficient energy
(7) Controlled thermonuclear fusion
(8) Nuclear fusion

A1 **Quality of life and management of living resources**
(1) Food, nutrition and health
(2) Control of infectious diseases
(3) The 'cell' factory
(4) Environment and health
(5) Sustainable agriculture, fisheries, and forestry and integrated development of rural areas including mountain areas
(6) Ageing

continued

Table 7.2 *Continued*

Technology areas in the 4th EU Framework Programme

A
10

Agriculture and fisheries: (1) Integrated production and processing chains, (2) Scaling-up and processing technologies, (3) Generic science and technologies for nutritious foods, (4) Agriculture, forestry and rural development, (5) Fisheries and aquaculture

B　**Targeted socio-economic research:** (1) Science and technology policy in Europe, (2) Research on education and training, (3) Research into social integration and exclusion

E　**Training and mobility of researchers:** (1) Research networks, (2) Access to large-scale facilities, (3) Training through research

C　**Cooperation with third countries:** (1) Scientific and technological cooperation in Europe, (2) Cooperation with non-European industrialized countries, (3) Scientific and technological cooperation with the developing countries

D　**Dissemination and optimization of results:** (1) Exploitation of research results, (2) Dissemination of technology to enterprises, (3) Financial environment for dissemination of technology

the R&D themes under four major programmes instead of 14, as in the FP4. The key actions intend to mobilize a wide range of scientific and technological disciplines required to address a specific problem, and to overcome the barriers that exist between disciplines and organizations.

The structure of FP5 implies three answers to the question of technological priority. First, it makes a choice in favour of integration, defining four major technological fields only. These fields are further specified in the key actions, problem-oriented science and technology topics with wide R&D content. With respect to FP4, integration is thematic but also organizational, since the thematic fields of the former Framework Programme had lost their management autonomy and were integrated into the new structure.

Second, the programme makes a choice in favour of interdisciplinary approach, since many disciplines are recognized within each thematic programme and key action. In the 'City of Tomorrow', for instance, city and regional planning coexists with environmentally clean technologies and car engine technologies. Bringing together many scientific fields is intended to exploit current technological advance, while keeping track of the problems and challenges of everyday life in Europe.

Third, FP5 highlights the dominant research and technology fields of our era: life sciences, information technologies, industrial technologies, and environmental sciences. These fields reflect the approaches of integration, and provide the necessary interface between academic categorization of R&D and the phenomenology of the practical problems.

Technology areas in the 5th EU Framework Programme

D **Improving human research potential and the socioeconomic knowledge base**

B **Confirming the international role of the Community**

C **Promotion of innovation and encouragement of SME participation**

Framework Programme 5 seeks a balance between technological advances and the challenges of contemporary life. The need to sustain Community policies and to have immediate meaning for the citizens of Europe is seen to reorient the science and technology fields. As happened with the modification of the regional policy from Regional Technology Plans to Regional Innovation Strategies, we witness the same move from technological objectives towards demand-led objectives and approach.

In the on-going and still non-concluded discussion on FP6, seven priority thematic areas have been selected. They cover most of the areas of FP5 but more interest is shown in health and food sectors. These are:

- *Genomics and biotechnology for health*, to exploit breakthroughs achieved in decoding the genomes of living organisms, more particularly for the benefit of public health and citizens and to increase the competitiveness of the European biotechnology industry.

- *Information society technologies*, to stimulate the development of the Information Society and allow European citizens in all EU regions the possibility of benefiting fully from the development of a knowledge-based society.

- *Nanotechnologies, intelligent materials, and new production processes*, to exploit leading-edge technologies for the knowledge, and intelligence-based products, services and manufacturing processes.

- *Aeronautics and space*, to consolidate the position of the European aerospace industry vis-à-vis increasingly strong world competition, and improving safety and environmental protection.

- *Food safety and health risks*, to develop a system of production and distribution of safe and healthy food and control food-related risks, relying in particular on biotechnology tools.

- *Sustainable development and global change*, to strengthen the scientific and technological capacities in this field and make a significant contribution to the international efforts to understand and control global change and preserve the equilibrium of ecosystems.

- *Citizens and governance in the European knowledge-based society*, to mobilize European research capacities in economic, political, social, and human sciences with a view to understanding and addressing issues related to the emergence of the knowledge-based society.

Critical Technologies at the Beginning of the Twenty-first Century

Framework Programmes reflect R&D priorities of the European Commission and the Directorate General responsible. All leading industrial nations, however, have made serious efforts to capture future technological trends and outline the course of critical technologies; included are studies of the MITI in Japan, the US government, the Federal government in Germany, and other OECD countries.

Particularly interesting is the foresight initiative on science and technology at the start of the twenty-first century, commissioned by the German Federal Research Minister. An interdisciplinary working group carried out the initiative under the auspices of the Fraunhofer Institute (Karlsruhe). The study adopts a comparative approach, examining research previously undertaken in Japan and the US, and identified 87 critical technologies grouped under nine headings. These areas were expected to affect the solution of societal, ecological, and economic problems in the immediate future. Grupp outlines, as follows, the structural logic of these technologies (Grupp 1994).

Advanced materials are expected to play a critical role in multiple sectors on safety, environmental protection, and comfort. The trend is towards producing materials with predetermined characteristics and the methods evolved from 'trial and error' to the design of tailor-made materials. More specific technology fields in this area are, among others, high-performance ceramics, polymers and metals, gradient materials, materials for energy conversion, organic magnetic and electric materials, surface materials, diamond layers and films, molecular surfaces, meso-scale polymers, and multifunctional materials.

Nanotechnology is an emerging technology field challenging traditional engineering concepts by developing processes at the atomic and molecular levels. Interdisciplinary cooperation is important and the applications will probably reach into the fields of tailor-made materials, biological technical systems, single-electron tunnelling, nano-scale materials, manufacturing in micro- and nano-scales.

Microelectronics represents the major technological revolution of the late twentieth century, exerting a strong influence in most technology areas. In the twenty-first century, high frequencies, high data transmission, and superconductivity applications will radically change the field of micro-electronics. Emerging technologies in this field concern information storage, signal processing, microelectronics materials, high-speed electronics, plasma technology, superconductivity, and high temperature electronics.

Photonics is the combined use of microelectronics, opto-electronics, integrated optics and micro-optics, and is well suited to all types of pattern recognition, parallel search procedures, and artificial neural networks. Individual subjects in the field include laser technology, luminous silicon, broadband telecommunications, photonic digital technology, optical computing, as well as microsystems engineering, and sensor technology.

Software and simulation is an important asset for Europe with growing applications in new theoretical and applied fields such as modelling and simulation, molecular modelling, bio-informatics, non-linear dynamics, artificial intelligence, fuzzy logic, data networks. Today's proximity of software to information technology hardware is expected to extend to molecular electronics and biotechnology.

Molecular electronics or bioelectronics cover a field of research in which highly complex electronic systems operate on the basis of molecular switching elements and networks. The combination of biology and electronics is transferring models from the operation of the human brain to electric and electronic processes. Applications concern biosensor, neuro-technology, and neuro-informatics.

Cellular biotechnology covers the area of biotechnology but it is highly probable that over the next few years cell biology will be established as an independent subject bridging molecular genetics, biochemistry and medicine. The general heading of cellular biotechnology includes topics of molecular biotechnology, catalysis and biocatalysis, bionics, biomedicine materials, renewable resources, environmental biotechnology, and plant breeding.

Information, production and management engineering does not coincide with traditional production and management as subdivisions of business administration, but it relates to the mastering of technology and innovation. Important issues are the environment for technological innovation, the organizational innovations, the bridging of research, development

Table 7.3 Production relevance of emerging technologies

	Construction	Energy	Food	Medicine	Exploration, recycling	Environment	Transport
Advanced materials	✓	✓	✓	✓	✓	✓	✓
Nano-technology	✗	✓	✗	✓	✗	✗	✓
Micro-electronics	✗	✓	✗	✓	✗	✓	✓
Photonics	✓	✓	✗	✓	✗	✓	✓
Microsystem engineering	✓	✓	✓	✓	✓	✓	✓
Software and simulation	✓	✓	✓	✓	✗	✓	✓
Molecular electronics	✓	✓	✓	✓	✓	✓	✓
Cellular biotechnology	✓	✓	✓	✓	✓	✓	✗
Production/management engineering	✗	✗				✓	✗

Source: Adapted from Grupp (1994), Appendix A.

and production phases, and the development of advanced knowledge management techniques including modelling in manufacturing, production logistics, and lean production systems.

The contribution of the above technologies to the solution of important societal problems may be diverse. Industrial and production applications cover a wide range of sectors; the technologies regarded as more generic, however, are those in the fields of advanced materials, microsystem engineering, molecular electronics, and cellular biotechnology (Table 7.3).

A more futuristic account of the changes that we should expect in the above fields of science and technology and the effects on economic and social issues is given in the forecast of emerging technologies made by George Washington University. The forecast was a continuous assessment of major technological advances, based on the scanning of relevant information sources, trend analysis, and the Delphi survey. The results highlight some important trends for the coming three decades that will be characterized by major technological advances.

- In *manufacturing*, we are likely to see the mass customization of many products around 2011. Automation and computer-integrated manufacturing should proceed, such that the proportion of factory jobs will decline from its current percentage of about 20 per cent of the workforce to less than 10 per cent by 2015. There is a 64 per cent likelihood that helpful robot servants will arrive in 2016.

- In *materials*, composites will enter product designs by 2016. Promising advances in nanotechnology and microscopic machines would lead to the development of self-assembling and intelligent materials around 2026 or 2027. Advances in high-temperature superconductivity may finally see practical application in commercial applications by 2015.

- In *food production*, by 2008, genetic engineering should allow the routine production of new strains of plants and animals. In 2015, the majority of farmers will have adopted organic or alternative farming methods, and the use of chemical fertilizers and pesticides will have declined by 2012 to less than half of current usage. Precision farming and hydroponics will be commonly used by 2015, whereas automated farming and urban greenhouses will not appear until 2020. Panellists agreed that the consumption of artificial meats, vegetables, bread, and other foodstuffs could become common fare by 2022, but they gave this only 39 per cent likelihood.

- In *medicine*, computerized medical systems, including provisions for home and self-care, should be commonly used by 2007. Holistic health practices are becoming more accepted and will be well integrated in medicine by 2009. Gene therapy will help eradicate inherited diseases by 2013. Growing genetically similar or cloned organs and constructing synthetic organs are likely to arrive in the years 2018 and 2019, respectively.

- The fields of *energy* and the *environment* are inherently difficult to separate, especially because there seems to be a convergence in environmental awareness and alternative energy use. By 2010 or so, we should expect manufacturers to adopt 'green' methods, and a significant portion of energy usage will be derived from renewable sources and biomass. In these years consumers will recycle about half their household waste. Around 2016, additional improvements in fossil fuel efficiency will reduce greenhouse gas emissions by one-half. At the same time, the majority of manufacturers may operate within industrial ecology parks and use recycled materials for their projects. Though the impact on society would be great, the likelihood of advanced energy systems such as hydrogen and fusion coming online in the 2020s is low.

- In *transportation*, technologies that may have the most direct impact on daily lives are in the field of transportation. Before people commonly drive advanced electric cars in the 2010s, hybrid vehicles combining the advantages of electric and internal combustion systems will be on the road by 2006. By 2017, high-speed rail systems will connect major cities of the developed world, led by Japan. Around this time, we will see automated highway systems and intelligent transportation systems commonly used to reduce traffic congestion, take control of route planning, and even do most of the driving. The panel gave a low probability to hypersonic aircraft, accommodating half of transoceanic passengers. These changes in transportation, coupled with changes in IT and telecommuting, may lead to clustered, self-contained communities around 2023.

(Halal *et al.* 1998)

Many of the elements described in the German foresight study are found also in estimations of future technology trends in Europe made by OECD (1998). It is estimated that at the beginning of the twenty-first century five industrial branches are expected to dominate the production landscape: (1) industries related to environmental issues (monitoring, recycling, waste disposal, measurement), (2) information technology industries (computer equipment, software, telecommunication services), (3) health industries (pharmaceuticals, medical equipment, medical services), (4) sports industries (brand name products, athletic equipment and infrastructure), and (5) tourist industries, including popular art, leisure crafts and hotels. Accordingly, a number of technological fields are expected to support and nurture development in these five broad industries, including:

- Advanced materials and ceramics.

- Computer technology and software, simulation, high resolution images, computer networks.

- Biotechnology, molecular biology and medicine technology.

- Energy technology.

- Technology of integrated production systems.

In these attempts to outline emerging technology fields and critical science and technology topics, two trends are clear. There is a consensus on the broad definition of critical technologies for the immediate future, which encompasses advanced materials, information technology, microelectronics and software, biotechnology and molecular biology, and management engineering. The second, and more important, is the trend of cross-fertilization. This is quite different from the old principle of technologies working in combination to respond to commercial applications in the production or civilian sphere. What is new is the belief that advances in a particular field of science and technology do not emerge from developments in the understanding and deepening of knowledge inside the field, but rather from the application of models and thinking coming from areas with no apparent thematic links. Technology foresight exercises imply that cross-fertilization is promising for all major emerging technologies, photonics, microelectronics, and biosciences.

Technological Priorities for the Less Favoured Regions of the EU

It is widely accepted that during the past decade, science and technology acquired higher priority in the development of the less favoured regions (LFRs) of the Union. Now more exposed to international competition from low-wage but technologically capable countries, these regions urgently need technology, training, and human resources, which will allow them to compete in terms of technology and quality, rather than price and labour cost.

For the LFRs, the challenge comes from the technology gap between the core and the less developed regions and the established structures of R&D, which threaten the process of regional convergence. There are indications of increased polarization between north and south in the Union, in terms of information and communication technologies. Furthermore, Objective 1 regions are characterized by a series of technological deficiencies, such as low RTD intensity, over-representation of the public sector and lower presence of the private sector, emphasis on basic research, low levels of technology transfer between the public and private sectors, and poor linkages to international R&D and innovation networks (Zitt *et al.* 1999; Landabaso 1995).

Given these conditions in the LFRs, the questions of technological priority, R&D, and innovation demand some urgent answers. Should these regions adopt similar technological objectives to the core regions? Or is it better to focus on technologies appropriate for the traditional industries, those usually dominating the productive sector? Or should they invest in the more advanced technologies as a bypass to catch up?

In May 1998, the European Commission addressed a communication to the Council, the European Parliament, and the Committee of the Regions in order to bring together regional development, R&D, and innovation into a single coherent framework (European Commission 1998b). The communication, *Reinforcing cohesion and competitiveness through research, technological development and innovation* (COM 275/98) points out that the R&D and technology gap between the European regions is far larger than the economic gap, and discusses a number of actions on the level of the R&D Framework Programme and the Structural Programmes to bridge this gap.

On the level of the R&D programme, it is noted that the FP5 introduced a series of key actions such as 'Sustainable management and quality of water', 'Sustainable development of agriculture, fisheries and forestry, including the integrated development of rural areas', 'Systems and services for the citizen', 'Sustainable mobility and intermodality', and 'The city of tomorrow', which are particularly relevant for LFRs. Additionally, the horizontal programmes are concerned with the linkages between core and LFRs, reinforcing the training and mobility of researchers, the promotion of innovation and dissemination of research results, and the extension of networks of excellence.

On the level of the Structural Programmes, the communication points out the progress made in the funding of R&D and technology projects during the 2nd Community Support Framework (1994–9) which showed spectacular increase in technology funding both in Objective 1 and Objective 2 regions. In terms of recommendations, the communication outlines three priorities, which may ensure that RTD and innovation interventions are integrated with the productive sector of the LFRs:

- Cohesion policy should shift from primarily promoting upstream research and technological capacity on its own, towards helping to turn R&D and innovation efforts into economic activity.

- Cohesion policy should improve networking and industrial cooperation. The complexity of the current technological development requires better integration between R&D and other business functions and feedback loops linking R&D, product innovation, production, and marketing.

- More interest should be taken in human capabilities, which are central to competitiveness and knowledge-based development.

The orientations of both the R&D and Structural Programmes suggest that technological priorities in LFRs are defined on the one hand in terms of appropriate technology fields, and on the other, in terms of linkages and networks with more advanced regions, partners, and institutions. The thematic topics highlighted in technology foresight exercises are valid, but in addition thematic fields primarily targeted to LFRs concern water management, sustainable development, agriculture, sustainable transportation and city planning. However, technological advance seems to be a question more of relationship than specialization. For the Structural Funds, in particular, the emphasis is laid on the integration between R&D and the production sector at the regional level, and on trans-regional R&D and innovation networks fostering European technological integration.

Regional Technology Intelligence: Technology Watch, Foresight, and Assessment

Technology areas defined by the European R&D programmes and national foresight exercises on future technologies may be extremely useful for understanding the advancement of science and technology, but seem to have limited use as a direct guide for regional technology policy.

The regions have the need for more detailed technological options and individual trajectories for innovation and technological development. However, the complexity of the factors that influence the integration of a region into the world economy and the chaotic advance in science and technological innovation make it irrelevant to choose standard technological objectives for every region. By contrast, it seems highly important to define specific technology objectives at the regional level, and to capture the trends in products, services, and technologies securing a 'foothold in the future' for the creation of a regional technology-based competitive advantage (Hamel and Prahalad 1994). Three major procedures and techniques for acquiring such technology intelligence are technology watch, technology foresight, and technology assessment.

Technology watch (TW) opens a window to the understanding of technology trends; it is a starting point for technology information, analysis, and assessment. TW is a practice of inquiry that pursues a comprehensive understanding of technologies by providing analytical frameworks to monitor and understand the changes, either in particular technology areas or in entire technological landscapes. The purpose is not so much to gather voluminous, detailed information, but rather to create 'insight', 'executive enlightenment', and awareness of what is going on in particular fields of science and technology (Van Wyk 1997).

Technology watch is a continuous observation and data mining rather than a one-off practice. The main task is to create a system for long-term technology information, benchmarking, analysis of technology trends, including opportunities and threats, and reporting. Given the number and complexity of the technology fields, the variable sources of information, the multiplicity of indicators and milestones, and the different methods for analysis, it is not possible to define a unique method of technology watch. Van Wyk (1997) has suggested, however, a four-step procedure.

Step one is the definition of the landscape that has to be observed. Technology watch is possible in defined technology areas only; to cover a wider technological landscape it is necessary to review more areas. A major problem at this initial stage is the correct classification of the technology area(s) that will be scanned. The options are many, since one may find many different classifications, according to scientific and technology areas, commercial technology areas, and technology directories by different organizations.

Step two is the definition of information sources. These sources include scientific and technical literature, science and technology columns of business magazines, reports of international organizations on new technologies, usually referred to as 'emerging', 'key' or 'critical', and patent databases. National foresight exercises may provide valuable input, as well as assessment and testing reports. Internet resources are most valuable. The home pages of leading technology companies are a useful source of information, as well as information gathered with the help of search engines.[1] A key necessity in scanning is to establish a directory of sources that one should 'visit' periodically and monitor new elements and data.

Identifying indicators and landmark technologies that serve as milestones of technological advance is the third step. The definition of technology performance parameters has major importance in following the advances into given technology areas. After reviewing the relevant literature, Nieto *et al.* describe three categories of technology performance parameters (Nieto *et al.* 1998).

- In some studies, the technology performance has been estimated on the number of related scientific articles that were published. The underlying hypothesis is that increments in a number of significant publications about a determined technology, reflect increments in the level of understanding it, which normally is converted into product/process improvement (Roussel 1984).

- Other studies have measured the technology performance with criteria and variables of a commercial nature, such as the number of new products introduced into the marketplace (Becker and Speltz 1986). However, defining a parameter exclusively on commercial criteria is of little use when making technology decisions.

- Finally, some authors emphasize that the performance parameter must reflect technical characteristics or qualities that synthesize the most significant characteristics of the technology (Foster 1986; Lee and Nakicenovic 1988). Configuration variables that reflect intrinsic properties of the materials employed are a usual performance indicator of this type.

Observing landmark technologies and performance indicators and tracing their evolution creates an understanding generated from the rate and direction of change in a particular area of the technological landscape. This helps to stop one becoming lost in a sea of descriptive information and data.

Step four is analysis and evaluation. This is a domain of highly creative thinking, where procedures are not algorithmic, and intuitive judgement and individual flair are more important. Van Wyk proposes a thematic analysis in which the main objective is to identify, from the list of landmark technologies, those that are relevant to the organization concerned, and relate them to its core competences, overall strategy and vision (Van Wyk 1997). A matrix of landmark technologies and core competences may be very useful in this respect. The reviewer should consider each landmark technology or performance indicator in turn and define its impact on the core competences of the organization.

Watts and Porter, by contrast, propose an analysis based on bibliometrics, which exploits information stored in large electronic databases, such as the Engineering Index (ENGI), the US Patents, and Darwent World Wide Patents. This technique was developed by the Technology Policy and Assessment Centre at Georgia Tech, and used context indicators (i.e. geographical dispersion, economic dispersion, sectoral concentration, location of activity, maturation, applications, know-how availability) calculated from the inscriptions of the base (Watts and Porter 1997). The consecutive steps of the analysis are presented in Table 7.4.

The search starts from Boolean adjacency operations and experimentation, and with the help of indicators traces the current status of a technology in terms of its life cycle prospects, significant contextual influences, and product value chain potentials.

Technology foresight (TF) is a move forward, adding a prospective dimension to technology watch. The term was introduced by Irvine and Martin (1984) to describe a systematic effort to look ahead in science and technology with the aim of identifying the areas of strategic research and the emerging generic technologies likely to yield the greatest economic and social benefits. Grupp and Linstone (1998) point out that foresight takes into account that there isn't a single future, and depending on the action or failure to act at present, many futures are possible, but only one of them will happen. No doubt, the wording is inspired by quantum mechanics and the uncertainty principle of Heisenberg, nevertheless it points out the added value of the foresight exercise. The latter is supposed to look

Table 7.4 Steps in technology opportunities analysis

1 Search on the basic topical term(s) in multiple databases.
2 Download electronic abstracts from a prime, available database; examine cumulated keywords to refine topic understanding to generate good search algorithm.
3 Redo search in most advantageous database(s); download abstracts.
4 Examine keywords, title words, and abstract words and phrases; read abstracts to gain fluency with related activities, applications, key players, and dispersion.
5 Plot trends in overall activity, topic specific activity, institution-specific activity, etc.
6 Consider activity patterns by type (academic, government, industry) or other.
7 Model the technology life-cycle.
8 Cluster technological or other activity associated with the target.
9 Map key supporting technologies, institutional interests, etc.
10 Depict maps at different time slices.
11 Map likely future technological or competitive profiles, if appropriate.
12 Develop a technology decomposition tree, including tagging players, a breakout for key contributing technologies.
13 Perform analysis on special areas (e.g. gap analysis).

Source: Adapted from Watts and Porter (1997).

forward to the complex interaction between scientific communities with management views on competitiveness, technology investments, and market opportunities. The purpose is not a forecasting based on probabilistic predictions of future technologies, but a dialogue combining data analysis and communication between informed parties, experts, and stakeholders. Before describing, however, the dominant method of technology foresight, let us examine two characteristic examples.

- Japan has been conducting TF for a long period and in a variety of public and private organizations and contexts. Since 1971, the Science and Technology Agency has been conducting Delphi surveys at regular intervals, about every five years, to provide information for science and technology strategies and planning. Every TF survey projects 30 years into the future, and the Delphi method has been used throughout. The sixth survey began in 1995 and the results were released in June 1997. It was developed in three stages. First, major technological categories were set up, covering the fields of materials and processing, electronics, information, life sciences, space, marine and earth science, resources and energy, environment, agriculture, production and machinery, urbanization and construction, communication, transportation, and health and medical care. Since the beginning of TF exercises in Japan, the number of technological fields and the number of technological topics has been constantly increasing. Second, after breaking down the above technology fields, smaller subcategories, technologies and products were listed: 1,072 topics were defined with technologies expected to have a particularly great impact. Third, experts from R&D institutes, universities, and companies assessed the analytical topics and individual technologies. A total of 3,000 researchers have participated in the sixth survey, and 100 were involved in the design of the survey and the analysis of results (Kuwahara 1998).

- Another good example of TF is the French survey on critical technologies (Les 100 technologies clés) that had a narrower scope, but combined Delphi expert interviews with bibliometric studies and patent analysis. The initial questions were very pragmatic and concerned the more important technologies for the French industry, the European leadership in these fields, and the actions to be taken. The approach was very similar to the TF 'German Technologies at the Beginning of the 21st Century' discussed in the previous section (see pp. 162–4). The first step involved the definition of technology selection criteria. A steering committee was created which outlined nine selection criteria: actual and potential markets, impact on foreign trade, social and cultural acceptability, vulnerability, contribution to national needs, connection with the national industry, diffusion capacity, and assessment of competitiveness. The next step used these criteria to identify technologies; large groups were defined (life sciences, information technology, energy, managerial techniques, health, environment, communication, transport, housing, and infrastructure) which were further analysed in 136 technology topics. In the third step, each technology topic was assessed on the basis of bibliometric studies, patent analysis, and interviews with experts. Additional information was collected on markets, players, companies, and R&D programmes. In the final step, 105 technologies were identified as 'critical', accompanied by a short description, a ranking of the degree of development, and the relative scientific leadership in Europe. A good information base was produced, and the positive impact of this TF exercise helped to reorient industrial research subsidies of the Ministry of Industry in relation to the 100 critical technologies (Heraud and Cuhls 1998).

The distinctive characteristic of technology foresight is the Delphi method. It consists of experts' judgement by means of successive iterations (rounds) of a given questionnaire, to show convergence of opinions and to identify dissent or non-convergence (Grupp and Linstone 1998). The method is useful for long-range forecasts, 25–30 years, and the experts' opinions replace theoretical coherent frameworks suitable for extrapolations.[2]

The Delphi method is constructed along a hierarchical model. Level one includes the monitoring and evaluation committee that decides on the

Regional Foresight

Limousin (France): The region of Limousin is an early starter in regional foresight. Its first study (1987) provided scenarios for the development of the region to a 2007 time horizon. In 1997 a second foresight study was undertaken with a time horizon to 2017. The study was based on a three-step methodology: (a) a retrospective diagnosis aimed at analysing the role and impact at policy-making level of the first foresight exercise; (b) A prospective diagnosis to describe the most prominent trends at different scales and in different domains at global level, and to plot these trends by means of a gross impact matrix to describe the impact of the trends on the region and to investigate the different possibilities of action for the region. (c) Defining actions – here the objective was to develop a proactive plan to address the future.

West Midlands (UK): The West Midlands Regional Development Agency (Advantage West Midlands) started a two-year foresight exercise in late 1999. The exercise aims to support regional industrial competitiveness through the use of foresight, the exchange of best practice, and the utilization of a sound strategy for research, technology development and innovation. The exercise is tailored mainly for SMEs. It is designed as a mini-foresight exercise emulating the sector panel and steering group approach of the national foresight.

North-East England (UK): Foresight North East is a programme which was set up in 1996 and run since 1998 by RTC North. While serving as a contact point for national foresight, the programme [has] run several successful regional foresight activities using a variety of methods. Scenario workshops have proved very popular, both in relation to the offshore sector and vocational education. Opportunity mapping has occurred in Energy and Environment sectors. High tech seminars have been organized in IT, communication, chemical sensors, nanotechnology and other specialist areas. The choice of method is generally a matter for the committee or panel concerned.

The Basque region (Spain): Foresight activities linked to the Science and Technology Plan for the Basque Country promoted by the Basque Government are carried out periodically. The Plan is organized around eight industrial clusters (Aeronautics, Automotive, Energy, Environment, Telecommunications, Electrical appliances, Knowledge and machine tools). The clusters are responsible for analysing the trends in technology, with the aim of feeding into three types of S&T support programmes. In addition, a Technology Analysis Working Group analyses future trends in order to detect the main technological trends that will exert influence on the region, and these inform the core of the plan.

(Gavigan and Scapolo 2001: 21–2)

main technology fields that the exercise will cover, and the main concepts for the evaluation of the technology fields (i.e. role within the industry, social implications, national and international leadership, etc.). This usually leads to a dozen fields, more or less common in all national technology foresight exercises. A subcommittee is then set up for each technology field.

Level two concerns the work of subcommittees deciding on the further division of each field into more detailed technology topics. Once the topics are defined, each subcommittee discusses and selects the technology related questions and indicators for the specific technology field. The subcommittees also select the experts who will be asked to answer the questionnaire concerning each technology topic.

Level three is the work done by experts in each technology field and topic. The experts are asked to fill in questionnaires in successive rounds, and in each round they are informed of the answers given by the other experts. The main advantage of the method is that the experts can shift position, and this is a normal effect of communication and interaction between them. The rounds end when there is a stabilization of answers. In the end the result may exhibit bipolar views, since the method does not force consensus. In a famous Delphi exercise performed by the RAND Organization in 1964, the first round began with a blank sheet, and the panellists provided the first issues.

In Europe, the procedures adopted in Delphi exercises in Germany, France, and the UK, were highly influenced by the Japanese experience, and there was a good degree of bilateral cooperation. At the regional level, there was a very positive response to the initiative of the Technopolis of Bordeaux, and in many other regions (see Regional Foresight). In any case, the value of the method seems to be higher for public administration and the big companies, since both may use the results for framing their future technology plans.

Technology assessment (TA) adds a political dimension to technology watch and foresight. The roots of TA are in the 1960s when large-scale applications of technology began to affect the USA economy and society. The turning point was the creation in 1972 of the congressional Office for Technology Assessment (OTA) which was focused on identifying and analysing the potential negative consequences of technologies, and its demise at the end of 1995 (Herdman and Jensen 1997; Hill 1997). Technology assessment should be distinguished from technology evaluation. The first is more political and impact oriented, whereas the second is focusing on the comparison of defined technologies.

Various definitions were given to TA, which differ in the role of technology assessment, whether it is a neutral, fact-finding activity or whether it is normative and contributing to the development of technologies. Two typical definitions are:

Technology assessment is a class of policy studies, which systematically examine the effects on society that may occur when a technology is introduced, extended or modified. It emphasizes those consequences that are unintended, indirect or delayed.

Technology assessment is an attempt to establish an early warning system to detect, control, and direct technological changes and developments so as to maximize the public good while minimizing the public risks.

(Van den Ende *et al.* 1998)

The ideas and practices in TA have changed dramatically during the past 30 years, and three generations of TA can be distinguished, coexisting today, each with its own specific goals and methods (Berloznik and Van Langenhove 1998).

Early Warning TA represents the original discourse, giving emphasis on the prediction of the societal impact of scientific and technological development. It is usually part of a political decision process, which is interested in an informed opinion on aspects of a technological application or a major investment project. The practices of OTA followed this concept. It was clearly stated that Congress should 'equip itself with a new and effective means of securing competent, unbiased information concerning the physical, biological, economic, social, and political effects of technological applications, and to provide early indications of the probable beneficial or adverse impacts of the applications of technology' (The Technology Assessment Act of 1972, cited in Herdman and Jensen 1997). In this discourse, TA is considered as 'neutral' and 'objective'. Scientific rigour, reliability and validity of work, statistical significance, experimentation and control, guarantee an assessment that is not influenced by the decision-making process.

Constructive TA is a second generation of TA that emerged after the 1980s. In this case, the emphasis is upon the guiding of technological development and the active involvement of all possible actors taking part in the development, implementation, and use of technologies. CTA questions both the neutrality of the assessment and the assumption that it is possible to predict the course of development of a technology and all its societal effects. From this point of view, it proposes participatory procedures, and the broadening of the decision-making process about technological innovation by including as many relevant actors as possible.

Integrated TA is the most recent approach. In this case, TA becomes part of the technology development process, and scientists are engaged in it while working in the laboratory. The results of the assessment guide the design of the technology they are developing. The concept of ITA constitutes a transfer into the R&D labs of quality management principles and the culture of zero-defect quality management. The major objective of ITA is to increase the efficiency of R&D by reducing the negative aspects of a technology in its initial stages.

The methods applied in TA are diverse. The rule is that in different approaches of TA, different methods are used (Van den Ende *et al.* 1998). In Early Warning TA, the methodological focus is on impact analysis made by experts in the specific fields. These methods include analyses of technological options, life cycle analyses, market studies, construction of scenarios, and forecasting. In Constructive TA, the methods shift towards intervention to assure the participation of the interested actors in the innovation process. Participatory TA is a typical method of this kind, based on discussions, meetings, and workshops. Integrated TA forms part of the research process. During the evolution of the R&D, researchers reflect on and if possible examine the consequences of the technology they are developing. The results are used as a feedback to avoid negative or unwanted consequences.

These three techniques (TW, TF, TA) are not exclusively for developing technology intelligence. They may prove very efficient in bridging the gap between the determination of generic technology fields and the definition of specific technology topics corresponding to the profile of a geographical area.

Technology foresight exercises in Japan, Germany, France and elsewhere show a convergence at the level of generic technologies that are considered most important, since the same cluster of 10–12 technologies appears at the ground level of critical or emerging technologies. This cluster comprises information technologies, microelectronics, advanced materials, industrial technologies, life sciences, nutrition and health technologies, biotechnology, energy technologies, environmental sciences, and production and management engineering. However, the gap between the foresight exercises grows larger at the next stage of analytical technology topics within the above generic fields. At this level, the regional specificity becomes decisive. The choices increase from tens to hundreds, and technology watch methods or Delphi foresight may be fruitful in defining a smaller group of appropriate technologies for a particular region.

Technology Intelligence and Innovating Regions in Europe

As mentioned, technology and innovation have become major priorities for the development of the less favoured regions of the European Union and this is clearly reflected in the new generation of regional development programmes for the period 2000–6. The guidelines for the Structural Funds of this period, and the communication of the European Commission on competitiveness through research and technological development, point out that the cohesion policy should give an increasing priority to promoting RTD and innovation capacities, integrating all fields of intervention of the structural assistance. Part of this concern are the RIS-RITTS initiatives which are opening new ways in the intervention of the Structural Funds and guide the European regional policy towards actions for R&D, technology, and innovation.

Based on the principles of RIS and the concept of regional innovation systems, we have used the term 'innovative region' to characterize regions that apply regional strategies in order to strengthen or further develop the respective regional innovation system (Komninos 1998). Autio points out that a regional innovation system is a social system composed of interacting entities: the knowledge application and exploitation entity and the knowledge generation and diffusion entity. The interactions within and between organizations composing the system and its entities generate the knowledge flows that drive the evolution of the regional innovation system (Autio 1998). Innovation-driven projects and the innovation environment formed into an Innovative Region address the structural deficiencies of small firms and the regional technology organizations: the shortcomings related to the capacity of firms to identify their needs for innovation, the scarcity of technological intermediaries, the poorly developed financial systems, the lack of dynamic business services, the weak cooperation between the public and the private sectors in the field of technology and innovation, the low participation in international RTD networks, the scarce linkages of multinational companies with local suppliers (Landabaso *et al.* 1999).

In the process of constructing an effective regional innovation system, Landabaso *et al.* very accurately point out the need for:

An 'intelligent cell' to trigger a learning process in a regional economy. The regional government (and its development-related agencies) can play a major role in articulating and dynamizing a regional innovation system, understood as the process of generating, diffusing and exploiting knowledge in a given territory with the objective of fostering regional development.

(Landabaso *et al.* 1999)

Technology intelligence tools (technology watch, foresight, and assessment) applied during an RIS exercise may support decisively the tasks of the above 'intelligent cell'. In hybrid forms, it already happens. Many RIS projects have developed innovation-related intelligence to monitor the progress of the plan, to capture the characteristics of the regional innovation system, and to evaluate the contribution of specific projects and actions. These efforts, however, do not apply the systematic techniques, the communication processes, and the institutions of technology intelligence. They rely on simplified technology and innovation watch systems that do not cover the interests and initiatives of all the actors involved in the RIS exercise.

We should insist that technology intelligence is not a matter for the public administration only. It concerns all the actors of a regional innovation system: the companies that use the technology, the technology suppliers, the R&D institutions, the technology intermediary organizations, the innovation financing institutions, and the public administration. Each actor may have different objectives and apply different techniques. What matters is the cumulative capacity to manage technologies and follow the state of the art in technology and innovation. From this point of view, technology intelligence is based on the diffusion and use of appropriate techniques, including technology watch, foresight, assessment, benchmarking, and others.

The demand for knowledge management and software related to technology intelligence is important. In the beginning of 1999, we conducted a survey to measure the demand for knowledge and innovation management techniques at the regional level. The survey was part of a trans-regional project concerning the *Dissemination of Innovation and Knowledge Management Techniques* and covered six European regions: Central Macedonia, the Basque Country, Crete, Norte, Thessaly and Wales.[3] In each region, the survey was based on three sources of data and analysis: desk research involving the results of RTP and RIS projects and data describing the respective regional innovation systems; interviews with local technology intermediary organizations and experienced consultants in the application of innovation management techniques; and interviews with 40–60 small companies in each region with a structured questionnaire covering innovation and technology issues and the use of systematic techniques and methodologies. The survey showed a very high demand for technology intelligence tools. Technology watch is the most sought after among 25 innovation management techniques in the region of Norte, while it holds a prime position in the other regions. Equally important is the demand for benchmarking, technology assessment, and technology audit.

While the users of technology intelligence belong to the entire landscape of the regional innovation system, the institutions for the promotion and application of technology intelligence are rather limited. Larger companies may develop technology watch adapted to their needs; the same is true for finance institutions that need technology assessment in order to select products for risk capital and innovation funding support. However, appropriate institutions for the application of technology intelligence are mainly the intermediary organizations, such as innovation observatories, relay centres, technopoles and technology parks, and technological institutes. A positive contribution to the diffusion of the results to the entire regional innovation system may also come from established technology networks, clusters, and producer associations.

Technology intelligence cannot guarantee that the actors comprising a regional innovation system will become more adept in dealing with technology. It can contribute, however, to informing regional authorities and RIS committees of the most relevant science and technology fields, and to permitting companies and organizations to stay close to the state of the art in R&D, technology, and production. No doubt, this is a major step towards technological innovation.

PART III

Intelligent Cities

Islands of Innovation meet the Digital World

8 Intelligent Cities
Islands of Innovation become Digital

We live, it is said, in a learning society, where individuals continually need to reassess the appropriateness of what they know in order to survive and get a job. Just as in the past it was the changes in technology and technique that determined how people adapted their jobs, be it techniques in agriculture or industrial production, today the emphasis is more directly on applications of new knowledge and insights.

(C. Landry *et al.*, *The Creative City in Britain and Germany*)

Towards the end of the twentieth century the technologically aware metropolitan and regional administrations of Europe, the USA, and Japan saw a further opportunity for the development and prosperity of cities in the 'information society'. A series of pilot projects and applications attempted to improve the abilities of cities to manage information, transmit knowledge, and use information technologies. Included were virtual reality applications, websites and IT web pages for cities and regions, telecommunications applications between groups of users in a city, metropolitan area networks linking the municipal government and the local education and research organization with high speed communication, fibre optic cables and administrative applications for cities such as automated budgeting, automated property registers, integrated personnel management, automated social security, automated environmental information, email applications, advertising multimedia and e-commerce applications, knowledge management tools, search engines for researching specific subjects, thematic databases, guides and lists of information, professional directories and lists of businesses and organizations, digital representations of historic cities and areas, lists and representations of monuments and cultural heritage works, digital directories of addresses for issues relating to cities on the Internet, and so on. These applications promote the informatization of cities and regions offering better communication capabilities, more complete representations of city spaces, more accurate and up-to-date information, and useful knowledge and information management engines and tools.

A small number of the aforementioned applications opened new roads for intelligent cities and regions.

Cities, Globalization and Knowledge-based Development

During the 1980s, new forms of capital accumulation and the formation of the hegemony system appeared in western societies. The rupture of the previous social and economic systems, which had dominated during the post-war years, may be traced on the levels of production organization, skills and the division of labour, consumption models, income distribution, revenues and social stratification, regulatory policies and institutions, as well as on the spatial division of labour and the urban and regional systems.

The French regulation school and the American flexible specialization literature provide some excellent insights into this global restructuring and transition of the western societies (Gottdiener and Komninos 1989; Leborgne and Lipietz 1990; Lipietz 1984; Piore and Sabel 1984). The old phase, as well as the new one, is associated with a specific form of productive relations, technology, consumption norms, and conflict resolution practices. Growth and relative prosperity occur when these elements mesh together and form a coherent and stable environment for capital accumulation. Conversely, it falls into crisis when the conditions for harmonious growth are ruptured. The current period of international order is understood as a structural break, an organic crisis resulting from the collapse of the Fordist regime of accumulation and the associated mode of regulation. The new period is based on the globalization of the economies, on flexible accumulation strategies, and on new hegemony projects of popular capitalism. These were counterposed to the Fordist modernization strategy of the 1960s and to the social democratic, One Nation welfare state project, first established through the post-war settlement (Jessop 1989).

It is important to underline that the current globalization of the economy, the enterprises, the regions and the cities, does not appear through a smooth continuity and organic replacement of the old regime by a new one. On the contrary, the changes were forced by strategies and projects that offered creative solutions to the contradictions and the reproduction obstacles of the old regime. Once again, we should note that the concepts of agency, strategy, and project are key concepts for understanding the post-Fordist transition. The major contemporary social projects are associated with the transition towards a knowledge-based economy and society, which is taking shape by: (1) the reorganization in terms of flexibility, and innovation in the sphere of production, (2) the supra-national institutional regulation in the sphere of policy, and (3) the new state of knowledge, and post-modernist cultural values.

The contemporary growth, planning, and design of the European cities are substantial parts of these projects. Cities were affected by industrial decline, the diffusion and restructuring of the productive system across the national space, de-concentration of the urban population, a growing unevenness in income and the social polarization of housing provision, and finally, the degradation of social equipment and urban infrastructure (Komninos 1986). Almost paradoxically and along with decline, restructuring has also given birth to new urban landscapes: on the one hand, the so-called 'silicon landscapes', such as technopoles, high-tech industrial parks, industrial districts, corridors and routes of development outside the city, which correspond to expanding industrial sectors and to new forms of cooperation among industry, universities and the state; and on the other hand, the selective build up and renewal of central city areas associated with the growth of producer and financial services.

These developments permit us to understand that city restructuring is not only the effect of the new up and coming projects (flexibility, globalization, post-modernism). They are also fields of experimentation and creativity, where these same projects are co-formed and further elaborated. For instance, the project and the debate about post-modernism have been largely constructed in the field of architecture and urban design. The advances in productive cooperation and the new 'space-time compression' economies owe a lot to cities like Prato and the other communities of flexible specialization, which constitute prototypes and social experiments on new forms of coordination and integration. The understanding of the growth patterns in cities like Grenoble, Toulouse, Turin, Munich, the western Crescent, and central Scotland have seriously contributed to the wider productive reorganization and flexibilization. In many places, pro-growth coalitions are expressed mainly through city planning schemes (Turin, Toulouse, Montpellier) and urban planning has become a central module in many industrial modernization strategies.

The involvement of city planning and design in the shaping of major social projects at the turn of the twentieth century has important repercussions throughout the whole city-making theory. It becomes more and more difficult to agree with linear conceptualizations of the city as the outcome of a given economy, political arrangement and cultural values. The structuralist view of the determining roles of separate structures (economy and ideology on space) seems rather inadequate to capture the complexity of today's urban development. Important progress has been made since the neomarxist 'production of space' thesis in favour of a 'co-formation' approach, where the making of a city is not considered as the product of economic relations and ideological values, but part of the social projects for the construction of the dominant, economic and cultural relations and practices (Castells 1989; Scott and Soja 1998; Gottdiener *et al.* 1999; Sorkin 1992).

The seminal book by Peter Hall, *Cities of Tomorrow: An Intellectual History of Urban Planning and Design in the Twentieth Century*, describes such a point of view: the process of translating ideals and plans of pioneers and key individuals into reality (Hall 1988). Much of what has happened in the world's cities during the post-war years, he argues, can be traced back to some spatial models and key ideas of a few visionaries, often ignored or rejected by their contemporaries. Starting from the Victorian city and the garden-city vision, Hall comments on an important number of urban planning concepts: the City-beautiful movement, Albert Speer's plans for the reconstruction of Berlin, the Lutyens-Baker plans for New Delhi, the Corbusian Radiant City and its quasi reconstructions (Brazilia, Pruitt-Igoe), community architecture and urban renovation, Frank Lloyd Wright's decentralized Broadacre City and the soviet de-urbanist anti-bureaucratic visions, the suburbia and the non-place urban realm, the urban schemes of 'Image-engineering' in Boston and Baltimore, and the Docklands plans. These city plans and design schemes rely on specific principles and ideas: high-rise densification and the least space per habitat, the creation of small self-governed communities, city dispersal and decentralization, the monumentality of the form, the arts and craft form concept, the standardization and object-type notion, the instrumental logic of the form, and so on and so forth. Some ideas and design principles were realized; others were not. The lesson from history is that the visions and ideas that were turned into reality were connected with wider successful social strategies. Those that remained as plans and ideas were associated with social projects that were also rejected.

The widespread ideas of Mies van der Rohe, Le Corbusier, CIAM, De Stilj and neoplasticism, the Deutsche Werkbund, for example, owed a lot to the successes of the Fordist, Keynesian and Roosveltian strategies over their corporatist and statist rivals. On the other hand, we should link the deviations from the garden-city vision to the demise of the anarchist social project. And yet, beside the apologies of Leon Krier, it is difficult not to associate the failure of the national socialist version 'New Tradition' with the failure of the Third Reich. It is equally difficult not to associate the failure of the soviet de-urbanist's visions with the rejected strategies over popular consumption in the USSR.

A logical question, following this line of thinking, concerns today's social projects and regulations with which contemporary urban planning is associated. What are the major ideas shaping today's planning and the life of cities in Europe and the US? To this question, David Harvey's book, *The Condition of Post-modernity*, gives a genuine reply.

There has been a sea-change in cultural as well as in political-economic practices since around 1972. This sea-change is bound up with the emergence of new dominant ways in which we experience space and time. While simultaneity in the shifting dimensions of time and space is no proof of necessary or causal connection, strong a priori grounds can be adduced for the proposition that there is some kind of necessary relation between the rise of post-modernist cultural forms, the emergence of more flexible modes of capital accumulation, and a new round of 'time-space compression' in the organization of capitalism.

and,

Since the metropolis is impossible to command except in bits and pieces, urban design simply aims to be sensitive to vernacular traditions, local histories, particular wants, needs, and fancies, thus generating specialized, even highly customized architectural forms that may range from intimate, personalized spaces, through traditional monumentality, to the gaiety of spectacle. All of this can flourish by appeal to a remarkable electicism of architectural styles.

(Harvey 1989)

The preliminary assessment of Harvey is that the concern of post-modernism for difference, for communication, the complexity and nuances of interests, cultures, places, and the like, exercise a positive influence. Post-modernist thought gives a radical edge, since it has been particularly important in acknowledging the differences in subjectivity, gender and sexuality, race and class, temporal and spatial geographic locations and dislocations. However, while it opens a radical prospect by acknowledging the authenticity of other voices, post-modernist thinking immediately shuts off those other voices from access to more universal sources of power by ghettoizing them within a language game. This political silence avoids facing the realities of the political economy and circumstances of global power and comes close to complicity with the aestheticizing of politics upon which it is based. Such a controversial cultural and political attitude, coupled with the revival of entrepreneurialism and neo-conservatism might challenge the title of the new city regulation suitable at the time of flexible accumulation. 'Flexible post-modernism' as a mix of fiction, fantasy, fictitious capital, images, ephemerality, chance, flexibility in production techniques, labour markets and consumption niches, and the stable institutions favoured by neo-conservatism, is opposed to 'Fordist modernity'. The opposition indicates how two different regimes of accumulation and their associated modes of regulation might hang together, each as a distinctive and relatively coherent kind of social formation.

The association between contemporary urban planning and design models, the cultural project of post-modernism and the flexibility project, is fundamental to an understanding of the current situation of western cities. The general relation between accumulation regimes and regulation modes is that the former is not given, but it is achieved through compromises and institutional practices. Within the theory of regulation there is no place for necessity, but the open game of institutional forms and compromises may or may not create equilibrium (Lipietz 1984). In the field of post-Fordism, this signifies that flexible production and accumulation strategies depend heavily upon institutional and cultural regulation. The planning of cities is not supposed to serve a given flexibility but it has to contribute to constructing it along with its built urbanity and social compromises. What is asked of urban planners today is not to represent a given order of ideas or values, but to invent urbanities for flexible economies and information-based technologies. If we put it in terms of regulation, they are asked to invent city models to regulate flexible agglomerations and innovative environments for knowledge-based development. For the moment this is an open question and may take many different answers. But the debate has already begun and some answers are already given (see Global Affairs Institute 1999).

Smart Communities in the US

One of the new major movements for transforming cities in relation to new knowledge and technology conditions is the Smart Communities (SCs) movement in California, USA, which focuses on promoting the philosophy and applications of the information society at the level of cities and regions.

A smart community is simply a community in which government, business, and residents understand the potential of information technology and make a conscious decision to use that technology to transform life and work in their region in significant and positive ways. The rationale for the movement stands on the human interaction and social cooperation that are needed for making a smart community:

Market forces may generate new technologies, but they do not give rise to smart communities; only people do – people with a vision, with a commitment to change, with a willingness to work together with others in their community to achieve a common purpose.

(Smart Cities Guide Book 2001)

The primary purpose of the movement is to promote the concept of smart communities through seminars, forums, and conferences, the media and the Internet. Furthermore, the California Smart Communities Institute, located at San Diego State University, is working to promote the concept at the level of local authorities and consults communities in finding the most appropriate and effective applications.

The technological foundation of a typical smart community is an informational network that links various users in a significant, common purpose. The network generally consists of three elements: (1) infrastructure, (2) access points, and (3) applications. The infrastructure is the medium over which the information travels via telephone wires, copper or fibre optic cables, and wireless or satellite communications. The access points are the gates at which the users can enter into the network using personal computers, workstations, television set-top boxes, or kiosks. The applications are the uses to which the network's information and resources can be put.

Despite the early efforts focused on new (and heavy) telecommunications infrastructure, the actual trend is towards simpler solutions, in which significant infrastructure enhancements may not be necessary to implement most smart community initiatives. A minimum solution is, for example, to integrate local telephone, cable, and other telecommunications providers into the developmental process of a smart community in order to use the capabilities of existing telecommunications infrastructure, and open the network to the widest possible reach.

The creation of access points is a more pressing concern in most SCs because the computer remains the primary interface with the information highways. Moreover, not just any computer will suffice as a network interface. It has to be relatively powerful, have a speedy modem, and an Internet connection. A number of smart community ventures, like Northern California's Net at Two Rivers, Seattle's Public Access Network, and the Los Angeles Freenet, have made enhanced access to the Internet or the local information network one of their primary objectives, typically through free or discounted Internet accounts or publicly accessible kiosks in libraries, community centres, and public buildings.

Once the infrastructure and access points are in place, communities turn to the development of online applications, which constitute the core of most smart community projects. The Internet itself provides the access to a rich and growing base of information. No smart community is trying to replicate this resource. On the contrary, they are trying to supplement the Internet's global information base with data and applications pertinent to the specific community. One community may choose to embark on a programme to provide citizens with more specified information and services via the Internet. Another community may want to promote itself economically via the Internet with the goal to ameliorate its position in the global economy. Another community may want to connect its schools and libraries to the Internet and better prepare its students for their chosen careers. In all the cases, geographical areas turn to telecommunication technologies and information technology applications to promote economic development and job creation, and to improve the quality of life (Caves and Walshok 1999). Some characteristic cases presented on the Smart Communities website[1] include:

Blacksburg, Virginia is a small university town with fewer than 40,000 residents, but with the highest (proportionally) use of the Internet. The diffusion of information technology was based on the willingness of the public administration, the local university, and private industry to explore how they could work together to create an 'electronic village'. More than 40 per cent of the town is now on the Internet, 62 per cent use electronic mail, all school children who desire it have free email accounts and direct access to the World Wide Web, 65 per cent of local businesses advertise on the Internet with websites and online services.

San Diego University launched the International Centre for Communication in 1990, which, together with the City of San Diego, some years later formed a public–private committee to promote online delivery of government, health, and educational services. Part of the initiative is the creation of an electronic application to sustain the growth of San Diego businesses.

San Francisco Public Library together with its numerous public, private, and non-profit partners are transforming local libraries from traditional book repositories to comprehensive community centres offering a wide range of cultural, educational, health, and information services available free to the public over the Internet and public broadcasting television. Part of this effort is the first interactive television service (Response TV), in which viewers can use a telephone line to add information on a television screen and to participate in interactive community polls.

Smart Valley is an association of more than 75 Silicon Valley companies and organizations working with community leaders to launch technology projects that enhance the quality of life in Silicon Valley. The vision is to create an 'electronic' community by developing an advanced information infrastructure linking all sectors of the community, education, health care, local government, business, and the home. Among the various projects figure the connection of 150 Silicon Valley schools to the Internet, the diffusion of teleworking, online employment search, and the creation of an election website for the Silicon Valley voters.

The aforementioned indicative applications show the spirit of smart communities. These projects relate to the development of skills within a community in the sectors of knowledge and the use of IT/multimedia technologies rather than technology transfer. Without doubt, there is a technological dimension present, but the main emphasis is on motivating the human community to adopt innovations. These applications introduce new means of (electronic) communication, education (distance learning), work (teleworking), information (the Internet), management (automation), service provision (online), and so on which must be accepted too, so as to be assimilated by the largest part of the community. This aspect of acceptance and dissemination of applications is of primary importance, and makes the project communal (urban) rather than individual and technological.

The creation of a smart community is the result of planning on three levels: (1) at the level of technical infrastructure, (2) in terms of tools and applications, and (3) in terms of institutional regulations which permit/facilitate these applications. Figure 8.1 illustrates these levels together with the people and agencies that coordinate the development programme.

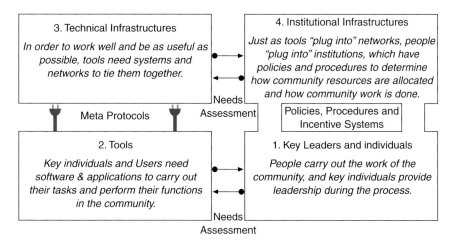

Figure 8.1 Planning a smart community
Source: Smart Communities Guide Book (2001), Implementation Guide.

The first planning duty is to identify and mark out those people/agencies who will undertake the project. In some areas, the starting point from the creation of a SC was one person who was later supported by a group. In other cases, a local government authority, a university or a non-profit company took the initiative. The most successful projects, nonetheless, were based on groups of people who balanced the advantages of personal handling of the project (speed, cohesion) with the advantages of collective handling (wider support base, location of resources, continuity).

Planning the technical infrastructure is a basic component and condition for the development of tools and applications. The first task is to find out what exists through a process of infrastructure mapping. Technical infrastructure includes the information transfer network and the access points to it. The Internet is the most commonly used communications platform, a fact that significantly limits the requirements for a new and expensive infrastructure. Critical elements are the range of communications and the ability to transfer large volumes of data. In certain applications that require large quantities of data, such as image or video processing, the usual capabilities provided by telephone networks are inadequate. If there is no technical infrastructure available, then developing a new infrastructure becomes the focus of the project. This task can slow down the process, which is why it is important to use the infrastructure that is already there.

Defining and developing the tools is an essential step. Simple tools include electronic mail, teleconferencing, and the promotion of activities or products via websites, whereas more complex tools are required to provide health, education, and business consultancy services, and so on, online. Since infrastructure is becoming standardized and the Internet is proving to be the main means of communication and data transfer, the core interest in planning is to be found in tools and customized applications for the provision of services online, and for distance work and education.

Finally, institutional regulations are focused on the combining of traditional and modern forms of communications, providing services and work, and intervene in the acceptance of the latter. For example, the application of e-commerce requires regulations for electronic means of payment, which credit institutions must accept. The application of tele-education requires the adaptation of educational mechanisms and agencies, which will certify the validity of distance educational services. Telemedicine requires that the system for providing health care be redesigned within a specific area. Consequently, institutional regulations are needed to permit and facilitate SC applications, to guarantee the validity of the procedures put in place and to ensure the financing of electronic services.

The level of dissemination of information society applications in the communities of California is significant. Research by Caves and Walshok (1999) in cities with 45,000 plus residents showed levels of dissemination in excess of 50 per cent. Nonetheless, the applications are still relatively simple and are limited to the dissemination of information via the Internet rather than the provision of advanced services online.

European Digital Cities

The European version of smart cities was presented with the Digital Cities Programme, which placed emphasis on the development of telematic services rather than on the dissemination of network applications via the Internet. European Digital Cities (EDC) started life as a programme of the European Commission in 1996 for promoting telematics applications in matters related to cities and for laying down the principles of the information society at the level of cities and regions.

Five networks of cities contributed to the creation of the EDC programme:

- *The Telecities Network* connects cities with shared interests in the development of telematics and information society applications.

- *The POLIS Network* is a union of 55 cities and regions from 17 countries in Europe that collaborate on matters of transport and environment and exchange best practice and innovative solutions.

- *The Car Free Cities Network* is a network of 60 cities that are attempting to ensure a healthier environment with less atmospheric pollution, environment-friendly transport systems, improved transport safety and more effective use of energy.

- *The Eurocities Network* represents 90 European metropolises from 27 European countries and 27 associated members whose main mission is

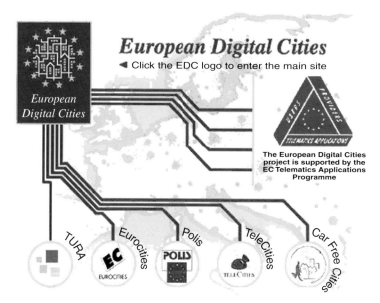

Figure 8.2 The European Digital Cities programme
Source: European Digital Cities (2001).

to improve the quality of life in cities and to promote European urban policy as a main factor in European integration.

• *The TURA Network* includes cities that have implemented telematics applications via the corresponding EU R&D Programme.

The European Digital Cities programme is an open network that enables local government authorities to acquire information and experience in telematics applications. The main fields of interest, which are connected to corresponding thematic groups within the network itself, are: telematics and employment, economic development with an emphasis on small enterprises, the quality of life for disadvantaged individuals, information channelling and administration of cities, training and education, the environment, health, and tele-democracy. The network exchanges experiences and best practice from individual projects and applications, explores the socio-economic repercussions from the implementation of telematics technologies in cities, and exploits the synergy of the cities in order to develop joint telematics infrastructures and technologies for more intelligent cities.

This activity was developed using classic networking methods such as conferences, collaboration between cities and regions, and exchanges of experience. In the most characteristic examples of projects implemented are applications for information dissemination systems in cities, telematics in transport and the environment, and the electronic delivery of a wide range of services (European Digital Cities 2001).

Information dissemination projects provide access to thematic databases and inventories which can be useful to the population of a city, to enterprises and businessmen. The projects EPITELIO,[2] INFOSOND,[3] and MAGICA[4] include telematics applications in information dissemination, and services associated with the transfer of information such as teleconferencing, tele-education, messaging services, and simple tele-working applications.

Telematics projects designed to support transportation within cities are a second discrete category of applications in the EDC network. Characteristic examples are the projects CAPITALS,[5] CONCERT,[6] and EURO-SCOPE,[7] whose objective is to automate transportation services (payment of tolls, parking), manage the urban transportation system (optimization of the fleet, operation of infrastructures) and disseminate information to users about the best manner in which to use urban infrastructures and transport networks.

However, the most significant category of telematics applications in cities relates to the online provision of services. Most projects, and indeed the most interesting applications fall into this category, projects such as DALI[8] on decentralization and the online provision of municipal services, EQUALITY[9] providing safety and alarm services, INFOCITIES with remote education, culture, and health services, the PH-NET[10] telemedicine project and the PERIPHERA[11] project providing telematics services to groups faced with social exclusion and persons with special needs. Despite the lack of homogeneity in the services provided, these projects gathered experience about online service provision for disparate problems in cities and this allowed for the generalization of telematics applications in many aspects of the life of a city.

The first phase of the European Digital Cities programme was completed in 1999. Applications implemented to date show that there are tools entering into the critical field of knowledge management and technological innovation that would permit a substantive contribution to the goal of 'intelligent cities', in other words the implementation of IT technologies in the field of technological knowledge and automation of procedures related to technological development. The building blocks for just such an effort have already been set: the development of thematic databases and the use of telematics tools in transferring information, online education, training and consultancy services, and the management of technological knowledge in specialized areas of research and science.

An equally important contribution of the EDC programme has to do with its focus on the development and provision of services rather than on networking and telecommunications problems. It has been found that the Internet and existing telecommunications networks based on telephone lines or ISDN lines provide an adequate basis of infrastructure on which the very telematics application itself can be developed. Before long, wireless Internet communications will provide extremely high speeds to every point of the city. We will experience online services via 10 Mbps or more wireless Internet connections, which will radically alter the content of communications. The essential problem, though, is the content of the communication and the online services on offer. In the EDC programme, and its different emphasis compared with the Smart Communities movement, services were placed at the centre of the effort to achieve digital cities. With this it was recognized that the main added value of digital cities relates to services that can be provided to citizens to aid the functioning of the city.

Intelligent versus Digital Cities

A digital city is not made of bricks, steel and concrete, but of computers, telephone lines, electronic connections, and bits (Mitchell 1995). In a digital city each resident has a computer and a modem with which he connects to the city system. Thus equipped the citizen can wander its roads, make purchases using e-commerce applications, read books in libraries, book tickets at the theatre for a show playing the following month, or watch the latest James Bond movie from the comfort of his armchair (Table 8.1). In a digital city, a large part of the functions of the real city (and especially the functions related to information and images) are performed at a virtual level.

A characteristic digital city application was developed in Amsterdam (DDS 2000). In Digital Amsterdam, from the moment it was turned on, the residents had online access to the minutes of meetings of the town council, to official police documents, they could log on to the Internet from the digital city's Central Station, visit art and science museums, explore sex shops and could even rent areas or offices to promote their products or their work. This virtual city was connected to the life of the real city but had its own rhythm and was self-determining in virtual space.

Some representative cases of digital strategies for European Cities were also discussed at the first PACE-Telecities conference on public administrations and business in the new economy, including experiences from The Hague, Stockholm, and London.

Wilbert Stolte, vice mayor of The Hague, pointed out that there could be no urban policy, in any field, without the inclusion of an information and communications technology dimension. It is rather easy to understand this is the case of urban development, spatial planning, and mobility, but the same holds for education, social cohesion, and the quality of life. Stolte presented The Hague's municipal strategy for the information society, which is based on the principles of every citizen connected, a transparent city hall, and support for the economic profile and identity of the city. At the centre of this digital city initiative is <http://www.Residente.net>, a

Table 8.1 IBM's application for a digital interactive city

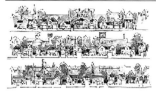

IBM is offering its services to develop an Interactive Community, on the WWW, for the developer's/builder's project.

An interactive community is one in which a community is connected not only by physical proximity, but also electronically through the technology of the WWW and the Internet. This community could be offered, via electronic means, information and services that are particularly relevant to the community, such as:

- **News:**
    - Today's news from the community.
    - Selected regional news as they pertain to the community.
    - World news.
    - Login for your personalized news service.
- **Information:**
    - Hours of operation of regional amenities.
    - Transit schedule.
    - Maps and trip wizard (suggests a route to a destination).
    - Traffic information.
    - Weather.
- **Events:**
    - What's happening in your community today!
    - Coming attractions.
    - Electronic box office.
- **Businesses:**
    - Community map with businesses in the area.
    - Community yellow pages.
- **Services:**
    - Medical.
    - Baby sitting.
    - Animal shelter.
    - Walk safe.
    - Community's handy man.
    - Community interactive shopping.
    - Booking of facilities within the community.
- **Community electronic bulletin board:**
    - Interest groups.
    - Community classifieds.
- **Schools:**
    - Contact your school.
    - Parent–teacher white board.
    - Students' bulletin board.
    - Assignments.
    - School clubs and extra curricular activities.
- **Let's go out:**
    - Restaurants.
    - Clubs and bars.
    - Parks.
    - Movies.

Source: http://www.can.ibm.com/smarthomes/community.html

portal built through a joint initiative of the municipality and two telecom operators and supported by the EC's TEN-Telecom programme. The site gives all citizens a free email address, which allows communication with the municipality and participation in the democratic process. Members of the <Residente.net> may build virtual communities, discussion platforms, and develop their own homepages. The portal also includes a virtual shopping centre, and information on cultural and sports events. The municipal vision of the information society has been developed in a participatory process together with many citizens and companies through a series of workshops. For the moment, the ideas and projects behind the digital city initiative have been well accepted, but in the immediate future the accent will be placed on the development of services through partnerships, networks, and cooperation (PACE-Telecities 2000).

Carl Cederschoid presented the e-strategy for Stockholm, which includes applications in areas such as municipal services, e-democracy, control and management of the city administration, e-structure, competence development and education, procurement and outsourcing. The strategy plays an important role in Stockholm's goal to advance the preconditions for the use of new digital technology within the city administration, the private sector and throughout the city as a whole. In facilitating access to municipal services, information in the modern society for the citizen will be accessible when needed or requested. In principle, all official documents can be made available for citizens on the Internet and this is just the lowest step on a process for more integrated services. In the end what is expected is a series of services, including elections and teledemocracy, via the Internet. Cederschoid also explained the recent developments in the Stockholm district of Kista, located 12 km from the city centre, which was established as an ordinary industrial park and quickly became 'Mobile Valley' with high-tech companies such as Ericsson and Microsoft establishing themselves there. Now in Kista, Sweden's Royal Institute of Technology is setting up a university focusing on information and communications technologies, which will host about 10,000 students studying, conducting research and cooperating with the companies in the area. This in turn will accelerate the urbanization of Kista changing its character of a traditional working area without many of the services that the contemporary society requires for work or education. Modernizing Kista means connecting the adjacent housing areas to the growing centre for new technology and getting new land uses, restaurants, libraries, theatres, cinemas, and pubs, into the area (PACE-Telecities 2000).

Another, more removed, case of a digital city is Singapore, where with the vision of an 'intelligent island' an extensive IT infrastructure has been developed. Defining Singapore's future as 'IT 2000 – A Vision of an Intelligent Island', the government has embarked on a massive programme to build up the necessary infrastructure. The programme is comprised of three elements: (1) good IT education at the school level, IT vocational training, and awareness, (2) efficient IT infrastructure including the world's best telecommunication, and wide household coaxial connection, and (3) IT-based economy, and wide applications of e-commerce, electronic transactions, protection of intellectual property rights in cyberspace, etc. (Mahizhnan 1999). Despite the name, the above cases and intangible infrastructure constitute a digital communication and exchange environment rather than an intelligent city. Let us explore exactly what this distinction means.

Among the wealth of information society applications dealing with issues related to cities and regions, there is one category of applications that can rightfully claim the title 'intelligent city' or 'intelligent space'. It is where the creation of a digital/virtual space is combined with a real community of people and producers characterized by a high level of knowledge and innovation use. In cases such as these, IT applications and knowledge management tools are built atop a real island of innovation. Hence, the intelligent space includes two intertwined components: (1) a human community within a defined geographical area which is developing institutions and social networks that favour knowledge and innovation, and (2) an infrastructure based on IT and management tools that optimize the management of knowledge, technological development, and innovation.

Consequently, we use the term 'intelligent city' to characterize areas (communities, neighbourhoods, districts, cities, regions) that have the ability to support learning, technological development, and innovation procedures on the one hand, with digital spaces and with information processing, knowledge transfer and technology tools on the other hand. In this sense, every digital city is not necessarily intelligent. But, every intelligent city has a digital component to it.[12]

However, it is not enough to develop an infrastructure for transferring information in order to characterize an area as intelligent. Cable network and communications capabilities are not proof of 'intelligence'. We attribute intelligence to various faculties and intelligence is often identified in terms of competence, talent, IQ, and social adaptation. Even from the perspective of computation, the intelligence of a system is characterized by its capabilities for information gathering, understanding, making inferences, making predictions, and applying it to the understanding and solving of new problems. This is much more than communication and exchange of information.

From this viewpoint, the main problem in an intelligent city is to interconnect its three basic elements: the island of innovation, the digital communications environment, and the tools/technologies for managing knowledge. Today the know-how for the construction of innovation environments exists, as well as the know-how for the construction of digital environments and cities. However, those applications that connect these aspects and create an integrated and functional 'digital–real space', are rather limited.

One of the first experiments to create an intelligent environment was done in Prato, Italy. Prato is one of the most well-known industrial districts in central Italy with the largest concentration of spinning mills in the world. The city is specialized in and produces woollen fabrics with more than 10,000 small enterprises operating there applying flexible and specialized work methods in one phase of fabric production. The average number of employees in this industry is low, around six per enterprise. A characteristic of the productive system is the cooperation networks and the flexible combinations of enterprises, which coordinated by the buyers (*impannatori*), undertake to perform production orders. In order to assist these cooperation networks, the European Community funded a digital application that would facilitate flexible combinations of producers. In part, the telematics network replaces the role of the buyers and the person-centred procedures for selecting producers to collaborate on performing an order, so lacking in transparency. Thanks to the digital network every producer can potentially become a buyer and seek associates in different stages of making a product (Lymberaki 1991).

An analogous application, this time in the field of technology transfer, was developed at the Kyoto technology park, Japan. Kyoto Research Park is part of the central area of Kyoto and it is intended for the promotion of scientific research activities and technological cooperation between industry, government, and academia. At the beginning of the 1990s, the Park was designated an intelligent city. This corresponds to a digital technology service offering 'venture incubation' operations 24 hours a day, and an international information exchange network and support services for R&D-oriented companies (Kyoto 2000).

In these examples we notice that the connection between the innovation island and the digital application occurs at the level of basic services and relations that characterize the corresponding innovation environment: in relations between producers who are the heart of the industrial district, and in technology transfer services which are the centre of the technology park. A generalization in the reasoning means focusing the intelligent city on the basic functions of the island of innovation: IT technologies and virtual spaces should be developed in relation to the functions of research, funding technological development, technology transfer, new product development services, and technology collaboration for the implementation of innovations.

In digital cities the connection between the digital and the real space occurs in all functions of the city where this is technically feasible and has social utility: in transport, at work, in the home, in services and entertainment (Figure 8.3). For each function of the city transferred into virtual space, a part of its real, its true substance and the relations connecting it to other functions is transferred into this virtual space. This allows part of the functionality to be achieved in virtual space. For instance, I do not have to move to visit a bank if I can visit it in virtual space and do exactly the transactions I usually do in real space. I do not have to wander in order to discover an empty parking place in the city centre, if I can visit a virtual parking centre and be informed where the vacancies are. In these cases the benefit for the city and its citizen do not lie solely in movement but also in the physical infrastructure, the real space, and in the functions' equipment that operates in virtual space.

In an intelligent city, by contrast, the connection between real and virtual space is more limited. The principle of transferring real functions to the virtual spaces is maintained, but concerns only functions relating to knowledge, research, training, and technological development. These functions, as they incorporate a large degree of information, are a field ripe for the use of IT, knowledge management, and remote communication tech-

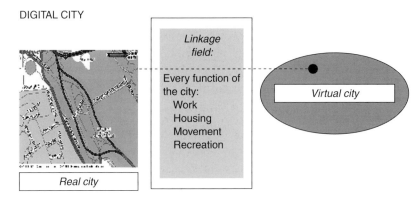

Figure 8.3 Functional links in a digital city

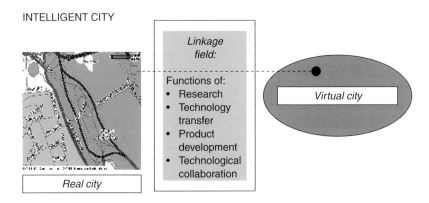

Figure 8.4 Functional links in an intelligent city

nologies. The primary functions, which can be performed in virtual space, are the five principal functions forming the innovation environment such as research and technological development, funding of innovation, technology transfer, product development services, technological networking and cooperation.

Components of an Intelligent City

It is clear from the previous section that an intelligent city is an island (community) of technological innovation integrating real and digital innovation development functions. The functions of an intelligent city relate to the production of knowledge (R&D), technology transfer, funding innovation, new product development services and the production process, technological collaboration activities, and networking. These functions are performed in parallel in both spaces, with direct human interaction in real space, and via IT and telecommunications technologies interaction in virtual space.

There are three basic components of an intelligent city: (1) the island of innovation formed by a community of people, production, exchange and other activities, (2) the virtual innovation system which includes knowledge management tools on the one hand, and the IT system for online provision of information and innovation services on the other hand, and (3) the connection between the real and virtual innovation system, in other words, the use of the latter by the island's scientific community. These elements relate to both spaces, the real and virtual, and connecting them together creates a new real–virtual innovation system.

The island of innovation is a reference point for the intelligent city. Simple forms of islands of innovation are clusters of industries or services, the flexible industrial district, the science park, the technology park, and the innovation centre. More complex forms are created by adding the aforementioned islands together in technopoles and regional innovation systems. Each island of innovation refers to a real community of people, scientists and producers, and to an environment within which social relations transform scientific knowledge into new products and where a constant renewal of production processes and exchanges take place.

The virtual innovation system has two dimensions, knowledge management technologies and the informational system for online operation of knowledge and innovation functions.

- Technologies and methods for managing innovation make up part of the main innovation processes such as producer–user channels, production chains, collaborations with research institutes, spin-offs, technology transfer, and so on. They are supported by rules and conventions built on institutions that manage knowledge and technology flows. A significant role is played here by intelligent agents and knowledge management tools. These intelligent agents and tools are software entities that help people and businesses to handle information in smarter ways, to become more productive, more innovative and more competitive. Intelligent agents are being employed today in business applications in the manufacturing, health, financial, retailing and many other industries, in electronic commerce and the Internet (IBM 2000).

- The informational system includes IT and communication tools and technologies. The transfer of operations from the innovation environment to virtual space is not a simple projection of real functions into virtual space. Digital or virtual applications promote the automation of technological innovation functions but at the same time radically reconstruct those functions. At this level, communication solutions provided by the Internet such as web applications, data transfer, search engines, multimedia applications, online services, remote education applications, and so on play a primary role.

Connecting these two elements together (the real and virtual innovation system) requires that the functions of the island of innovation be reconstructed so that it is feasible to make them work in the virtual space. This means that the 'digitizing' of a function, such as technology transfer for example, is not a simple projection of the function in virtual space. It presupposes the 'de-materialization' of the function, its deconstruction down to its basic elements, codification of its base procedures, and reconstruction with the use of methods and technologies that can replace the complexity of direct human interaction and the creativity of human thought in handling the unexpected, circumstances that do not follow the rules, in resolving unknown problems. Consequently, reconstructing the functions of an island of innovation with the prospect of their being supported by composite digitalization applications and IT is a particularly complex procedure, which requires ingenuity and special methods, and techniques. Knowledge and innovation management techniques play a definitive role at this point. These are techniques, methods, and tools for handling knowledge that intervene and facilitate technological innovation processes.

Figure 8.5 represents the fundamental elements of an intelligent city: the five structuring functions of an island of innovation, the virtual environment of innovation created by digital configurations of these functions, and the linkages between the real and virtual innovation spaces.

Let's consider Figure 8.5 a little further, taking as an example a characteristic island of innovation, that of the flexible industrial district, the knowledge functions of the district and the connection between the real and virtual innovation space.

A flexible industrial district is a closed community of producers which includes four basic social groups: (1) buyers or product designers, (2) spe-

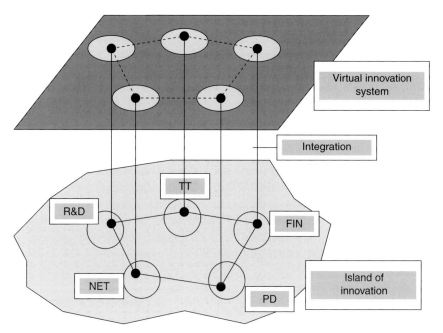

R&D: Research and development
TT: Technology transfer
FIN: Financing of innovation
PD: Product development
NET: Networking

Figure 8.5 Components of an intelligent city

cialized enterprises in different production segments of an industrial sector, (3) specialized craftsmen, and (4) home workers. A product batch starts from the buyers'/designers' group and who achieve a production agreement/order and determine the quality specifications and price. Then the buyers allocate parts of the overall work to specialized enterprises which undertake some part of the overall production process. These in turn use their own workforce but also external, specialized craftsmen and home workers. Within the district competition is intense. The buyers have good market and quality knowledge and impose high standards on the enterprises they cooperate with. Workers' fees include a combination of salary and participation in the profits. The most skilled workers use their participation in the profits to create their own enterprises. Unions ensure wages and conditions of work at a collective level. These contracts provide for large margins of flexibility in times of high and low rates of work. Flexibility is increased with seasonal contract work and part-time work. An enterprise with a large workload decentralizes (shares) parts of its production with other enterprises and forces wages down. By contrast, at times when there is a slack workload, enterprises work below cost to maintain relations with the buyers and designers.

The knowledge and innovation functions in the district mainly relate to the creation of new products, but also to their production conditions such as new machinery and new forms of cooperation between producers. To a large degree innovation is determined by the skills, knowledge, and information channels between the groups comprising the district: skills to design new products, skills for the renewal of production models, high-level ability to process materials and the quality of the finish, good information about the trends in the market, and the optimum allocation of the overall project to individual subcontractors. Among other things, the innovation and knowledge processes include: (1) codified and tacit product design knowledge, (2) tacit material and machinery handling knowledge, (3) information on markets, producers and products, (4) interactive communication networks involving producers and users, and (5) information on the availability of enterprises to produce at any moment in time, as well as methods for optimizing inter-firm collaboration.

A virtual environment for support of the innovation and knowledge system in the district can be described as a combination of communications networks, remote services, information from databases on market trends and interactive relations between buyers, enterprises, producers, and users. This system may provide exact and on-time information in relation to a series of parameters for optimizing decision planning and product development such as: (1) new trends in design due to fashion, quality, and consumer behaviour, (2) market trends, changes in demand and the level of prices, (3) new production technologies and materials and energy saving methods, (4) information on suppliers and optimization of outsourcing, (5) online searches for and selection of partners and subcontractors, and (6) online communication with users, and so on. It is clear that such a system may be a significant factor in making the decisions of buyers/designers easier as well as those of specialized enterprises, which are the motive force behind innovation in the district.

The connection and integration of the three levels referred to above (district, knowledge and innovation functions, informational system) creates a new real–virtual district where knowledge and communications relations are optimized by using IT and knowledge management technologies. This real–virtual application increases the ability of the community of people composing the district to ensure the ongoing creativity, non-standardization, constant innovation and a high competitiveness of its products. Under no circumstances can the virtual–digital component be separated off and replace the creativity of the district. Its role is complementary in relation to the real community of creators and producers.

However, how feasible are these virtual constructs? Already a series of research projects funded by the TURA (Telematics for Urban and Rural

Areas) programme, as part of the EU's 4th R&D Programme (1995–9), has created many focused tools and methodologies. Below, four projects from the TURA programme are presented in summary form with telematics applications in the field of innovation, improving workforce skills (SYRECOS), outsourcing (TELEMART), service provision (TIERRAS) and re-engineering (CWASAR), which show the ability to develop digital applications and services in the context of knowledge and innovation management.

- SYRECOS (Système Régional d'Echange de Compétences et de Services) is an application capable of providing a system and new practices to answer the problem of finding skills. On this issue the company has two choices. First, to search for training and allow members of the company to acquire the needed skills. Second, to appeal to external skills using consultants, research centres, universities, and other relevant institutions. Both functions are supported by SYRECOS. The approach is to design and validate two systems, the first one dedicated to continuous training and post-training actions, and the second to support the regional technology transfer. The project is based on two suites of software both using web technologies. The regional tele-service for continuous training software is based on an Oracle database, and allows the user to manage and publish training offers for a region or a professional sector. The technology transfer tele-service is developed in Java technologies, and supports the access to about 80 technology advisers in 24 different organizations, which help more than 1,000 small companies across the Languedoc Roussillon region.[13]

- TELEMART (Telematics Marketing of Teleworkers) is an online work brokerage system, which can locate and contract business services. Using the World Wide Web, the TELEMART brokerage service helps clients identify suppliers who are able to undertake the work and simplifies outsourcing with the placement of requests and orders with one or many suppliers. The system comprises four main component services and secure access based on public key authentication: (1) supplier offer catalogues, (2) enquiry and order processing, (3) online payment, and (4) comprehensive customization management. The following end users have been involved in the system. *Service operators*, who are responsible for developing the TELEMART service at a national level and operating field trials with the participation of teleworkers, suppliers, and customers. *Suppliers*, who operate a network of teleworkers and have introduced service offers within the TELEMART catalogue. *Teleworkers*, who undertake outsource work managed by a supplier with which they contract. *Customers*, who may identify an existing provider of services and may try online the service he offers. TELEMART is implemented as a series of separate marketplaces all under a single brand, all with their own identity. A client can source from any or all of these marketplaces without it being apparent that a particular broker is contracted to a particular operator, i.e. the catalogue and transaction services are seamless across all the marketplaces. The database behind the system is implemented on an Oracle Enterprise Server, protected by a military B1 specification trusted gateway 'virtual vault'.[14]

- TIERRAS (Trans-European Research on Telematics Applications or Regional Development Strategies) is a project aimed at building a permanent partnership among a group of European regional authorities directly committed to support experimental telematics services as part of their regional development policies. The regions involved are Emilia-Romana, Midi-Pyrénées, Wales, and the Balearic Islands. The project was based on the principle of embeddedness in regional development policies. The project gave the opportunity to develop and test common tools in order to provide four main families of telematics services: tele-information, tele-registration and payment, tele-training, and tele-support. These services were aimed at individuals interested in participating in the local system, and small firms as determinant actors of regional economic development.[15]

- CWASAR (Cooperative Wide Area Service Architecture) is a telematics project for the promotion of competitiveness of the European industry. The system consists of a large computer network connecting a multitude of independent commercial, governmental, research, and educational organizations of different sizes. The key services to be provided include a continuous electronic fair, finding business partners, conducting business transactions such as ordering, booking, contract negotiations, as well as transfer of documents such as text, hypertext, engineering data, and multimedia documents. The main goals of the project are to establish the conditions of functionality of such a system, i.e. to establish a significant user community, to define the technical architecture providing the system's functionality, and to define the security architecture. The general functional architecture adopted consists of a user front-end, a database, a protocol suite, and the security custodians.[16]

We can talk of an intelligent city when a virtual innovation environment is created atop the real island of innovation, which facilitates and supports the functions of the real system. The content of this component, the virtual innovation environment is definitive for the character of an intelligent city. The ability to integrate the real space with the virtual space is determined by the development of knowledge management processes at both levels. These processes create the connecting tissue of the real–virtual system. In the real space, handling of innovation is done via interpersonal communication and institutional relations, whereas in the virtual space it is done via telecommunications technologies.

A large number of characteristics and relations of the real innovation system are codified and transferred in the virtual space. Users entering the virtual space handle relations and processes belonging to the real innovation system. Of course, these actions are not completed in the virtual space. Validation is needed by real subjects that are represented in the virtual space. This connection, however, between the real and virtual levels is a key issue for the whole construction.

The relations between the real and virtual innovation system are illustrated in Figure 8.6. This figure shows that different models of innovation environment (flexible industrial districts, science parks, technopoles, regional innovation systems, and others) may be connected with the same virtual innovation environment.

The basic processes leading to innovation remain in the real system. What is transferred to the virtual level is a series of tools and technologies to manage the innovation processes, which are applicable to all basic innovation environment models. These tools, which constitute the core structure of the virtual innovation environment, fall into three categories:

- Tools, methods and technologies for knowledge management and development of innovation such as technology audits, technological evaluation, benchmarking, re-engineering, and so on.

- Telematics and online communication tools and technologies, in essence applications on the Internet such as web pages, search engines, databases, watchdogs and authentication engines, and so on.

- Online services and utilities that offer real services to users and suppliers of technologies, information, and other useful applications on knowledge management and innovation.

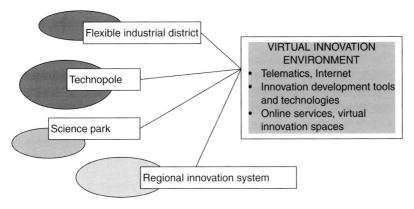

Figure 8.6 Interconnection between the real and virtual innovation environment

These elements of the virtual system can be adjusted to serve the different structures in each innovation environment. They can also serve the spatial cohesion relations of a flexible industrial district equally as well as the institutional formations on which a regional innovation system is based.

Is the creation of an intelligent city fully feasible after all? Or is what was described above simply a metaphor, a replica of intelligence in an environment that remains stationary and soulless? Is there evolution in Archigram's vision of the living city and in that of the interaction between the built city and humans professed by modernism? Do the citizens and organizations based in an intelligent city, as described, become better able to solve problems, adapt to their environment and thus more intelligent?

Our answer to these questions is in the affirmative. What has been described is the beginning of a course that may lead to a radically different urban environment from that which we experience today. There is no doubt that thanks to the virtual, i.e. the digital component, processes in an island of innovation may become easier, i.e. speeded up, processes such as the development of knowledge, technology transfer, the creation of new products and procedures, networking and collaboration. All of this is of great importance for the new economy of knowledge and the conditions for prosperity in the twenty-first century.

The typical city at the end of the twentieth century where the functions of industry, services, trade, housing, recreation, education and so on dominate is gradually conceding its position to a new urban system where the basic components (universities, exchange malls, industrial districts, science parks, recreation zones, etc.) operate on two levels, in the three-dimensional natural world and the virtual space of the Internet. The integration of these levels creates a reality much more complex than before but with increased capability for supporting individuals and organizations hosted by them. The merging of the real and digital innovation environment creates a new dimension marking the beginning of intelligent cities.

9 Real–Virtual Technopoles

One of the worst definitions of artificial intelligence is by Barr and Feigenbaum in their reference text, *The Handbook of Artificial Intelligence*, 'Artificial intelligence is part of computer science concerned with designing intelligent computer systems, that is, systems that exhibit the characteristics we associate with intelligence in human behaviour – understanding languages, learning, reasoning, solving problems, and so on'. This is poor that it links artificial intelligence only with the subject of computer science. Secondly, it points only to computer systems, no others.

(Kevin Warwick, *March of the Machines*)

Real–Virtual Relations in Technology Parks

Technology parks and planned technopoles offer a promising field for testing the integration between the real and virtual components of an innovation island. Systematically organized and to a higher degree than the flexible industrial districts and the regional innovation systems, technology parks are innovation islands produced after detailed planning of the infrastructure, activities, and services. The planning procedures pave the way for the development of a virtual component upon the real park.

Many technology parks have already developed digital applications and platforms to make their services more friendly and open to a wider audience. We could mention the portal to the Swedish technology parks (http://www.swedepark.se), the portal to the Finnish technology parks (http://www.tekel.fi), the portal to the Greek science and technology parks (http://www.portal.urenio.org), the technology watch system of the Thessaloniki technology park (http://mercury.techpath.gr), the virtual documentation centre of the Andalusia technology park (http://www.pta.es), the online marketing service of the International Association of Science Parks (http://www.iaspworld.org), the virtual discussion forum of the UK Science Parks Association (http://www.ukspa.org.uk), and others. These applications, and many others that an interested student may find on the web, allow for investigating the relationships between the real and the virtual dimensions of the parks.

A technology park represents a community composed of three groups: the innovative companies, the R&D institutes, and the technology transfer organizations. Their location in the limited area of the park is a positive condition to gain in communication and identity. To the companies, the location within the park provides a brand name of high technology, quality premises with a distinguished address in the amorphous urban sprawl, formal and informal interaction with researchers and technology managers. To R&D institutes, the park supplies mechanisms for technology diffusion, whereas the vicinity to innovative firms may enhance joint projects and new ideas for applied research. To technology transfer organizations, the park ensures inputs of technology, both from the innovative companies and the research institutes. Overall, the park creates the conditions for internal communication and cooperation between the three groups, and external diffusion of technology and innovation towards the surrounding area.

The driving force of the developmental dynamic of a park is the circuit between the premises and the technology. Companies and institutions choose to locate in the park because it is a place for innovation and technological development. The investment in land and premises, and the location of innovative companies and R&D organizations, advances technology resources giving birth to a technology-intensive cluster. On the other side, the investment in technology increases the value of the real estate property, raises the prices and the return rate of investments in land and premises. Premises and technology go together, each contributing to the value and performance of the other.

A virtual technology park is a digital application linked to the community and the actors of the real park. It is composed of knowledge management tools, Internet or intranet infrastructure, multimedia applications, databases, and intelligent agents, which fall into two categories: knowledge management tools supporting the technology transfer functions and services of the park, and telematics tools supporting the internal and external communication and exchange.

The virtual technology park is a replica. It reproduces the functions of a technology park in a virtual/digital space. Users may approach the virtual park and get some of the services that the technology park provides. A lab may acquire information on patents through an online technology watch system; a bank or risk capital fund may evaluate a new product or technology with the help of online technology evaluation tools; a small company may find partners to participate in an R&D consortium; a researcher may retrieve information into rich online databases. A virtual park is more or less a set of online tools for technology dissemination and innovation development.

The integration of the real and virtual park opens a new dimension since the synergy between the community of people and the digital tools upgrades the performance and interaction of the park's actors. This is a knowledge-based integration, valuable to the entire human community of the park and to external customers.

- To the people working in the promotion of the park's land and premises, for instance, the virtual park is a tool for marketing, promotion, and advertisement. They can reach new customers and increase the international presence of the park; they can promote wider the location and related services or target the promotion on specific groups.

- The technology transfer and training departments have an additional tool of communication and demonstration. The virtual park is a gate, which the customer can open and reach technologies and services. Some of the services may be reached online. For all the technologies, demonstration becomes easier and more convincing.

- To the companies, the virtual component consolidates the relationships of cooperation with other companies inside the park, strengthens the local innovation cluster, and gives additional promotion and marketing power.

The new entity, created by the integration of the real and virtual park, is an intelligent entity, an intelligent park and environment, offering additional problem-solving capacity to scientists and innovators for the management and creation of new products or processes. The combination of knowledge management tools and the Internet is the powerful engine of this new intelligent environment. As in previous major technological innovations (railways, telegraph, electricity) the intelligent environment is going to bring about novel elements in the everyday life of work. For instance, as electricity introduced a new generation of machines, and railways allowed for the rapid transportation of people and goods across the country, the new combination of knowledge tools and the Internet is going to supply the last worker of a learning community with the most advanced thinking and problem-solving capability, and amplify its intellectual power.

The intelligent technology park, as with any type of intelligent environment, be it district, city, or region, is the outcome of a two-step process: (1) of the creation of a virtual park with the help of innovation management tools and Internet technologies, and (2) of the integration of the virtual and the real park, so that the community of people in the real park make use of advanced knowledge management and knowledge creation technologies online through the web.

A Virtual Network of European Technology Parks

Some of these ideas were tested in the research project OnLi which was financed under the 5th R&D Framework Programme of the European

Commission.[1] The project links technology parks, university labs, and technology transfer centres of Finland, Germany, Greece, and Portugal wishing to develop telematic applications and to offer online services in the areas of innovation management, technology transfer, and spin-off support to European companies.

The network consists of a well-balanced mix of technology parks and innovation-led organizations. The four technology parks (Thessaloniki, Tagus, Oulu, Ostfalen) make up the core of the network. Coupled with the service-oriented technology parks, which bring with them experience from their regional companies, are a university research laboratory with wide experience in the field of innovation, and a private technology transfer organization well versed in project management and the practicalities of innovation management. The network also brings together expertise from all corners of Europe. This not only addresses the point of validity and sustainability of the scope of the network, but also ensures that companies from countries with cultural proximity to the countries involved can start using the On-Line Innovation services right away.

- Thessaloniki Technology Park is a member of the International Association of Science Parks (IASP) and a partner of the Hellenic Innovation Relay Centre (HIRC) belonging to the network of Innovation Relay Centres of the European Commission. The TTP provides services of regional development, technology transfer, contract research, international technology transfer, and contract education, and manages the incubator building.

- OuluTech Ltd commercializes technology-based ideas, inventions and research results in Finland and abroad, including the obtaining of patents, further product development and marketing. OuluTech also helps to start up enterprises based on research and product development, and to transfer innovations to be utilized by already established enterprises. Its principal activities include the commercialization of innovations and research results, business development, seed financing, and technology services for small companies.

- Taguspark is a science and technology park in the Lisbon region of Portugal. Taguspark was launched in 1992 as a central government initiative to act as a tool for economic and technology development. A private managing company, with mixed capitals, was set up at that date to manage the development of Taguspark. The business and innovation centre attracts, selects and helps the development of technology-based companies from their very beginning (the idea) up to being a mature company able to implant itself in one of the park's plots.

- The Ostfalen Technology Park is based on Magdeburg's Otto-von-Guericke University in Germany, and helps the park's tenants to establish a solid base for innovation-led production and marketing. The mission of the park is to support young innovative entrepreneurs, in all the stages of the business cycle, from the creation of innovative products to manufacturing, and marketing.

- The Urban and Regional Innovation research unit (URENIO) is an institution of the Aristotle University of Thessaloniki for the promotion of research and provision of scientific and technological services. URENIO's research focuses on cities and regions, that base their development on R&D, technological innovation, technology-intensive companies, technology infrastructure, knowledge and information networks. The central research theme of the unit is the regions and the environment of innovation, including flexible industrial districts, science parks, and technopolises, innovative regions, and virtual innovation environments and intelligent cities.

- The Hellenic Centre for Technology Transfer SA (HCTT) is a private organization established in 1999. HCTT is a consortium of two companies (Euroconsultants SA, Intratech) with considerable experience in technology transfer, and two European Technology Transfer organizations (Technology Transfer Centre of Estoro Commercio Piemontesi, Product Development Centre of Wales). The centre is active in all aspects of technology transfer based on the Total Project Concept.

The organizations composing the OnLi Network are working together along the concept of 'intelligent cities', meaning to develop a virtual innovation environment and integrate it with the technology practices of the real parks. The working method is to decompose the technology transfer functions of an ideal technology park in separate modules, and then each member of the network focuses on the development of a specific virtual module of technology transfer. At a later stage, adding and customizing the virtual modules, a global virtual technology park is produced.

Table 9.1 Partners and focus of the OnLi network

Partners	Thematic focus
Thessaloniki Technology Park SA	Technology watch
OuluTech Oy Ltd	Technology clinics
Science & Technology Park Taguspark SA, Lisboa	Financing of innovation
Technologiepark Ostfalen	Marketing of innovation
URENIO research unit, Aristotle University of Thessaloniki	Technology evaluation
Hellenic Centre for Technology Transfer SA	Technology audit

Overall, the network constitutes a pilot action and the lessons learned from each implementation can be transferred to a number of other thematic areas and technology parks. On-Line Innovation provides a test bench for a number of creative services related to providing consulting advice, self-evaluation, and training online. It is also testing new approaches and ways to promote innovation to SMEs and encourage their participation. Testing of the online offer of services currently available by the technology parks is limited to each park's region where the greatest chances for customization exist. The Internet is quickly becoming a standard technology for SMEs. It is critical that those involved in innovation management utilize this tool effectively. The easy access to information provided by the Internet, coupled with the increased use of the web as a tool for SMEs in Europe, familiarizes entrepreneurs with the use of services offered by technology parks and technology transfer organizations, and hence promotes and encourages participation in such types of actions. OnLi is not aiming to replace technology parks but rather to increase their effectiveness, profile, and visibility with SMEs in Europe and enhance their usefulness through the use of enhanced information technology means. The virtual applications are adapted to the specific requirements of each region and used in a virtual one-stop shop. This customization allows users to work within an environment more tailored to their specific needs.

Each technology park participating in the network is developing a three-level application combining technology transfer services, virtual tools for innovation and technology transfer, and integration of real and virtual practices.

- OnLi starts from the description of services currently offered by the four technology parks. These cover the main domains of technology transfer: technology watch, technology evaluation, technology audit, technology clinics, innovation financing, and promotion of innovation. Each network partner focuses on one area corresponding to existing expertise and services.

- The second level is the creation of a virtual system, composed of Internet and innovation management tools, through which the users can instantly access online innovation management tools, technology matches, training, consultancy, self-evaluation, success stories, best practices, and information links. The system integrates fragmented expertise and creates a showcase for European best practices with each partner integrating their expertise. The virtual application includes also *general information* on issues relating to innovations and technological developments in specific thematic areas, *access to case studies* and best practice, *links* to other websites providing relevant information, *database* screening and analysis of information on new technologies available on various databases, *online consultancy* services relating to the establishment of innovative firms, and promotion of innovation within the organization, and *online training* on issues relating to the above mentioned thematic categories.

- The third level is the integration of the real and virtual innovation services, and mainly the adaptation and adjustment to the particularities of the environments of the participating partners. It is a critical step towards achieving full, online, consultancy services. The need for online consultancy and real-time problem solving is well documented in the literature. Even though the state of the art in Internet technology might allow such a service to be provided, the technology is still at an immature stage and has not yet become mainstream. What is more important in this case though is that companies and end users are not familiar with these services and are often opting for training and guidance.

The process for achieving the above-described construction of four intelligent parks is illustrated in Figure 9.1. The *definition of technology transfer modules* is the starting point. The selection of six modules (technology watch, technology evaluation, technology clinics, etc.) corresponds to typical practices of technology transfer, and is based on the suggestions of the partners and the shortlist of practices already in use. Technology audit, for example, is a key element of technology transfer and a series of structured questionnaires and interviews are used as auditing tools.[2]

Once the core modules of technology transfer were selected, the network started to work on the construction of the virtual system. The first task was to create a toolbox including online software entities for technology transfer. All the partners contribute with the selection of appropriate methodologies and software. The *virtual toolbox* was developed with the combined effort of partners, and was composed of six tools covering the areas of technology watch, technology evaluation, audit, technology clinics, innovation financing, and marketing of innovation (see, www.newventuretools.net).

The toolbox is addressed to companies and technology intermediaries, and the user may work at different levels of complexity. For instance, a small company with a low level of technical expertise may use online the technology evaluation tool and assess technologies available on the market through a cost–benefit approach. A more experienced consultant or technology broker may use the tool to examine existing and potential technology processes, and look further at the implementation and functioning conditions.

The toolbox is the central piece in the construction of the virtual technology park, but the parks have to take a step forward and customize the toolbox to the specific environment each one is working on. The four parks have adapted all the tools to the particularities of the operating environment in their countries considering differences in the business and

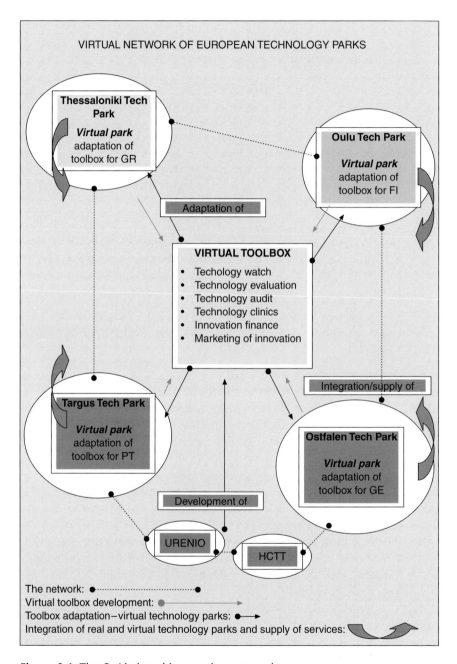

Figure 9.1 The OnLi virtual innovation network

socio-economic environments. The result of this stage is a web-based application, a virtual technology park upon each park, including tools adjusted to the partner-country peculiarities, the web linking software tool, and a training tool software.

The final step is the *integration of real and virtual parks*. Each of the four technology parks of the network is connecting the virtual toolbox for technology transfer services to the real technology transfer practices. Integration is to prepare the personnel, procedures, services, and marketing profile of the technology parks to work with the virtual modules. It means training personnel, promotion of the new online services, making of demos, and organizing demonstration meetings with customers. At this stage, the human community of each technology park, but also the managers of companies located outside the park, may use a virtual environment that multiplies the efficiency of their work and supplies them with advanced capability to resolve technology transfer problems in the areas of technology watch, technology evaluation, marketing, financing of innovation, and others.

Making a Virtual Park: The Module of Technology Evaluation

The overall construction, the virtual technology park, is composed of a number of modules corresponding to main technology transfer functions. Each module combines innovation and knowledge management tools, and Internet communication tools that allow its use from distance and online. Apart from the technology transfer modules, the virtual park also includes multimedia promotion material, links to relevant innovation sources, portals to Internet addresses, search engines, and other Internet tools. It is clear that two technologies converge to build the virtual technology park modules: knowledge and innovation management tools and technologies, and Internet and web communication technologies. The latter provides the platform on which the innovation and knowledge management tools operate.

Thus the construction of the virtual technology park follows a modular approach, guaranteeing an open architecture and the possibility of future enrichment and extension.

Here, as a case study, we will discuss the process to develop one module of this kind, the online technology evaluation module. The same process is valid to create other technology transfer modules, from financing of innovation to marketing of new technologies and products. First we will describe what technology evaluation is, and the main techniques used to evaluate technologies or new technology-based products. Then we will look at the digital transcription of technology evaluation methods and the creation of a virtual space to perform a web-based technology evaluation.

Technology evaluation is a set of principles, methods and techniques for effectively examining the potential value of a technology and its contribution to a company, region, or industrial sector. It is one of the most significant methodologies in innovation and technology transfer, utilized in screening new ideas, assessing innovative or non-innovative products and technologies. It is a powerful technique for an organization in examining new ideas, identifying and analysing causes or potential change, developing and planning possible solutions, and finally selecting and implementing a proposed technology.

Technology evaluation may be understood in a variety of ways. First, as a group of studies that systematically examine the effects on society that may occur when a technology is introduced; second as an attempt to establish an early warning system to detect, control, and direct technological changes; or third, as a process used to analyse alternative technologies that provide information and help the actors involved to develop their goals. A thorough evaluation assesses the technology and its device's value from technical, market, and consumer perspectives and reconciles the results within a valid methodology.

For the investigation of the available technology evaluation methodologies and tools, we used the Science Direct database of Elsevier, a major online database including about one million articles with a fairly good representation of engineering and technology issues. From the articles included in the database, four technology evaluation approaches were identified: (1) technology benchmarking, (2) failure analysis, (3) lifecycle analysis, and (4) cost–benefit analysis. Every approach is built on exclusive tools and technologies, necessary for the evaluation process.

Technology benchmarking is a method for comparing the performance of an organization with best practices and technology applications of others. Application of benchmarking focuses on the detailed understanding of your own processes, and then compares your own performance with that of others analysed. Comparison may also involve best practice based on standards and specifications stemming from the systematic study of science literature, and business literature with the scope to identify relevant information and technologies. In many cases, dedicated journals provide indicators that compare characteristics of similar products/technologies that make a comparison easier.

Project teams conduct process or technology benchmarking. The first step is to specify a process or a series of interconnected processes to be studied. Next a benchmarking partner, or a group of partners, with superior performance in the process being examined is identified. The high performance process of the partner is then studied. In this way a performance gap is established and the elements that have led to the superior performance are understood. The final step is to formulate an improvement plan and implement the actions necessary to close the performance gap (O'Reagain and Keegan 2000).

Table 9.2 Evolution of benchmarking

Performance benchmarks	■ Key output measures ■ Balanced scorecard ■ Leading indicators
Process proficiency	■ Processes inventoried ■ Process ownership ■ Process improvement
Best practice mastery	■ Best practice understanding ■ Sharing ■ Adoption
Best practice models	■ Best of best practice models

Source: Adapted from Camp (2000).

Over the past 15 years, the evolution of the benchmarking practice came through the search for performance benchmarks, the interest in process proficiency, the understanding and mastery of best practice, and the development of best practice models.

Overall, benchmarking is a culture of looking outward (outside the organization, at a company, industry, region, or country) to examine how others achieve their performance levels and to understand the processes behind excellent performance.

Failure analysis is a laboratory-based evaluation method which takes samples of different technologies and evaluates them, using appropriate destruction or other tests. The concept is very close to the evaluation of products with respect to quality standards. In both cases, a sample of technologies/products is brought to a laboratory where it is tested either against other technologies and products, or against standards and specifications.

A good example of the method is given in the evaluation of wire bonding technologies in high-power multi-chip IGBT modules (Hamidi *et al.* 1999). These modules for power transmission in industrial and traction applications are operated under severe working conditions, and one of the main failure mechanisms encountered in modules subjected to thermal cycles is wire bond lift-off, due to the large thermal expansion coefficient mismatch between the aluminium wires and the silicon chips. The evaluation focused on the testing of aluminium wires of different qualities assembled on the chip with different wire bonding technologies. The process includes:

- The definition of the problem: Several hundred thick aluminium wires (0.3 to 0.5 mm) are used to electrically contact the chips in a module. The wires are connected to the aluminium metallization on the silicon chips using an ultrasonic bonding process. Due to thermal expansion mismatch between aluminium wires and silicon chips, the thermal cycles applied to the device during operation lead to bond fatigue and lift-off. The question is whether wires with different characteristics and different bonding technologies may increase the lifetime of the bond and provide better bonding parameters.

- The creation of modules that will be subject to tests: In order to test the reliability of the bond connection on the chip, different IGBT modules were assembled. Four types of aluminium wire from four different suppliers were selected. They were connected to the chips with two different technologies: the first solution consisted of direct-bond-on-chip, and the second placed a molybdenum plate soldered on top of the chip and subsequent wire bonding on this plate. Thus, a number of test-modules were created combining wires with different qualities and different bonding solutions.

- The execution of the tests: All the test modules were subjected to a power cycling test using the same test equipment and under the same conditions. The modules were open and a number of bonding parameters were measured. The tests were stopped if one of three predefined failure criteria was reached.

- The failure analysis, which examines and explains the test results. At the beginning the analysis focuses on the behaviour of the test modules vis-à-vis the failure criteria. For example, certain modules presented a lower temperature and longer lifetime than the others, which are very significant observations. Then, a detailed failure analysis was made for each module. It included, among others, optical inspection, electrical measurements, scanning acoustic microscopy inspection, and electronic microscopy imaging. From these investigations, a number of significant conclusions were drawn on the failure mechanisms and the lifetime of the test modules, which indicates the advantages of one technology over the other.

Failure analysis is an extremely well defined and precise technology evaluation methodology, and may provide accurate comparative information on

Table 9.3 Technology evaluation: Testing modules

	Direct-bond-on-chip	Bond-on-molybdenum plate
A Al 99.99% + Ni	Module A1	Module A2
B Al 99.999% − Ultra pure and soft	Module B1	Module B2
C Al 99.998% + Ni	Module C1	Module C2
D Al 99.99%	Module D1	Module D2

technologies in various fields of science and engineering. The application presupposes available laboratory and testing infrastructure and tools.

Life cycle analysis is an alternative evaluation method looking at the life cycle models that have been used in different fields of industrial studies in order to explain the evolution of industries, products, and technologies. The assumption is that the life cycles of technologies and products follow similar patterns of living beings. Therefore, changes are easily predicted and life cycle models may capture the maturity of a technology and the trends of its evolution.

In life cycle analysis four stages can be distinguished in the evolution of a product or technology: introduction, growth, maturity, and decline (Nieto *et al.* 1998).

- Introduction: a new product/technology is introduced into the market-place. Only one or two firms have entered the market, and the competition is limited. The rate of sales growth depends on the newness of the product. Generally, a product modification generates faster sales than a major innovation. The technology performance of the innovation increases slowly.

- Growth: a new product gains wider consumer acceptance and the objective is to expand the range of available product alternatives. Industry sales increase rapidly as a few more firms enter the marketplace. To accommodate the growing market, modified versions of basic models are offered. Successive incremental innovations increase the technology performance rate of the product.

- Maturity: industry sales stabilize as the market becomes saturated and many firms enter to capitalize on the still sizeable demand. The possibilities of increasing product contributions are limited. Innovations are less frequent. The technology performance rate stabilizes.

- Decline: the product/technology becomes obsolete, its market is null, and its use value is covered by other products, more advanced or more suitable to consumption habits.

The relationship between the product cycles and the technology supporting the product is illustrated in Figure 9.2. The link between technology and life cycle seems far more stable than at the product levels. Given that the life cycle of the technology and the life cycle of sector often reveal the same phenomenon, some authors do not differentiate and integrate them into what has been named industrial technology life cycle.

A very useful tool for representing the technology life cycle model is the S curve model. This is a function that relates the accomplished effort in the development of a technology with the results that are obtained. It is called an S curve because, when the results are graphically demonstrated, the curve that is usually obtained is a sinusoidal line that resembles an S.

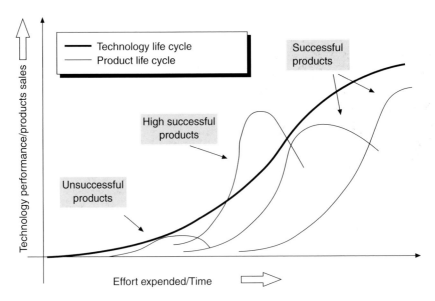

Figure 9.2 Relationship between the technology life cycle and life cycles of products
Source: Nieto *et al.* (1998).

The key issue in the application of the S curve model is the selection of the performance parameter. If the performance parameter were defined in a way that acceptably reflects all the technological improvements that may affect the contribution (quality, safety, and cost of the products), the S curve model would facilitate the understanding of the process of techno-logical change. In this way, when the S curve is used as a performance model of evolution of a specific technology, what it is demonstrating in reality is the speed at which incremental innovations in a given technology are produced. Therefore, if the performance parameter were defined ade-quately, the S curve model would provide reliable analyses from which significant recommendations for the design of technological strategies could be derived.

Cost–benefit analysis, finally, is a horizontal evaluation methodology. As technology has evolved, it has become more complex, seemingly at an increasing pace. Decision makers are left with the awkward problem of evaluating potential outcomes and choosing technologies to achieve these outcomes in the presence of this intense complexity. Decisions that are well intended can lead to losses in results as unexpected outcomes develop, or as outcomes have unexpected consequences. Decision makers therefore have a great need for a framework that structures information in a way, which makes the complexity more tractable, but still takes into account the implications of the complexity. Cost–benefit analysis is an analytical tool that has the potential to significantly advance this process.

Cost–benefit analysis (CBA) provides a means for systematically comparing the value of outcomes with the value of resources achieving the outcomes required. It measures the economic efficiency of the proposed technology or project. When all else is equal more efficient projects should be chosen over less efficient ones. When there are many options to consider during a decision-making task, it is useful to evaluate the options with a common metric. Cost–benefit analysis refers to any type of structured method for evaluating decision options (Bierman *et al.* 1981; Hull 1980; Keeny and Raiffa 1976; Phillips 1983).

CBA has become widely accepted among business and governmental organizations. Although CBA has definite limitations, especially in the non-standard way that the payoff function is derived and calculated, its potential for making decisions more rational is comforting to those who must make the decisions. In situations in which large amounts of money are at stake, the presentation of a cost–benefit analysis is the preferred way to demonstrate the reasoning behind investments.

For the application of CBA, inputs may be divided into parameter values and benefit and cost values. Parameters include the discount rate, the future rates of economic growth, the future rates of inflation, the estimations about the future rates of technological change. Benefit and costs include monetary values for marketed goods, monetary values for non-marketed directly used goods, monetary values for non-marketed passively used goods, goods for which monetary values cannot be measured.

An example of cost–benefit analysis is given by the comparison between three technologies for setting up a workshop for mechanical construction in the plant of Citroën at Meudon, France (Girard and Poncet 1982). The technologies compared were: (1) a flexible workshop based on high-level automation, (2) a flexible workshop based on the re-engineering of existing machinery, and (3) a traditional workshop. The question was to analyse which solution was the most profitable for the company, in terms of investment and profitability. A cost–benefit analysis was adopted, which systematically investigated both sides of the problem: the costs for setting up each type of workshop, and the benefits from its operation.

For the estimation of the costs of each of the three solutions, a series of assumptions were adopted:

- That the workshops produce the same type of pieces, selected from a representative sample of the production at Meudon.

- That the workshops produce the same number of pieces, but they use different combinations of materials, labour force, industrial space, etc.

- That the cost of initial investment is calculated for a given production output, the same for the three solutions, and the revenue from the sales of the products is equal in all the three workshops.

These assumptions permitted a calculation of the costs for setting up each workshop. The costs included the purchase of machinery, studies, materials for the production, costs of personnel, and financial expenses.

The calculation of costs gave the input for the second step of the method, which included the estimation of the benefits from each solution. The estimation was based on the annual cash flow for a period of 10 years, payback time, rate of internal return, and realized benefits. It appears that the flexible workshop based on high-level automation is the solution with the better performance and profitability. This evaluation is meaningful for any industrialist wishing to invest and looking forward at the modernization of the tools of production.

Online Technology Evaluation

Once the major technology evaluation methodologies were identified, the next problem to resolve was to examine which part of the methods might be transferred at a web platform and be applied virtually (online). Various parameters affect this possibility. It is the complexity of the methodology, the linearity or not of the evaluation process, the number of actors that participate and the level of interaction among them, the need for research and testing infrastructure. Depending on these parameters, some evaluation methodologies may fully operate online, while others may only be partially supported by web and digital applications.

Take the case of online technology benchmarking. It seems a very promising field for virtual application, and we have already developed an online tool. Technology benchmarking is a methodology of evaluation that can be executed virtually 100 per cent. Online benchmarking illustrates a way to create virtual innovation management tools and was a guide to build virtual cost–benefit analysis.

Online benchmarking application is based on the business excellence model and the Benchmark Index developed by the UK Department of Trade and Industry. Benchmarking starts with a questionnaire including quantitative and multiple-choice qualitative questions. The index has already been used to test over 2,000 companies in the UK, and has been further endorsed by the European Commission in a major project to assess the competitive performance of 1,500 companies in nine member states (Small Business Service 2000). The index uses a series of measures to track the performance of a company and is structured in seven chapters: (1) finance, (2) management, (3) engineering, (4) manufacturing, (5) quality, (6) delivery, and (7) marketing. The company has to answer these questions, and if needed is facilitated by an external adviser. We have also developed an alternative version of the index for Greek companies, since many of the British variables make no sense in the Greek environment. In any case, both questionnaires may be used to collect the initial data from the company.

The software that runs the application is a client-server and has two parts. Looking outward is a front-end, developed on an Internet platform. On the World Wide Web, the client finds a homepage with a number of modules corresponding to the Benchmark Index or the URENIO Benchmarking Questionnaire. Each module includes a series of questions that the company has to fill in. The second part of the software is the database. This is an Oracle database, designed with an open architecture and automated links to the front-end modules. Once the client feeds the modules of the Benchmark Index/Questionnaire with data, these are automatically transferred and stored in the database. The database contains routines and algorithms that produce the benchmarking comparison figures. The overall design of the software allows movement from the initial data to the comparison benchmarking figures online, with very little interference from the user.

The database cannot function without concrete data, and the generation of benchmarking reports is feasible for those sectors and activities that are well represented in the database. In principle, at least 20 entries (companies) are necessary at each cluster of the database as a reference (comparison) group.

After having resolved the design, development, and testing of the benchmarking database, we started to introduce data from companies. We performed innovation audits in 300 companies in Greece, following the modules of the URENIO Benchmarking Questionnaire. The audits cover the major industrial sectors and companies with more than 20 employees, in three regions of Greece: Central Macedonia, Thessaly, and Crete. The data from the audits are on a secure server, off-line, to assure the confidentiality of data and reports.

To use this online benchmarking application, a company has to enter into the website of URENIO and find the application into the Benchmarking section. The front-end opens with a username and a password, and contains the modules of the Benchmark Questionnaire. After answering the questions of the index (normally it takes about two days to gather this data for a company), the user prints a report to review the data entry and stores the data on the server. The administrator of the system transmits the data into the Oracle database, on an off-line server, and produces the benchmarking report. The user gets the report by email, which compares its performance with the performance of other companies held in the database. Altogether the evaluation gives an appraisal of the strengths and weaknesses and a detailed analysis of the position of the company with respect to various indicators, establishing whether the company fits to the upper or lower quartile of compared organizations, as well as the quantitative margins for improvement.

As it appears, most of the work is carried out virtually, without the physical presence and communication between the company and the benchmarking agency. The application is very friendly, and the understanding of the comparison diagrams is rather easy. The next step for the company is to get in touch with specialized consultants and technology providers to resolve the highlighted weaknesses.

Online failure analysis is a more complex case. Due to the need for laboratory tests and equipment, the automation and online application of the method is rather limited. In the evaluation of bonding technologies, for instance, the bulk of the work concerns the laboratory tests upon different modules, the inspection of the modules after the test, and the interpretation of the results. The technologies available today do not allow the dematerialization of the testing and inspection processes. Therefore, it is not feasible to transfer the tasks of failure analysis on a virtual level, and implement the methodology online.

Online cost–benefit analysis may be an extremely useful tool for technology parks. Technology parks are advised by SMEs on the status of numerous innovation and technology projects that are requested each year. Decisions must be made on which projects are in the best interest of the SME. To make those decisions, each project request must be evaluated on both its own merit and its relative importance to other SME initiatives. In order to effectively evaluate each request, the technology parks must formalize the project requesting and justification process.

In this case, starting from a number of parameters regarding the cost of the money, the inflation rate, the rate of return, etc., it is feasible to design a template structuring the costs, and feed with the appropriate data. Then, using a 'free of intellectual property rights' database and suitable algorithms, it becomes possible to automate the estimation of the benefits. The complete sequence of tasks, including the initial parameters, the introduction of cost data, and the calculation of benefits, is functional on a web platform and may be used online, as an Internet application. We have developed such an application in the framework of the OnLi project.

The URENIO-CBA tool is a web-based application that includes the modules presented in Figure 9.3 and is described below:

The central web page of the application is a public address that includes two elements: an information module, and the CBA tool.

The information module updates companies, consultants, and experts about evaluation and assessment methods, tools, news and includes a public discussion forum on relative issues. Users can be informed and see case studies on the evaluation of innovation. The user can also submit a request describing his/her needs on assessing an innovative project. A technology consultant in the technology park may direct the solution, if it is appropriate, to the URENIO-CBA application.

The URENIO-CBA tool is open to the public. In the beginning the user receives a couple of fully analysed examples where he/she can understand what exactly the application is about and what he/she can get from it.

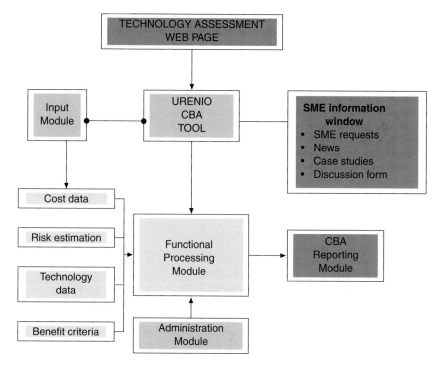

Figure 9.3 Architecture of online technology evaluation

There is also a page interface where the user can find all the information needed for applying the tool. When the user decides to use the tool, it is entered into the administration module. In the administration module, the user must fill out a form requesting information and provide a user name and a password to the application. The relationship is one to many. A single user can access many cases, if he possesses the owner rights.

Following this is the main input module, which includes input templates for project details, costs, benefits, technology difficulties, and risks. An online guide directs the introduction of data and the measurement units. Once the data has been introduced, a functional processing module utilizes the input data and processes the functional requirements of the tool. At the end, the user gets a report presenting cost–benefit estimations for different scenarios and technology solutions, and a sensitivity analysis for these solutions.

The two cases presented here (online benchmarking and online cost–benefit analysis) outline a methodology for building virtual applications suitable for other innovation management techniques also. Technology watch, technology audit, and innovation finance may generate analogous virtual tools along the same methodology, direction, and concepts. This is, however, one part of the OnLi virtual network objectives.

The other part is about integrating the real and virtual aspects of the parks participating in the network.

Intelligent Parks: Integrating Real and Virtual Technology Transfer Functions

The creation of a virtual component on a technology park opens the way towards intelligent parks. The bond between the real and virtual park leads to a substantial increase of capability in handling information, learning and managing innovation processes. In fact, this is the very meaning of intelligence:

We attribute intelligence to various faculties. Intelligence is often identified in terms of competence, talent, schooling, IQ, and social interaction. From the perspective of computation, the intelligence of a system is characterized by its flexibility, adaptability, memory, learning, temporal dynamics, and the ability to manage uncertain and imprecise information. Capabilities such as information gathering, understanding, making inferences, making prediction, and applying it to understand and solve new problems efficiently are observed to be critical features of such systems.

(Warwick 1998)

And

In an intelligent environment, the user and the environment work together in a unique manner, the user indicates what he wishes to do, and the environment recognizes his intentions and helps out however is appropriate. If well implemented, such an environment will allow the user to interact with it in a manner that is most natural for them personally. They should need virtually no time to learn to use it, and should be more productive once they have.

(Hammond *et al*. 1998)

Our definition of the intelligent technology park follows the concept of the intelligent city, described in Chapter 8, but also with the properties of 'intelligence' and 'intelligent environment' highlighted above (see also Hugeland 1989). An intelligent technology park: (1) is a community of people and technology-intensive activities, (2) where much of the technology transfer (location, spin-offs, brokerage, networking, etc.), which constitute the core activity of the technology park, is supported by virtual tools and knowledge management techniques, and exercised by a virtual technology park, and (3) supplies the human community of the park with advanced competences, tools, and methodologies to deal with the problems of technology development and transfer.

The interaction between the technology-minded human community of the park and the virtual/online technology transfer tools creates an intelligent environment that enhances the problem-solving capacity of the park's human community. In this sense, the meaning of intelligent environment and park is not a metaphor. The adaptation and use of the virtual park by the scientific community of the park supplies the latter with advanced competences, memory, interaction, and other faculties that we usually recognize as intelligence. The park becomes an intelligent environment with the full meaning of the term.

Another way to describe this real–virtual integration is through the concept of collective learning. Collective learning refers to that learning which becomes possible through membership of a particular milieu. Collective learning is the creation and further development of a base of common shared knowledge among the individuals making up this milieu. In this case, collective learning gives the possibility to use the particular skills of scientist and manager through a process of virtualization and the opening of these skills to all the members of a particular milieu, that coincide with the users of the virtual park.

Part of the knowledge collectively shared by the human community of the technology park is tacit knowledge. It is said that there is a critical qualitative difference between information, which is codifiable (and commodifiable) knowledge that can be transmitted mechanically or electronically to others, and tacit knowledge in the form of know-how, skills and competences that cannot be codified. Such tacit knowledge may be unique to particular individuals but it is often collective rather than simply individual, locally produced and often place specific. It therefore can only be purchased, if at all, via the labour market and not in the form of turn-key plant or other forms of 'hard' technology (Hudson 1996). The virtual technology park and the knowledge management tools incorporate mainly codified knowledge, but the digital interaction between the staff of the park and internal or external customers gives an advantage to share tacit knowledge through the simplification and ease of direct interaction.

Defining the intelligent park with respect to the knowledge operations of the scientific community of the park, the properties of the virtual park toolbox, and the integration (customization) of the toolbox to the needs of the park's community, we turn away from two mainstream conceptions in the actual debate on cities, virtuality, and telecommunications.

Intelligent technology parks are not about visualization. It does not concern applications of digital/virtual cities that look at the formal characteristics of a city mainly to visualize and present the complex urban environment on the web. For instance, the homepage of the Virtual City Resource Centre opens to a number of cases that illustrate this orientation. We take three examples, but the others are also in the same direction:[3]

- *Bath produced by CASA* at Bath University constructs a three-dimensional computer model of Bath. Bath City Council supported the project, and since its completion the model has been used by the city planners to test the visual impact of a number of proposed developments on the city. This is a good example of the use of VRML to produce virtual models of cities.

- *Ottawa by Wizard Solutions* is a VRML model including good use of viewpoints and embedded URL links to www pages. The VRML 2.0 version also features a 3D sound source and tour-based viewpoints. Although no social aspect is included in the model, the use of embedded information and moving tour viewpoints illustrates a good representation of a basic virtual city.

- *Siena by Construct* makes good use of textures to create the atmosphere of an Italian city. Construct has made imaginative use of hyperlinks and level of detail to create one of the few representations of urban form that creates a true sense of place.

This direction of virtual cities is about walking around the city on the web, looking at city maps, finding locations, participating in discussion groups, linking to Amazon to buy books, getting information and weather reports. Virtual city projects deal primarily with the visual media, and to an extent with numerical and textual media on computers. In this sense, the virtual city is the city in multimedia (Batty 1995).

The second mainstream conception is related to telecommunications, information highways, and the city. In particular, it examines the effects that virtual/digital cities signify for the 'death of distance' and 'vanishing of space'. Graham attempts to debunk five prevailing myths of the current rhetoric on telecommunications, including the myth of urban dissolution as new telecommunications and virtual tools allow urban functions to decentralize.

To Pascal, cities therefore will 'vanish' as their chief *raison d'être* – face-to-face contact – is substituted by electronic networks and spaces. New rural societies will emerge, as people exercise their new freedom and locate in small, attractive settlements that are better suited to their needs.... However, it is now becoming very clear that, as Jean Gottmann put it, 'it does not necessarily follow [from improvements in telecommunications] that the compact city has been made obsolete and that settlements will disperse throughout the countryside'. Teleworking, for example, is growing. But it is being adopted as a way of making work patterns around large cities more flexible rather than as a way of supporting some mass migration of full-time teleworkers to electronic cottages in remote locations.

(Graham 1997)

Contrary to conceptions of virtual spaces as multimedia and telecommunication phenomena, we argue that the essence of intelligent technology parks is knowledge management. However, the creation of a virtual component upon a technology park does not guarantee by itself advancement in the technology transfer practices of the park. On the contrary, it is the integration of the virtual means with the technology practices that makes the park's personnel capable of resolving more complex and knotty problems.

Going back to the model of the technology park as a cluster of innovative companies, R&D institutions, and technology transfer organizations, the virtual and intelligent components reorganize all practices and relationships of tenant organizations. Land planning and real estate management may become more effective with the use of advanced management, promotion, and networking tools. R&D may benefit from the use of virtual technology watch, foresight and assessment systems that upgrade the technology intelligence and inspection capability of research institutions. Much more than any other practice, technology transfer may gain from the widespread use of innovation and knowledge management techniques, which in the form of new software escort the practices of the engineers in the technology transfer units and departments.

Interaction and integration between the real and virtual dimensions of a technology park make the difference in terms of intelligence and problem solving capacity. The first step in this integration between virtual and physical spaces is to learn to use the virtual park. It is mainly about training in knowledge management tools. The second step is customization, thus adaptation of the virtual park to the environment that a park operates. This is fine-tuning of the initial tools, feeding of databases, matching to regional links and institutions. The third and higher degree of integration is the enrichment of the virtual component by the development of new tools coming from practices of the parks' scientific and technological community.

10 Real–Virtual Regional Innovation Systems

Real–virtual regional innovation systems allow discussion of the general form of relationship between the real and the virtual dimension of an island of innovation, and the methods to enhance innovation through knowledge management tools and information technologies. Starting from the technology dissemination practices of the project InnoRegio (seminars, audits, pilot projects for technology demonstration) we investigate the conditions that make a real–virtual innovation environment operational and useful to companies, technology suppliers, and technology intermediary organizations.

InnoRegio is a project supported by the European Commission in the framework of Recite II Programme (DG Regional Policy). Following a competitive open call in which 300 proposals were submitted, the project was selected with a three-year schedule. It is a large innovation diffusion project covering six European regions, with the scope to investigate new approaches that might sustain regional innovation systems, based on knowledge management, Internet (web) applications, and technology dissemination practices. The fundamental assumption is that the main functions of a regional innovation system (R&D, innovation finance, technology transfer, product and process development, and technology cooperation) may be greatly enhanced by the use of: (1) innovation and knowledge management techniques, and (2) web-based information technology applications. These tools allow creating a *virtual innovation environment* that is complementary and supportive to a real regional innovation system. Innovation management technologies and techniques, and web communication tools may help technology-driven organizations (high-tech companies, technology producers, technology brokers, technology advisers) to transform scientific knowledge to products and apply technological innovations.

InnoRegio follows the concept of 'Intelligent Cities' discussed in Chapter 8. It opens a research agenda towards real–virtual innovation environments that may be particularly important to less favoured regions. Virtual and online innovation may contribute to upgrade existing regional innovation structures, and bring tested solutions, technologies, and innovations to the most distant small company and technology intermediary organization.

Regional Innovation Strategies and Dematerialization of Infrastructure

Regional innovation strategies (RIS) with a series of applications in the regions of Europe, the European network of RIS regions (see, www.inno-vating-regions.org), national RIS networks in many member states, thematic networks for innovation, trans-regional innovation projects (TRIPs) and the connection of RIS to the structural funds, are currently the dominant regional policy for innovation and technological development in the European Union. The dynamic of RIS and the multiple networks for the promotion of innovation, rely to a great degree on a bottom-up planning philosophy. This does not relate solely to the priority given to the regional dimension in relation to the national, but also, and more so, to the involvement of a large number of actors in each region that contribute to the promotion of innovation and which create multi-level, multiplication effects.

Each RIS is an innovation environment, an island of innovation. In this environment, the business is the final organization that implements innovations using internal and external resources. Internal resources are human resources, financing and the equipment owned by the enterprise. External resources relate to financing institutions (such as venture capital, development incentives, etc.), to technology transfer (from research institutes and technology intermediary organizations), the provision of specialized services (consulting, market research, patenting, marketing, advertising), suppliers and producers of new products or machinery. External resources are raised from the corresponding regional innovation system and the objective of each RIS is to make the system richer, friendlier and more effective. These external resources are both hard, in the sense of equipment and infrastructure and soft in the sense of staff specializations, knowledge in the region, relations of collaboration and trust, management skills and so on.

The two relations mentioned above: 'innovative enterprise – external innovation conditions' and 'hard–soft infrastructures' working inside the environment of innovation are among the most definitive for shaping the innovation dynamic. These issues have been discussed at length in the

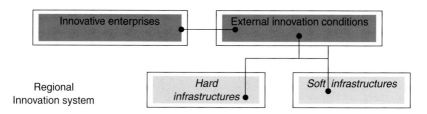

Figure 10.1 Innovative enterprises and innovation environment

literature on the role of infrastructure in innovation, on incentives for rein-forcing demand for innovation, the transfer of technology, and innovation networks (Camagni 1991; Cicioti 1998; Tolomelli 1990).

To achieve a favourable innovation environment is the main aim of each RIS initiative. Nonetheless, it seems that soft actions contribute to the objec-tive more than large hard infrastructures. The priority of soft infrastructures has been documented both in major empirical studies such as the 1st and 2nd Community Innovation Surveys and in recent theories about innovation (Conceicao *et al.* 1998; Edquist 1998; Edquist and Hommen 1999).

Field research undertaken in the framework of the regional innovation strategies in different areas of the Community clearly show that the prior-ity of businesses is to demand soft interventions such as financing mechan-ism, technology collaboration networks, access to sources of technology, and best practice.[1] This is only to be expected and absolutely in line with more recent theories on innovation such as the systemic theory of innova-tion, innovation as a learning process, and the collective systems of know-ledge and innovation.

Studies by Lundvall in particular have contributed to our understanding of the role of soft infrastructures in innovation with the emphasis on learn-ing processes and national systems of innovation (Lundvall 1992; Lundvall and Johnson 1994). The national system of innovation has been described as the range of institutions that contribute to innovation and the linkages among them. In the main these include, national R&D structures, manage-ment and labour milieu, national infrastructure, governmental policy, financial frameworks, and cultural practices. As already noted, the import-ance attributed to learning and institutional mechanisms is reflecting the experience of small states that are unable to invest public resources in a wide range of technology areas and which have a small number of large multinational businesses. Consequently, they are forced to select certain areas of technological innovation and to organize proper systems for mon-itoring and transferring valuable know-how and innovations.

Systemic relations have been advocated as the priority of the soft aspects of the innovation environment. In the evolutionary theory of innovation formulated by Schumpeter and Freeman, the systemic dimension appears as feedback between producers and users of technology (Freeman 1995). Following this, in the theory of national systems of innovation, the innova-tion system is formed from a plethora of agencies, universities, research centres, technology transfer institutes, consultancy firms, human resource management organizations, public and private sector financing agencies, technology demonstration organizations, and IT and high-tech enterprises, among others. Systemic relations concern the flow of information and know-how, collaboration relations and joint projects, the influence exerted on the formulation of research and technology policy, as well as the infor-mal relations of trust and the formation of a culture of innovation. This entire environment, the flows and relations, the individual and collective procedures for learning, are soft, but exceptionally definitive for the dynamic of technological innovation (Edquist 1998; Hall 1994).

With the abandonment of the linear model of science–technology–innovation, the importance of large infrastructures for research and technology in the formation of the innovation environment was replaced by the multi-sided, hierarchical or polycentric innovation networks which are much closer to the market and the daily procedures of learning and technology transfer (Conceicao *et al.* 1998; Forrest 1999; Utterback 1986; Rothwell 1992). This is even more pronounced at the level of a region where learning and the transfer of technology are the main sources for acquiring technological knowledge. In each region, technology transfer ensures wider technological knowledge than that available via endo-regional technological development. The relatively small size of the regions, sectoral specialization and the frequently limited presence of research and technology development institutes, raise technology transfer to the most significant source of innovation.

Empirical data and theoretical analysis thus converge on the conclusion that soft infrastructures (services), soft technology support actions (rather than large hard R&D infrastructures), and learning procedures are the central component of the environment promoted by regional innovation strategies. This understanding has opened the road for the implementation of programmes for the diffusion and transfer of know-how, the development of technological collaboration networks, the financing of innovation and technological modernization, which are projects in high demand by enterprises (Cooke *et al.* 1996; Edquist and Hommen 1999). Moreover, it makes the meeting between RIS and the digital world, the Internet, and knowledge management technologies reasonable for the development of a virtual innovation environment and for further 'dematerialization' of the innovation environment.

Nonetheless, a general trend has been noted in European regional policy and the structural interventions, in particular to finance hard infrastructures in the regional innovation system, at the expense of soft actions and soft infrastructures. No doubt this arises partly from pressure group interests in the member states, which find investments in hard infrastructure more profitable than investments in soft infrastructure. It is also partly due to the eligibility regulations for expenditure by the European Regional Development Fund. This policy creates a contradiction between the priorities for technological development (where soft actions are of great importance) and projects and infrastructures, which are implemented in full via the structural funds. It should be noted that cost–benefit in soft technological actions (technology diffusion, technological collaboration networks, training in innovation) is particularly favourable, since such actions are low cost but with high added value in the innovation cycle.

Another obstacle to the development of soft actions, interactive learning structures and institutional mechanisms for the dissemination of know-how at a regional level, is that research has not yet led to operational management models for technological knowledge within the regional innovation system. The focus is on the description of cases studies and the typology of regions rather than on elaborated models for effective management of regional learning and innovation processes.

InnoRegio: A Trans-regional Innovation Project

The above two challenges, the contradiction between the importance of soft infrastructures (learning processes and systemic technology relations) in regional innovation strategies and the financing of hard infrastructures on the one hand, and the limited research on interactive learning processes on the other hand, were the context behind the InnoRegio project. This is a pilot project for technology dissemination and the strengthening of the regional innovation system via knowledge management methods, learning procedures, and virtual applications promoting innovation.

InnoRegio is a follow-up of regional innovation strategies (RTP-RIS-RITTS) applied in the regions of Central Macedonia, Crete and Thessaly (Greece), the Basque country (Spain), Norte (Portugal), and Wales (UK). With its emphasis being placed on soft infrastructures and the virtual world, InnoRegio attempts to provide an answer to the issue of the dematerialization of regional innovation infrastructures. This problem relates to the identification of basic functions of the regional innovation system and the transfer/execution of these functions on a virtual level with the aid of IT and telematics technologies. The importance of dematerialization lies in boosting the effectiveness and the operation of the regional innovation system.

The project focuses on the capacity of the organizations comprising a regional innovation system (companies, technology producers, technology brokers, consultants, etc.) to learn, manage, and implement technological innovations. The central issue is the learning of *Innovation Management Techniques and Technologies* (IMTs) that facilitate the technology-driven organizations of a region to deal with innovation and technology. These techniques/technologies cover the entire process of innovation, including R&D, technology transfer, business skills, networking, and finance. They are developed by numerous research and technology projects, namely the Innovation Programme of the European Commission, as well as projects on knowledge management, world-class manufacturing, and business excellence.

The expected result of InnoRegio was a large-scale dissemination and pilot implementation of IMTs in six regions, including:

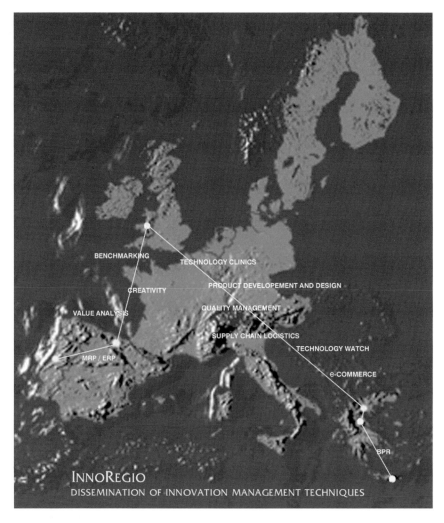

Figure 10.2 Innovative region project (InnoRegio)

- The development of *25–30 techniques and technologies* appropriate to enhance innovation in companies, technology transfer organizations, technology providers, and R&D institutes.

- The organization of *training* on these techniques for 2,400 companies and technology intermediary organizations.

- The application of *innovation diagnosis and action plan* to 600 companies.

- The co-finance of *pilot implementation* of selected techniques to 120 companies.

Table 10.1 InnoRegio: Participating authorities per region

	Central Macedonia	Basque country	Crete	Norte	Thessaly	Wales
Local authority	■ Region of Central Macedonia	■ Industry, Commerce and Tourism Department of the Basque Government ■ Association for the Promotion of Industrial Change	■ Region of Crete	■ Government's Regional Co-ordination Commission	■ *Region of Thessaly*	■ Welsh Development Agency
University	■ U*RENIO Research Unit – Aristotle University of Thessaloniki*		■ *Technical University of Crete*	■ Northern Portugal Universities Association	■ University of Thessaly	■ *University of Wales – Cardiff Business School*
SME organization	■ Confederation of Industries of Northern Greece	■ Syndicate of Companies of Alava	■ Chamber of Commerce and Industry of Chania ■ Agency for the Development of Tourism in Crete	■ Porto Industrial Association	■ Association of Industries of Thessaly	■ Pembrokeshire Business Initiative
Technology transfer organization	■ Thessaloniki Technology Park	■ *LEIA Technological Foundation*	■ Mediterranean Agronomic Institute of Chania	■ *Agencia Innovacao*	■ Metallurgical Industrial Research Agency	■ Snowdonia Business Innovation Centre ■ Business in Focus

The lead partner per region is in italics.

- The creation of *virtual innovation environments and a network of Internet websites* (one in each region) to provide online information for demonstration and implementation of these techniques and technologies.

The implementation of the project included four stages: (1) the feasibility verification study and the definition of the work programme, (2) the development of innovation and knowledge management techniques, (3) the dissemination and pilot application of techniques, and (4) monitoring and evaluation.

The structure of the work programme and the inter-regional partnership appear in Figure 10.3. The starting point was the *search and study of IMTs* that may be useful to companies and technology suppliers. The aim was to gather information and best practices on methods and techniques elaborated by European projects or by relevant international organizations while, in parallel, proceed to the acquisition or creation of the necessary know-how for the IMTs' implementation in the regions concerned. The implementation of benchmarking, for example, is not feasible without the construction of a reference database including indicators of best practice in management and manufacturing, which allows a given organization to benchmark against other organizations.

The dissemination of IMTs was the next stage and was based on relevant practices that bring technology know-how to companies and suppliers. First, the innovation development methods and tools were discussed in *training seminars*, in which selected and high-profile technology providers (consultants, brokers, information technology companies) presented IMTs to target audiences.

Innovation audits followed the training seminars and the sensibilization on IMTs. The audits were structured and covered issues related to financing, management, engineering, marketing and products, and supply chains. Five to seven days were spent per audit and company, and the conclusions were of two kinds. First, the organization received a report highlighting strengths and weaknesses in innovation, and an action plan on the appropriate IMTs that could possibly upgrade its innovation capability. Second, the data and indicators from the audit were fed into a database to create reference material for benchmarking. Thus, benchmarking reports could be generated with respect to international data as well as to regional and national data.

Linked to the audits was the third step of IMT dissemination, the *pilot applications* and demonstration. From the action plans generated through the audits, a number of cases are selected, in which InnoRegio co-financed pilot applications of IMTs for demonstration and experimentation. In each region, the project supported different pilot applications in order to test the widest possible range of tools.

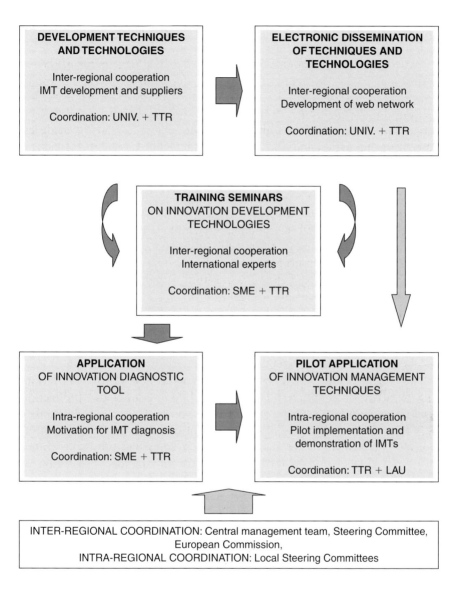

Figure 10.3 InnoRegio: Workflow and intra-regional cooperation

A *network of websites* assists the dissemination of IMTs. Six regional websites are creating a virtual innovation environment for the dissemination of IMTs in which one may find information on techniques and technologies, e-learning applications for distance teaching, the problems that these techniques may solve, the costs and benefits of their applications, the steps and conditions for implementation, companies/organizations that use

241

such technologies, and the national or international organizations capable of facilitating the implementation (see, www.urenio.org).

So, a full cycle of technology dissemination was accomplished, in real and virtual spaces, including training, auditing, and implementation and demonstration. The steps in this dissemination were based on inter-regional and intra-regional cooperation. The purpose of the inter-regional cooperation was to ensure supply with high-quality innovation management skills, taking advantage of the available expertise and know-how in the six cooperating regions. The added value of the intra-regional cooperation (between universities, companies, technology intermediary organizations, technology transfer agencies, local authorities) was to increase the motivation and participation in the project, bring together technology users and suppliers, and spread effectively innovation management to all the components of the regional innovation system.

Deconstructing Innovation

At the level of methodology, the InnoRegio project focuses on the regional innovation system. On the one hand it explores the practices, methods, and technologies for developing innovation and, on the other hand, it creates an interactive learning environment in innovation with the use of IT and the Internet. The emphasis is clearly on the soft side of innovation, on practices and methods for the renewal of products and production processes, which springs from the often cited contradiction in public policy to substitute real multipliers of the ability for innovation with major infrastructures where the outer casing (buildings, infrastructure, area, equipment) dominate and significantly cover over soft factors. Promotion of these aspects is expected to improve the targeting and reduce the cost of political interventions and infrastructures for innovation, shifting the centre of gravity of policies from the external form to the content of the public action. In a further step, InnoRegio focuses on practices and methods for innovation that become available through virtual innovation environments, which support learning and the dissemination of appropriate tools and practices.

The aforementioned approach involves a deconstruction of innovation so that its entire process can be analysed in terms of its individual functions and then in terms of its typical practices. Here, following the reasoning discussed in previous chapters, a deconstruction of innovation is introduced on two levels: at the level of its individual functions and at the level of subjects and practices that correspond to each function.

[Innovation] = [Functions of innovation] = [Subjects + Practices]

The full process of innovation includes the *functions* of research, financing, technology transfer, new product development, and technology collaboration networks. In turn each function includes organizations and practices. With the intermediation of organizations involved in the innovation process the initial and composite functions can be broken down into a large number of *typical practices*. The empirical form of these relationships is shown in Table 10.2, where innovation is broken down into five basic functions and then into a number of subjects (organizations involved), typical practices and tools.

Table 10.2 Innovation: Components, organizations, and practices

	Function	Organizations involved	Typical practices and tools
INNOVATION	Research and development	▪ University labs ▪ Research institutes ▪ Technology providers ▪ Company R&D departments	1 R&D management 2 Technology watch 3 Technology forecast 4 Creativity development 5 IPR management (patents) 6 Marketing of innovation
	Innovation finance	▪ Venture capital funds ▪ Commercial banks ▪ Technology transfer funds ▪ Regional development funds	7 R&D financing 8 Technology assessment 9 Product assessment
	Technology transfer	▪ Science and tech parks ▪ Innovation centres ▪ Liaison offices ▪ Industrial and technology bureaux ▪ Technology brokers ▪ Consultants	10 Technology audit 11 Benchmarking 12 Technology brokerage 13 IPR management (licensing, copyright) 14 Technology clinics
	New product and process development	▪ Manufacturing companies ▪ Companies in the service sector	15 Product design/ development 16 Product cycle management 17 Business process re-engineering 18 Quality management 19 CAD-CAM 20 MRP II
	Optimization of networks and inter-firm relations	▪ Manufacturing and service companies	21 Value analysis 22 Supply chain management 23 Outsourcing 24 Just-in-time delivery 25 E-commerce

Research and development, for example, as a basic function and component of innovation can potentially be performed by many organizations (university laboratories, public research institutes, R&D divisions of enterprises, and so on) which apply state-of-the-art tools and methodologies for R&D management, technological forecasting, the development of creativity and so on. At any stage of R&D development, all organizations are obliged to follow more or less the same methodologies and typical practices.

Likewise, technology transfer is a function that is performed by a range of technology transfer organizations (from technology parks to innovation centres and industrial liaison offices) and which is executed by typical practices of benchmarking, technology audit, technology brokering, technology clinics, and the purchase and sale of technology (licensing). When missing or inadequately implemented, technology transfer is incomplete, regardless of the size of the hard infrastructure and the equipment owned by the technology intermediary organization.

The deconstruction of the individual functions of innovation leads to an equivalent set of typical practices, which codify the existing state-of-the-art for the development of innovation. A total of 25 typical practices are mentioned in Table 10.2. This list is open-ended and dynamic since practices are being transformed as well as the list changing with the removal and addition of practices. The practice MRP I for example was replaced by the MRP II and ERP technologies, while recent publications have examined new approaches to maximizing production chains (Fernandez-Ranada *et al.* 1999).

Thus the methodological viewpoint of InnoRegio focuses on the deconstruction of innovation on the one hand into basic functions, components and typical practices, and, on the other hand, on the maximum possible use of IT and telematics technologies for learning and applying typical practices and tools. The network of six websites operating in the regions covered by the project serve this very goal. In its simplest form this network transfers information about innovation methods and technologies; service that is already accessible with the online presentation of more than 20 applications and practices for developing innovation. The next step is for certain of these practices to be fully or partially automated, thus opening the road to their online implementation with the assistance of telematics and tele-working methods.

The typical practices highlighted in Table 10.2 coincide with the methodologies, tools, instruments, and technologies that innovative firms are using to deal with innovation. We call this family of methodologies *Innovation Management Techniques and Technologies* (IMTs). Innovative firms and organizations can be identified by their research and development activity. Alternatively, companies that have developed or introduced at least one new product or new production process over a three-year period are also considered innovative. A new product or process was considered an innovation only if there was a substantial investment of new knowledge and a change in the knowledge base of the firm. The result is the transformation within the organization (enterprise, service organization, research laboratory) of the production processes, the products, and the organization. IMTs represent the instruments and tools that may facilitate these processes for the successful introduction of innovations.

Since the 1970s, public and private sectors have begun to focus on the use of innovation management strategies and tools to gain economic advantage on the global market. Ohmae and Porter have stressed the importance of current international innovation management strategies. Ohmae in particular described prevalent strategies by which companies make use of technology to gain control of the customer, suppliers, and other companies (Ohmae 1982; Roberts 1998). IMTs operate in the fields of R&D, innovation finance, technology transfer, product/process development, and technology networking, which are recognized as important subprocesses in the global strategy of the company.

Major sources of knowledge on IMTs are the Innovation Programme of the European Commission, which has supported original research in this field, and the literature on business excellence and world-class manufacturing.

The *Innovation Programme* of the European Commission gave an important push to the research on innovation management techniques. These are methodological approaches applied in firms either internally or through the use of external advisers with the aim of providing either an overall diagnosis of the firm's innovation practices or focusing on specific themes to align business strategies with technological competencies and challenges.

This programme, particularly via the action line 'Promotion of Innovation Management Techniques', has supported a number of projects to raise awareness and develop trans-national experiences for schemes promoting these methodologies, to spread good practices and strengthen the experience and professionalism of practitioners in this area. The main objectives of the Community projects were:

- To develop experience and raise awareness in the design and monitoring of support schemes promoting IMTs.

- To create a body of experience by the implementation of a large number of innovation consultancy assignments in companies.

- To disseminate results to facilitate the harmonization of methodologies and provide added value to regional and national schemes and their operations, public or private.

- To establish trans-national, national and regional groupings of organizations so as to allow the movement of skills to those areas most in need.

245

- To build practical experience in the design and monitoring of public support schemes for the promotion of IMTs.

Innovation Management Tools, published in 1997, was the first report presenting 18 IMTs. These tools were tried and demonstrated in the framework of the MINT projects of the SPRINT Programme of DG XIII-D (Table 10.3). The main conclusions relating to the development and their use were:

- IMTs do not deal with technology alone but integrate other issues such as culture, communication and organization in firms.

- Many IMTs deal with general strategy, process and product development, and on analysis, decision-making, and implementation.

- The tools reviewed are stronger on management participation than on employee participation.

- IMTs poorly serve micro-enterprises (below 15 employees).

- An all-purpose IMT does not exist. Instead a success factor is the efficient combination of methodology, consultant, and client firm. An effective combination of internal issues (resources, competencies, goals) and external business context (customers, suppliers, competitors) is of utmost importance.

- Clear and realistic objectives as well as early tangible results lead to longer-term commitment for the tool.

Innovation Management Techniques in Operation was a second report published in 1998, which described 10 more IMTs that have already been

Table 10.3 Methodologies included in *Innovation Management Tools*

- ADVIA. PC based software tool for business planning and budget simulation	- Product/market/technology scans
	- BUNT methodology for company plan and development
- TEKES MINT methodology for auditing	- FRAM methodology aiming at implementing a profit rise of five percentile units in firms with 5 to 35 employees
- Technology clinics for technology transfer	
- ANVAR innovation diagnosis	- Value analysis for technological diagnosis
- APRODI innovation training	
- Innovation factor analysis	- Strategic approach to technology for SMEs
- EOMMEX diagnosis	
- FORBAIT generic innovation diagnosis	- STIN analysis for auditing and action plan
- INNOVARE, quality management audit	- PERA profile diagnosis
	- PERA self diagnosis methodology

Source: Adapted from European Commission (1997a).

tested in companies by various national and regional organizations in several European countries, and have been validated according to their usefulness and applicability as innovation management tools. They were selected from among 24 projects funded by the Innovation Programme of the European Commission. The IMTs chosen were clustered into three groups: those that tackle company problems of internal origin (inward looking), those designed for problems with an external origin (outward looking) and, finally, those that responded to more general problems related to the company's capacity to confront change and manage it efficiently (forward looking).

Several of the IMT action line projects have been so successful that they have attracted the attention of national or regional authorities, which, in some cases, decided to continue (and in some case develop further) the scheme started by the Commission's funds.

World-class manufacturing and *business excellence* literature are further major sources of knowledge on IMTs. The term 'world-class manufacturing' was coined by Richard Schonberger to describe a manufacturing philosophy followed by many of the major successful Japanese manufacturing companies. Actually the term WCM has come to mean the pursuance of best practice in manufacturing and management (Schonberger 1986; De Toni *et al.* 1998).

The past two decades have seen the emergence of a number of striking innovations in the technical and organizational character of leading manufacturing firms. On the technical side there is 'information technology' and 'systemic automation' including 'flexible manufacturing systems' and 'computer integrated manufacturing'. On the organizational side, some major changes are the 'just-in-time' and the 'total quality control' systems which, together with other work process organization patterns developed in Japan, have introduced a new culture on product development and new

Table 10.4 Methodologies included in *Innovation Management Techniques in Operation*

DIAGNOSTIC	▪ Innovation profile diagnosis
INWARD LOOKING	▪ Value analysis ▪ Business process re-engineering ▪ Project management and development ▪ Product design and development
OUTWARD LOOKING	▪ Benchmarking ▪ Marketing of innovation ▪ Technology and competitive watch
FORWARD LOOKING	▪ Total quality management ▪ Creativity tools

Source: Adapted from European Commission (1998c and 1998d).

relationships among workers, between workers and management, and between firms and their buyers and suppliers (Calderini and Cantamessa 1997; Goel and Singh 1998; Takikonda and Rosental 2000; Veryzer 1998). Major areas of the new manufacturing practices include: (1) production scheduling and planning, (2) quality management, and (3) supply chain management (see URENIO 1999).

Production scheduling and planning, despite the comparatively recent introduction of a number of industrial databases and software tools for automated scheduling, is still largely generated by hand, using paper, pencil, and graphical aids (Gantt charts). Knowledge and intuition gained through years of experience are the principal tools employed by the scheduler, and improvement in quality and consistency of the production schedules led major manufacturers to develop or purchase database systems that track raw materials and work-in-process inventories. These database systems usually incorporate software tools automating some aspect of schedule generation up to a degree. Classification of these tools is based on the scheduling philosophy that is employed and the most important tools are listed below:

- *Manufacturing Resource Planning* is the most widely installed system in the industry today. It operates on fixed planning horizons and determines: (1) the quantities of each item that will be used in the production of the desired volume of end products, and (2) the item that must be purchased or manufactured to meet the predefined due dates for the end products.

- *Just-in-time Production* is a scheduling philosophy that dictates reduced materials inventories in order to achieve process improvements and reduce process variability. The major result of this approach is the reduced cost associated with holding of inventories. In addition, it improves process flow and floor control mainly by detecting early failures in the production system. The only actual disadvantage of the method is that it is purely descriptive with no available theory to assist in derivation of JIT methods.

- *Optimized Production Technique* consists of software (and hardware) packages and is an alternative to comprehensive MRP for production planning, materials planning, and resource scheduling. OPT works by sequentially examining at fixed intervals of time, how production resources should be used to meet requirements.

- *Resource-constrained Scheduling* is a more realistic paradigm that takes into account many more of the complexities of the scheduling environment. The similarity between the two problems is emphasized when both are viewed as networks. Therefore determining the best resource-constrained project schedule consists of a combinatorial optimization problem. Among the approaches most commonly employed to solve this optimization problem are branch-and-bound methods, dynamic programming, zero-one integer programming, and Lagrange multiplier methods.

- *Control Theory* seeks scheduling methods that either explicitly reflect the uncertain nature of the available information or give some guarantee as to the insensitivity of the schedule to future information. In practical terms, schedules are sought that are resistant to disruptions, to the absence or inaccuracy of status information and flexible to change. Control theory views scheduling as a dynamic activity, where the scheduling problem is actually one of understanding how to reschedule. Despite the fact that control theory only recently has been applied to discrete production scheduling, the underlying problem and fundamental issues are naturally described as a problem of control.

- *Discrete Event Simulation* has been used primarily as a means of testing fixed scheduling heuristics and dispatching rules. Since heuristics, plus priority rules, give better performance than plain priority rules, it is clear that flexible interactive simulation tools are useful for scheduling in manufacturing systems. The user of a simulation tool by reviewing the status of the job shop model, using his or her knowledge and practical experience, can stop, interact with the simulation model and try alternative scheduling approaches.

- In *Artificial Intelligence*, finally, the scheduling problem is viewed as the determination and the satisfaction of a large number and variety of hard and soft constraints, encountered in the scheduling domain. AI extends knowledge representation techniques in order to capture these constraints, to integrate constraints into a search process, relax them when conflicts occur, and diagnose poor solutions to the scheduling problem. AI research methods that are performed by heuristic rules guiding the search, thus finding the solution to computationally complex problems, are of great merit to scheduling applications. Similarly current research on genetic algorithms simulated annealing and learning systems hold potential for the improvement of speed and accuracy of various production scheduling approaches.

The *management of quality* is another discrete area of business excellence that is increasingly being introduced in successful companies, creating an holistic, or integrated enterprise. The concept of quality has evolved substantially from the days when it was difficult to convince any chief executive that he should place quality as a prime element in his strategy. Today, the definition of quality has grown to include more than product quality. It now includes costs, as a measure of process quality; profits, as a measure of company quality; and even work morale, as a measure of organizational quality. What was delineated by the term 'quality management' now covers many business strategies and tactics that permeate the firm, for example customer satisfaction, benchmarking, empowerment, partnership sourcing, business process, and quality function deployment.

The organization of the future will need to be a customer-sensitive, knowledge-creating, agile enterprise. It must provide value to every customer, where value is the customer's perception of total lifetime benefits minus total lifetime costs. It must continually exchange information and ideas with its customers and suppliers to deliver customized products and services. The organization must quickly reconfigure its products, services and processes, and it must integrate expertise from other organizations to remain competitive. Consequently, it will become critical to create an environment grounded in ongoing innovation and learning – one that will benefit from external uncertainty and unpredictability. Employees will need skills and knowledge to make empowered decisions and work in a variety of roles.

For the professional manager, the knowledge and application of quality tools and techniques will be mandatory. Total quality management (TQM) will be integrated into the way things get done every day. Managers will need to undertake organizational self-assessment based on quality principles and to be attuned to where both their own organizations and others are headed. TQM uses a number of tools and techniques that are well known and have been implemented in businesses throughout the world. These techniques include simple tools, such as: (1) affinity diagrams, (2) flowcharts, (3) tree diagrams, (4) check sheets, (5) cause-and-effect diagrams, or more complex and sophisticated methods, such as (1) force field analysis, (2) leadership, (3) customer focus, (4) employee involvement, (5) benchmarking, and (6) quality function deployment.

Supply Chain Management, is a third area of IMT development, and has only recently been recognized as a critical source of strategic advantage to business competition. The supply chain focus of today's enterprise has arisen in response to several critical business requirements, and there was a need for companies to reinvent themselves, and quickly, in order to win or avoid a possible decline in the development of the enterprise.

Over the past decade, the application of computerized information tools, the utilization of management techniques, such as just-in-time, total quality management and business process re-engineering, and the implementation of employee empowerment and cross-functional management philosophies have activated lean product design and manufacturing. These management paradigms have required companies to turn outward to their channels of supply and distribution in search of opportunities for cost and cycle time reduction and process agility. The four major business areas driving the supply chain management are:

- *Customer chains:* The needs of customers have changed. In the past, enterprises competed by selling product lines consisting of standardized, mass-produced products to customers who had relatively very little purchase choice. Today the customers expect to be treated as unique individuals and demand more from their supply channels with regard to high-quality, customized products and services, quick-response deliveries and information and communication technologies.

- *Information and communication chains:* Today as the value of accurate information grows and the speed of communication accelerates, information has increasingly begun to be seen as the fundamental source of wealth and competitiveness.

- *Distribution chains:* The dramatic changes that have been occurring in the marketing and distribution channel environment in the world economy, the rapid introduction of new products and services on an international scale and increased demands for quick-response delivery, led to the explosion of strategic alliances and partnerships on a global scale. The ability of companies to exploit the networking of marketers, designers, manufacturers, and distributors provided by today's information technologies, facilitates the creation of new forms of competitive-enriching collaboration and enhances the growth of supply chain alliances.

- *Logistics:* In the past, logistics was perceived primarily as an activity focused around product delivery and cost management. In contrast, today's best companies utilize logistics as a strategic, cross-functional, inter-enterprise management activity whose mission is to both plan and coordinate all inventory and delivery activities.

A major problem arising from the above literature is the difficulty of codifying the tools with respect to particular problems of an organization. IMTs are not static, unique, and unchangeable tools. It cannot be claimed that a closed set of developed, tried and proven IMTs exist for solving, one by one, the problems faced by companies. It seems difficult to find one-to-one correspondence between some specific problems of a company and a methodology that solves the problem. Instead, IMTs are usually considered in combination with other technologies, adapted and personalized to varying degrees for each specific case. Moreover, each time a methodology is applied in a specific setting, a variation of it is, to a certain extent, generated, a variant that could be proposed as a 'new' IMT (European Commission 1998c).

From the above vast literature and given the difficulties of codification, we identified a number of representative and promising IMTs, which constitute the core for learning and dissemination in InnoRegio. They are divided into four categories, following the fragmentation of the innovation

Table 10.5 Selected IMTs in InnoRegio

In the field of R&D:	In the field of product/process development:
1 Innovation factor analysis	10 Product design and development
2 Technology watch	11 Product life cycle management
3 Creativity	12 Business process re-engineering
4 Marketing of innovation	13 Management of quality
	14 Computer-aided design
	15 Material requirement planning
	16 Value analysis
In the field of technology transfer:	In the field of networking and cooperation:
5 Technology audit	17 Supply chain management
6 Benchmarking	18 Outsourcing
7 Technology evaluation	19 Just-in-time
8 Intellectual property management	20 Electronic commerce
9 Technology clinics	

process in R&D, technology transfer, product/process development, and technology cooperation.

- *Innovation factor analysis* is an overall diagnosis focusing not only on solving already known problems, but discovering 'new' problems. The main objectives are highlighting problem areas in firms, developing solutions/recommendations and improving the qualifications and skills of managers. The main business functions addressed are corporate strategy, management and product/process innovation. Two 'sub-tools' are applied within innovation factor analysis: a discussion guide for the diagnosis interview, and a survey/analysis guide for the assessment of the different innovation factors. The areas assessed are: products/markets, company strategies, technologies, subcontractors and procurement market, methods and instruments of innovation, and support for the innovation process.

- *Technology watch* is a systemic approach that exploits and transmits information that enables the company to create patents and introduce new products to the marketplace. The fields it detects include: new techniques, new machinery, new clients, new competitors, industrial property, patents, products, rules, regulations, differences between products and the company with respect to its competitors, R&D efficiency, competitive advantages, and new collaborators. Technology watch, the 'on-going verification of the state of the art', enables a company to keep track of how technologies evolve, in order to innovate and invest at the right time. The results of watch in SMEs are: (1) it helps them to avoid making a useless investment in the development of a product when the product has already been patented, (2) as a result of a patent analysis, the management can decide to launch a new product, and (3) it enables a company to participate in foreign calls for tenders.

- *Creativity* is the generation of imaginative new ideas, involving a radical novelty in innovation or a solution to a problem, and a radical reformulation of problems. Creativity is also defined as the integration of existing knowledge in a different way. All definitions require that creative solutions add value to business processes. Innovation results when creativity occurs within the right organizational culture, which provides the possibilities for the development of individual and group skills. Creativity can only be developed efficiently when it is tackled within a group or team. For this reason, most creativity techniques are undertaken within the framework of specific work groups, within companies or other organizations. The creativity process is a combination of external ideas, cultural and intellectual wealth and experience. Major creativity supporting techniques include: brainstorming – for problem solving; story boarding – for strategy and scenario planning used by groups; lotus blossom – for scenario planning and forecasting strategic scenarios; checklists – for product improvement or modification; morphological analysis – for product improvement and analysis of products/process; mapping process – for strategic management thinking in organizations; and excursion technique – for forcing groups to formulate strategies. Computer-based supporting techniques, such as artificial intelligence models and idea processor systems, are mainly used in research planning, product design, knowledge acquisition, and decision making. Fundamental concepts for all creative techniques are: the suspension of premature judgement and the lack of filtering ideas; the creation of analogies and metaphors through symbols, etc., by finding similarities between the problem situation and situations resolved; the building of imaginative and ideal situations – the inventing of the ideal vision; the finding of ways to make the ideal vision happen; the relating of things or ideas that were previously unrelated; and the generation of multiple solutions to a problem.

- *Marketing of innovation* determines and defines the types of action that must be carried out so that an innovative product or service will be successful in the marketplace. It tends to guide developments, so as to ensure definition of the product and introduce the product on to the market and control its penetration. It is generally included in strategic marketing, derived from the marketing of high-technology products and it is most valuable when the innovation product or service is still in the design process. The methodology consists of three main parts: (1) analysis or gathering and study of information with a view towards marketing decision-making. The analysis ends with market segmentation, which consists of representing the market by defining its limits, and the breaking it down into homogenous sub-sets. (2) Diagnosis, in which the segments to be acted upon are selected according to their interest and according to the company capacities. (3) Marketing plan, which defines the activities to be undertaken to launch the product on to the market.

- *Technology audit* is the overall evaluation of business activities for the description of the situation and the profile of enterprises, the identification of critical weaknesses in their operations, and the definition of problem-solving actions and priorities for development.

- *Benchmarking* is to compare a company's performance in a set of activities with that of similar enterprises, in order to allow it, as a result, to adopt better business practices and improve its competitive position. The use of the technique relies on identifying the best practices of an enterprise's competitors and in implementing the means either to reduce existing differences by adopting better business practice, or to maintain present competitive advantages. To this end, the measures to be adopted are: analysis of the company's processes, calibration of the best competitors' results, identification of how and why these results are obtained, use of this information to establish objectives and strategies, and implementation of the necessary means to achieve the objectives.

- *Technology evaluation* is a set of principles, methods and techniques/ tools for effectively comparing the potential value of a technology and its contribution to a company, a region, or an industrial sector. As mentioned it is one of the most significant methodologies in innovation and technology transfer, utilized in screening new ideas and assessing innovative or non-innovative products and technologies. Technology evaluation may be defined in a variety of ways: (1) as a group of studies considering technology impact that may occur when a technology is introduced, extended or modified, (2) as an early warning system to detect, control, and direct technological changes and developments so as to maximize the public good while minimizing the public risks, and (3) mainly as an analysis of cost and benefits from alternative technologies, which provides information and helps the actors involved in selecting and adopting one of them. A thorough evaluation examines different technologies and its device's value from technical, market and consumer perspectives and compares costs and benefits with respect to the goals of the actors involved.

- *Intellectual property rights management* focuses on patents, licensing, and technology purchase. Patents can only include certain subject matter. Inventions concern, in particular, new technical solutions, which offer practical means to resolve technological problems: products or processes offering new functional or technical features can be protected by means of patents or utility models. A patentable invention must comply with certain basic prerequisites. Both when applying for a patent and also during its lifetime, legal provisions and the rules of national patent systems have to be considered. Patents are geographically limited in their scope: a patent is only enforceable in the state in which the national patent office granting it has its legal domicile. In addition to national patent systems there are also regional and international patent systems.

Licensing is the financial exploitation of patents, according to specific contracts and agreements. Licences may or may not be exclusive. Licensing entitles the owners of patents to exploit their inventions: produce, dispose, and market or keep and use for the same purposes the products/processes protected by the patents, and prohibit a third party from exploiting their invention.

- *Technology clinics* are developed to diagnose and cater for the technology needs of small companies. Technology clinics were formed around a particular new technology capable of improving company productivity and quality. The aim of the methodology is to speed up both the application and the implementation of technology development projects. In addition, the method aims at encouraging the active use of external technology support organizations by the companies. The goal of a typical assignment is to solve a specific technology-related problem faced by the customer SME. The technology clinics act as an interface between experts from various research organizations and the SMEs. The most important outcome from the clinic concerns the support for decision-making for technological investments. Technology clinics enable SMEs to test new equipment and materials before the actual investment decision has to be made. As a result of the assignment, companies find out whether the currently applied technology should be replaced by a new one. Furthermore, some guidelines concerning the internalization or outsourcing of new technologies are provided. The technical solutions resulting from the assignments have a high potential for upgrading the competitiveness of SMEs, as they take the form of improved quality, cost savings, new products, and increased productivity.

- *Product design and development* form a set of tools that enable product innovation, improving their quality, functionality, image and differentiation, and thereby increase SMEs' competitiveness. These techniques may be classified in two large groups: (1) techniques and tools for design development, which provide the means to analyse the product concept in the context of its restrictions, and (2) computational techniques, which support design integration through shared product and process models and databases. The main goals of product design methodologies are to: help new products meet the specifications related to customers' needs, quality, price, manufacturing, recycling, etc.; reduce development costs and the time necessary for commercialization; coordinate and schedule the activities involved in the design and development of products within the entire set of activities, taking into account time, tasks, resources, manufacturing, etc.; and integrate the above objectives into a development strategy in line with the company's capacities.

- *Product life cycle management* is the investigation of the life cycle curve for each product and the strategic selection of necessary actions to pick the prime time life of the product: taking it out of the market or making appropriate transformations to lengthen its total time life or replacing it with a new or improved product.

- *Business process re-engineering* radically rebuilds the processes of the company so as to achieve radical improvements in time, costs, and quality. Reducing any actions that generate inefficiency, simplifying/compressing several earlier steps of a process into one, designing alternative processes, and incorporating customers' expectations to the definition of the process. The method is made up of several basic steps: (1) select the strategic added-value processes for redesign, (2) simplify new processes – minimize steps – optimize efficiency – modelling, (3) organize a team of employees for each process and assign a role for process coordinator, (4) organize the workflow – document transfer and control, (5) assign responsibilities and roles for each process, (6) automate processes using IT (intranets, extranets, workflow management), (7) train the process team to efficiently manage and operate the new process, and (8) introduce the redesigned process into the business organizational structure. Re-engineering brings a transformation to the whole company. Areas specifically subjected to the method undergo radical change, but it is also necessary for the other functional areas to be re-analysed in order to create a coherent whole. The process is useful for businesses with serious difficulties (whose structures fall below others and require radical change), for businesses with approaching difficulties (who risk being swept away by market changes, technology, and demand for quality if their processes are not modified), and also for businesses leading their market, where re-engineering allows them to stay ahead of the competition.

- *Management of quality* maximizes the value of each operation within the company and in relation to clients and suppliers, in order to improve the quality of each operation, product, service, etc. It includes a total supervision of quality issues: procedures within the company and world-class technological capabilities, encouraging employees, communication with clients and suppliers. It also includes *leadership*, reinforcing the role of senior managers focusing on the continuous improvement of company's quality and competitiveness, and *employee involvement*, the empowering of employees and recognition of their role, giving to employees control of their activities and responsibilities of their actions. Quality improvement is a concept applicable to the whole range of a company's activities and to its immediate environment. The process integrates both, the company's organization as well as that of its suppliers and distributors, as part of the value chain. In the market, quality is a synonym for excellence. Total quality, in particular, is a process of maximizing the value of each operation, process, product, service, etc. Every area of the company must be integrated into the quality process, and it is often necessary to revise or transform the operational and organizational structure of the company. The general objectives are to provide internal and external clients with products and services that permanently meet their expectations, and to eliminate the procedures that generate losses in terms of cost, time, and reliability regarding the product or service.

- *Computer-aided design* is defined as the use of information technology in the design process. A CAD system consists of IT hardware, specialized software, depending on the particular area of application, and peripherals. The core of a CAD system is the software, which makes use of graphics for product representation, creates databases for storing the product models and drives the peripherals for product presentation. The role of CAD is to help the designer to:

1 Accurately generate and easily modify graphical representation of products, view the actual product on screen, make modifications, present ideas on screen without any prototype – especially during the early stages of the design process.

2 Perform complex design analysis in a short amount of time: static, dynamic, and natural frequency analysis, heat transfer analysis, plastic analysis, fluid flow analysis, motion and tolerance analysis, and design optimization.

3 Record and recall information with consistency and speed.

- *Material requirements planning (MRP)* takes over the calculation of late acceptable start-time of each assembly for each product. MRP renders final product requirements of the main production programme into the demand for raw materials, parts and sub-products. This 'rendering' is based on a concise table of materials for each product, where demand, corresponding to level 0 (final product) of the material tree spans to lower levels and entails into parts' demands and, finally, of raw materials. MRP II is a method for the effective planning of all resources of a manufacturing company: it represents a group of software programmes designed to tie together disparate company functions to create more efficient operations in areas such as assembly, delivery of products, and services. It extends MRP and links it with the company's information resources such as human resource information system, financial management, accounting, and sales. MRP is being used in a variety of companies where a number of products are made in batches using the same production equipment. MRP is most valuable to companies involved in assembly operations and less valuable to those in fabrication. MRP does not work well in companies producing a low number of units on an annual basis. Especially for companies producing complex expensive products requiring advanced research and design, lead times tend to be too long and uncertain and the product configuration too complex for MRP to handle.

- *Value analysis* is aimed at determining the ways to obtain the maximum value from a product, process or service. It works to improve the relation between a product's functionality and price: minimizing manufacturing or rendering/optimizing costs of a product, process or service while at the same time preserving the functions by reviewing the nature of each product with respect to the design, the processes used in its manufacture and the procedures involved in everything from its conception to after-sales service. The methodology is to analyse a product, process or service to its basic components, to associate each of these components with the different functions they fulfil, to determine why a component is part of a product and whether or not it adds value and how to reduce its cost or, in cases where it adds no value, to eliminate the component/activity. The result of this process is quite often the innovation of functions and products: a new product or service that covers the same needs as before is created, and new functions are defined which must be fulfilled by new products or services. The technique can be applied to any area of activity of a company or organization (large and SME), as well as to each of the development phases of products or services where it is important to increase the cost/quality ratio. Numerous variations exist depending on how, where and when it is applied: manufacturing, product design and development, rationalization of industrial processes, machinery design, total quality management, administrative processes, after-sales services, and industrial design.

- *Supply chain management* is the overall evaluation of the supply chain focusing on the interaction between companies involved in the production and distribution of a product or service. Integration of actions related to the evaluation of suppliers, coordination and supplier associations, wastes and defects of inter-firm relationships, stock management, delivery quality, and purchase and cost transparency. Supply chain management integrates topics from manufacturing operations, purchasing, transportation, and physical distribution into a unified programme. It embraces and links all the partners in the chain: departments within the organization, vendors, carriers, third-party companies, and information systems providers. The fundamental objective is to add value, encompassing all activities associated with moving goods from the raw materials stage through to the end user. Strategic objectives of the method are: reducing working capital, taking assets off the balance sheet, accelerating cash-to-cash cycles, increasing inventory turns, etc.

- *Outsourcing* is the strategic use of external sources for the implementation of non-core activities in order to focus on core internal production activities. Finding sources not available internally, freeing internal resources for other purposes, gaining access to world-class capabilities.

- *Just-in-time* is an approach to achieving excellence in a manufacturing company, based on continuous elimination of waste and consistent improvement in productivity. Waste is then defined as all those things that do not add value to a product. JIT is a pull system, where raw material ordering, processing and assembly take place only when the system has a waiting order. The system produces the parts and products in the quantity and time required. In JIT systems very low safety reserves are kept. The main benefits from the application are to lead to zero stock levels, zero transportation time, zero preparation times, elimination of damages, zero delay time, and zero defective products.

- *Electronic commerce* focuses on product promotion and ordering by Internet, including the creation of electronic customers and distribution networks, distant commerce, business-to-business and business-to-customer e-commerce. The business to customer relation is usually carried out by systems that connect users to the company's website, and the systems are referred to as 'electronic shops'. The business-to-business is carried out by EDI and middle-ware systems. The most important benefit of the method is that it can keep companies from being thrown out of the game. A well-conceived website and a strong commerce application can put the company on an equal footing with larger corporations. The company can easily compete on quality, price, and availability. Exchanging transactions electronically, without human intervention, shortens the time it takes to complete each process in the supply chain and ultimately reduces overall cycle time. Thus a company can produce more without increasing overheads.

 Vendors and suppliers can access product specifications, order details, confirmations and updates, anything they need to complete a transaction, without the help of customer service or sales support. The method gives customers total control of the sales process: they can easily choose from all the products (better than a cumbersome catalogue); get up-to-the-minute, accurate product and inventory data; and shop anytime they like.

Through this deconstruction approach and with the use of innovation management techniques and/technologies,[2] the challenge of developing innovations is translated into the dissemination and implementation of different tools by organizations involved in the corresponding function. Innovation as a procedure equates to the application of methods which commence from technology watch and benchmarking and reach as far as the management of production chains and e-commerce. A self-evident condition for this change in the practice of innovation is the dissemination of IMTs and the training of enterprises and other organizations in their use and implementation.

Learning to Innovate in Real–Virtual Spaces

Learning and applying the typical innovation practices and IMTs can be done in many ways. At one extreme are the conventional methods with the involvement of external consultants, whereas at the other extreme there are distance-learning applications based on telematics technologies.

- For example, benchmarking is a technique that can be applied online with the assistance of a database system, user interface and automated processing diagrams. In this case the practice of comparative evaluation and the ascertainment of the position of the organization can be performed on a virtual level.

- On the contrary, business process re-engineering or value analysis requires the physical presence of an external consultant who works for a period of time on site in the organization and proposes the redesign of procedures in order to resolve problems that have been ascertained during the diagnosis phase.

- E-commerce requires the combination of an external consultant in the development phase and customization of the application, while after this the application will operate on a virtual level on the Internet.

These multiple possibilities for learning and using the physical and virtual spaces permit innovation to be connected to the world of IT, telecommunications, and telematics. There is a trend for the individual innovation practices to be transferred to or supported by IT and telematics technologies, and for the virtual space in which these take place, to be constantly widened (Demachak *et al.* 2000). A virtual innovation environment is being developed to support the procedures performed in real space, inside islands of innovation. One could assume that with the use of advanced communication tools the largest part of the applications will be transferred gradually from the real to the virtual space.

Motivation for Learning: Demand for IMTs

You cannot teach someone unless there is motivation and willingness to learn. In the case of IMTs, an indication of motivation was the active demand for use and implementation. The identification of demand for IMT learning and application in the six regions of InnoRegio was based on four sources of data and analysis. Included was desk-based research involving previous projects, and mainly the audits and consultation held during the RTP, RIS, and RITTS projects; interviews with local technology intermediary organizations (local enterprise agencies and innovation centres) with a close appreciation of the attitudes and needs of SMEs in their local area; meetings with the participation of SMEs to discuss the existing application of IMTs and preferences for new ones; and analysis of data gathered through a structured questionnaire submitted to 250 companies in six regions.

The analysis showed that firms have already incorporated, to some extent, several techniques, but there are still gaps in their efforts to achieve technological modernization, considering the high levels of demand for most innovation techniques.

- The most commonly used techniques concern the management of quality (ISO 9000 and diagnosis), environmental management (ISO 14000 and environmental evaluation), management planning and production scheduling, CAD-CAM, and project management.

- There is remarkable interest in some techniques that, as yet, are not widely used, such as customer management (satisfaction and inquiry of fidelity), employee involvement (communication plan, evaluation and satisfaction inquiry), product design and development, EFQM, benchmarking, and machine safety diagnosis.

- There is low knowledge and use for techniques usually bound with R&D and product development: innovation diagnosis, technology clinics, marketing of innovation, creativity, technology watch, and value analysis. Beside the low acquaintance with this family of techniques, the gap between the actual use and the demand of techniques from this category is the higher one.

The main reasons for the low use of IMTs are not really linked to the lack of companies' technological equipment, but above all, to the limitations of strategic management capacity, innovation management, and learning capabilities. The deficits are at the level of competencies in project management and industrial design and engineering, which are recognized as crucial by companies. There is a growing need for the use of new technologies to reduce the weight of labour cost advantages in global competitiveness and find out/create new sources of competitiveness. The deficit of strategy definition capability in companies could be resolved by the use of strategic diagnosis, technology watch, and benchmarking to upgrade the economic intelligence of firms.

There is also a need to improve the ability of companies to act at an international level, not as passive actors, but proactive, geared towards new product launches, new distribution channels, and identification of their products as company products (own brands). On many occasions, it is stressed that technological centres and intermediary activities are not adequate to cover SMEs' needs in the field of IMTs, and it is necessary to create new services and re-engineer existing ones. The priorities and needs of companies include access to technological information, development of international R&D cooperation, access to state-of-the-art and world-class technologies, and the widest use of technologies for the digital economy.

The final assessment of the most demanded IMTs in the InnoRegio regions is shown in Table 10.6. This table presents the ranking of demand on the one hand at the level of individual thematic units with the R&D and new product development/production process sectors at the top, followed by the technology transfer and inter-firm relations sectors. On the other hand, it also presents the findings on the most demanded techniques and technologies within each sector. At this point, the most interesting element is the convergence of findings from the research in the individual regions towards the highlighting of certain IMTs as the most important.

In the R&D sector, demand was identified in three cases. Innovation factor diagnosis as a diagnostic tool of the internal state of an enterprise, in combination with benchmarking, can lead to extremely significant conclusions on the possibilities for improving the capacity for innovation. On the other hand it lays the ground for the implementation of other IMTs such as business process re-engineering, value analysis, product cycle management, etc. Technology watch and creativity are exceptionally important for monitoring technological trends and the design of new products.

In the technology transfer sector, demand focuses on benchmarking and technology clinics methods. Undoubtedly benchmarking outperforms in relation to technology audit in identifying technological needs since it compares the processes in the enterprise with best practice and performance in the corresponding sector. In any event it is a leading methodology with connection to audit tools, business process re-engineering and the implementation of technologies (technology clinics) and the management of quality.

Table 10.6 Most demanded IMTs per region and thematic area

	IMTs for R&D	IMTs for new product development	IMTs for technology transfer	IMTs for technology cooperation
Central Macedonia	▪ Innovation factor diagnosis ▪ Technology watch	▪ BPR ▪ MRP – ERP	▪ Benchmarking ▪ Technology clinics	▪ Supply chain management ▪ E-commerce
Basque country	▪ Innovation factor diagnosis ▪ Creativity	▪ Product development ▪ Management of quality ▪ Value analysis	▪ Benchmarking	
Crete	▪ Technology watch ▪ Creativity	▪ BPR ▪ Management of quality ▪ Value analysis	▪ Benchmarking ▪ Technology clinics	▪ E-commerce
Norte	▪ Innovation factor diagnosis ▪ Technology watch ▪ Marketing of innovation	▪ Management of quality	▪ Benchmarking ▪ Technology/product evaluation	▪ E-commerce
Thessaly	▪ Innovation factor diagnosis ▪ Technology watch	▪ Management of quality ▪ Value analysis	▪ Benchmarking ▪ Technology clinics ▪ Technology/product evaluation	▪ E-commerce
Wales	▪ Technology watch ▪ Creativity	▪ Value analysis	▪ Technology clinics	

In the new product development/production process sector, demand was identified in matters of quality management, process re-engineering and improvements in programming with the introduction of IT. Clearly, the emphasis is on process-related technologies and with certainty we can claim that this is linked with the high representation of traditional industrial sectors in both the sample population and the regions.

Finally, in the field of inter-firm relations, the most demanded technique/technology was e-commerce. Production chain management and outsourcing are less known among enterprises.

Teaching Practices

As mentioned, the InnoRegio project has standardized the procedures for disseminating and learning IMTs in each region. Two parallel routes are available, learning in real space and learning in virtual space. In both cases learning is directed at the same objects, at actors in the regional innovation system (enterprises, research labs, business consultants, technology brokerage organizations), which are called upon to train themselves in and implement IMTs.

In real space the dissemination of know-how about IMTs includes:

1 *Dissemination via seminars*, with 12 seminars on the presentation of technologies to 400 organizations in each region (80 per cent businesses, 20 per cent research labs and technology transfer bodies).

2 *Application of innovation diagnoses*, with visits and work in 100 enterprises in each region in order to select the IMTs that are appropriate for each enterprise and preparation of a plan of action for implementing them.

3 *Pilot applications of IMTs*, in 20–25 enterprises/organizations in each region to demonstrate specific solutions and applications.

There is cohesion and deepening between the three levels. Each organization that is involved in the first level (1) has a 25 per cent probability of passing to (2) and then again a 25 per cent probability of succeeding to level (3). The incentive for participation is that InnoRegio covers 100 per cent of training costs in the first two levels and co-finances pilot applications by 50 per cent in the third level. The overall package is considered particularly attractive since it covers all preliminary work for the application and a large part of the application itself. The selection criteria is that of competitiveness: the best/most appropriate organization is chosen.

The philosophy being that the teaching is to provide state-of-the-art knowledge and to transform the relationship between teacher–trainee in a technology transfer relationship. In this case the trainee looks upon the teacher in the expectation of acquiring new know-how. This philosophy is implemented by selecting the best business consultants and IT providers to teach the IMTs and then support their application. Teachers were selected from major IT companies, consulting companies and technology parks to discuss innovation management techniques and technologies in terms of real implementation conditions, cases, cost, and benefits. If it is true that the enterprises learn better from enterprises and that leaders guide the market, then training by the best business consultants and IT companies is the optimum solution for the dissemination of new innovation management technologies.

Virtual Learning

Learning in virtual space is complementary to the dissemination of knowledge via seminars, diagnoses, and pilot applications. It involves the electronic dissemination of know-how, the provision of advice and the online application of IMTs via the Internet.

The core of the electronic dissemination of IMTs is a network of six websites in Central Macedonia, the Basque country, Crete, Norte, Thessaly and Wales, where a series of teaching and distance learning tools have been developed, such as:

- Web pages for online information about IMTs and technology providers.

- E-learning modules.

- Dynamic databases for the development of IMTs.

- Client-server software for the online application of some IMTs, such as technology watch and benchmarking.

- Virtual spaces created through the online operation of some IMTs (benchmarking, technology intelligence, e-commerce).

Certain of the IMTs are available more for virtual dissemination and application. In the simplest methods, information diffusion and cost–benefit analysis can be done just as well remotely. Other cases such as technology watch and innovation factor analysis and e-commerce are based primarily on the virtual space of the Internet and on IT tools. Our assessment is that the field of combined real and electronic dissemination and application will continue to expand and in the long-term IMTs' learning and use will be done more fully in real–virtual space.

The methodologies employed in InnoRegio create a virtual space, which is connected with the innovation system in each region where the project is being implemented. The deconstruction of the cycle of innovation into its basic functions, into management tools and organizations for the application of tools allows a radical transformation of the problem of innovation.

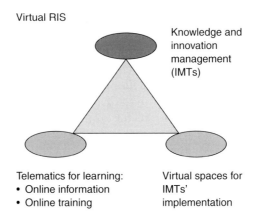

Virtual RIS

Knowledge and innovation management (IMTs)

Telematics for learning:
- Online information
- Online training

Virtual spaces for IMTs' implementation

Figure 10.4 Virtual regional innovation system: Three building blocks

In this new formulation of the problem, innovation is equal to the application of a series of typical tools/technologies by appropriate organizations. The application of IMTs is then done via learning, communication, and collaboration in both the real and virtual space thus creating a virtual RIS space atop the real regional innovation system.

A virtual RIS is a digital space for learning, technological collaboration, and application of innovation management consisting of three building blocks:

- The central block is composed of innovation management techniques and technologies which incorporate the knowledge and practices that enhance innovation at any stage, applied research and development, use of state-of-the-art technologies, tools for new product development, and networking technologies.

- Second is that these techniques and technologies are disseminated and transferred to users via telematics and virtual learning applications, including information portals, e-learning modules, online technical reports, demonstration material, links to databases and online libraries.

- The third element is a sum of the individual virtual spaces, which have been created in relation to the virtual application of the IMTs, such as virtual technology assessment, virtual benchmarking, e-commerce applications. These tools create their own virtual spaces and complement procedures realized at the real space of the regional system of innovation.

In Central Macedonia for instance, the pilot virtual RIS created combines multiple learning and IMTs' application procedures. An enterprise can consult websites on the Internet to obtain useful information on IMTs, monitor pilot applications and connect and get information from other related sites. The diagnosis of innovation in the enterprise is done semi-automatically and is supported by a tool in electronic format with the results of the diagnosis being fed into a client-server application that allows the export of benchmarking diagrams and conclusions from a database. A technology intermediary organization can request online benchmarking and follow a remote course in learning and using benchmarking. Pilot applications of technology watch and mainstream applications of e-commerce may be done to a large extent or completely via the Internet thus creating their own virtual spaces.

The reinforcement of the regional innovation system via the virtual dissemination and application of IMTs is due to the increase in interaction relations and the expansion of learning practices. The real and virtual dimension of the innovation system overlap and a new real–virtual innovation space is being created.

This solution for the creation of a virtual RIS atop the regional system of innovation, and particularly so the thinking on its dematerialization that is being introduced, can be applied to the creation of virtual spaces in other categories of the innovation islands such as industrial districts, technology parks, smaller islands based on innovation centres, or more complex technopoles. In these instances, the creation of a virtual space presupposes that the formative relations rooted into the district and park creation models, will be deconstructed with this being followed by the transfer of certain formative relations and functions to the virtual space. This is a rather general rule for the making of intelligent environments.

Notes

Introduction: Origins, Structure and Contents

1 Urban and Regional Innovation Research Unit.
2 European Regional Development Fund.
3 The term 'technology development' signifies the progress on the level of knowledge and technology, whereas 'technology-based development' signifies the social and economic progress made on the basis of knowledge and technology resources. 'Technological development' highlights both processes and their internal relationships.

Chapter 1: Innovation is an Island

1 See the survey on innovation of the General Secretariat for Research and Technology (1996).
2 Some support programmes for industrial districts and clusters, such as the 'Future of Greek Industry' drafted by the Ministry of Development, paid no attention to the minimum number of companies required to create a cluster, with the result that many supported clusters comprised only a few companies and the basic conditions of flexibility and innovation were lost.
3 The Kyoto Research Park, for example, has been defined as an 'Intelligent City', providing an international information exchange network and R&D support systems for technology-oriented businesses and organizations. Similar IT applications in support of innovation are found at the city of Prato, where the development of a local telematics network that supports inter-business collaboration is replacing the intermediating role of the *impannatori*.
4 For more see Porter (1990) in which these processes are fully developed.
5 GERD: Gross Expenditure on R&D. BERD: Business Expenditure on R&D.

Chapter 2: Districts and Technopoles in Europe

1 There is no indication in the bibliography, see Aydalot (1980: 151–8).
2 Areas eligible under Objective 2 of EC regional policy cover 16.8 per cent of the population of the Community and include regions in industrial decay, where: (1) the average rate of unemployment recorded over the previous three years is above the Community average, (2) the percentage share of industrial employment in total employment is equal or exceeds the Community average, and (3) an observable fall in industrial employment is also recorded.

Notes

Chapter 3: Technology Poles in the Less Favoured Regions of Europe

1 These choices were based on the results of market research on technological services in Crete which found that the main needs of businesses had to do with services connected with IT, market research, automation, improved productivity and the development of new products. On the other hand, demand for industrial facilities, due to the negative change in the number of industrial units and employments, was very limited.

Chapter 5: Regional Innovation Strategies in Europe

1 On the concept of regional competitiveness, Maskell and Malmberg (1995) argue that regions compete with each other, but regional competitiveness does not deal with competition in the usual economic meaning of the word. Regional competitiveness can be defined as the capacity of the region to attract and maintain firms with stable or increasing market shares in an activity, while maintaining stable or increasing standards of living for those who participate in it. This capacity is based on the resources available in the region, the physical structures established in the region through time (infrastructures), and in the region's specific endowment.
2 See for instance, *The Index of the Massachusetts Innovation Economy* (2001). Available online: <http://www.mtpc.org/theindex/index_99.htm>
3 Strengths, Weaknesses, Opportunities and Threats.

Chapter 7: Technology Intelligence in Innovating Regions

1 Search engines create their listings by automatically crawling the web, then people search through what they have found. If you change web pages, search engines eventually find these changes. Search engines have three major elements. First is the spider, also called the crawler, which visits a web page, reads it, and then follows links to other pages within the site. What the spider finds is collected and placed into the second part of the engine, the index, which like a giant book contains a copy of every web page the spider has found. Search software is the third part of a search engine. This is the program that sifts through the millions of pages recorded in the index to find matches to the terms of a search, and ranks them in order of what it believes is the most relevant. (For more on search engines and how they rank web pages, see Online HTTP. <http://www.searchenginewatch.com>).
2 Traditionally two mathematical approaches have been used for trend extrapolation. The first is continued exponential growth. This model suffers, however, from overstatement when projections are long term. The second approach is logistic growth or growth that conforms to the 'S' curve which traces the start-up phase, the midlife, and the maturation of a technology. A good example of such an application may be found in Nieto *et al.* (1998). The model is convincing when enough data are available to define the start-up phase.
3 InnoRegio is a follow-up project of regional innovation strategies (RTP-RIS-RITTS). The project focuses on the development and dissemination of innovation and knowledge management techniques and information technology tools in support of regional innovation systems. The aim is to develop and diffuse methods and techniques that permit the organizations composing a regional innovation system (companies, technology producers, technology brokers, consultants, etc.) to manage knowledge and implement technological innovations. These techniques cover the entire process of innovation, including R&D, technology transfer, business skills, networking, and finance (see also Chapter 10).

270

Chapter 8: Intelligent Cities: Islands of Innovation become Digital

1 See, http://smartcommunities.org
2 EPITELIO: Excluded people integration by the use of telematics innovative opportunities.
3 INFOSOND: Information and services on demand.
4 MAGICA: Multimedia agent-based interactive catalogues.
5 CAPITALS: Capitals projects for integrated telematics applications on a large scale.
6 CONCERT: Cooperation for novel city electronic regulating tools.
7 EUROSCOPE: Efficient urban transport operation services cooperation of port cities in Europe.
8 DALI: Delivery and access to local information and services.
9 EQUALITY: Extending quality urban service for added-value living using interactive telematic systems.
10 PH-NET: Public health network.
11 PERIPHERA: Telematics applications and strategies combating social and economic exclusion.
12 Most authors do not make the distinction between digital and intelligent cities. For instance, Mimos (2001) points out 'that there is no agreed standard definition for an Intelligent City. The Intelligent City concept is a merger of advanced technologies, urban planning methodologies and management functions. The technologies include telecommunication, electronics, IT, utilities, eco-technology, construction technology and architectural designs. Urban planning concepts are used to integrate these technologies to provide and create a habitat for mankind to sustain and manage both the operations of the technical systems and the socio-economic systems requirements of the habitants, the people management principles and functions are developed to operate the total systems. This requires information generation for decision making by managers of the city. The Intelligent City concept arose in response to complex social, economic, and political urban problems facing most modern settings. The need to improve the quality of urban life amidst increasing social, economic and environmental problems prompted technologists and planners in all areas to contribute to the creation of new and more holistic concepts for modern cities. Such improvements must cover all aspects of human life and thus consider living, working, leisure, socializing and other needs of citizens of modern settings. The technology of telecommunication, electronics, IT, utilities, eco-technology, construction technology and architectural designs must act in a concerted and holistic manner to create a healthy and efficient city community as well as living conditions and environment.'
13 See, http://edc.eu.int/TURA/projects/pages/syrecos.html
14 See, http://edc.eu.int/TURA/projects/pages/telemart.html
15 See, http://edc.eu.int/TURA/projects/pages/tierras.html
16 See, http://edc.eu.int/TURA/projects/pages/cwasar.html

Chapter 9: Real–Virtual Technopoles

1 OnLi: Online innovation: virtual network of European technology parks for innovative services, project of the European Commission, DG Enterprise, 2000–1 (see http://www.newventuretools.net).
2 The same approach of deconstruction was applied also in the project InnoRegio for the creation of a virtual regional innovation system, see Chapter 10.
3 See, http://www.casa.ucl.ac.uk/vc/cities.htm

Notes

Chapter 10: Real–Virtual Regional Innovation Systems

1 See www.innovating-regions.org, and in particular the links to innovating regions sites.
2 For a more analytical description of the above innovation management techniques and technologies see: Komninos *et al.* (2001).

References

Alison, D. (ed.) (1969) *The R&D Game: Technical Men, Technical Managers, and Research Productivity*, Cambridge MA: MIT Press.

Allen, J. (1988) 'What science parks and their tenants want from venture capitalists', in *Science Parks as an Opportunity for Property and Venture Capital Investment*, vol. II – *Venture Capital*, West Midlands: UKSPA – Peat Marwick McLintock.

Allesch, J. (1985) 'Innovation centres and science parks in the Federal Republic of Germany: current situation and ingredients for success', in J. Gibb (ed.) *Science Parks and Innovation Centres: Their Economic and Social Impact*, Amsterdam: Elsevier.

Amin, A. (1989a) 'Flexible specialisation and small firms in Italy: myths and realities', *Antipode*, Vol. 21.1, pp. 13–34.

Amin, A. (1989b) 'A model of a small firm in Italy', in E. Goodman, J. Bamford and P. Saynor (eds) *Small Firms and Industrial Districts in Italy*, London: Routledge.

Arufe, F. and Prieto, H. (1998) 'A network of towns: innovation and economic development', *Progress in Planning*, Vol. 49, No. 3–4, pp. 199–214.

Arundel, A. (1997) 'Why innovation measurements matters', in A. Arundel and R. Garrelfs (eds) *Innovation Measurement and Policies*, Luxembourg: Official Publications of the European Communities.

Asimov, I. (1997) *Chronology of Science and Discovery*, Heraklion: University Press of Crete.

Autio, E. 'Evaluation of RTD in regional systems of innovation', paper presented at *RESPOR* Conference of the European Commission, DG XII, Brussels, September 1996, and (1998) *European Planning Studies*, Vol. 6, No. 2.

Autio, E. and Laamanen, T. (1995) 'Measurement and evaluation of technology transfer: review of technology transfer mechanisms and indicators', *International Journal of Technology Management*, Vol. 10, pp. 643–64.

Aydalot, P. (1980) *L'Entreprise dans l'Espace Urbain*, Paris: Ecomonica.

Aydalot, P. (ed.) (1986) *Milieux Innovateurs en France*, Paris: GREMI.

Aydalot, P. and Keeble, D. (eds) (1988) *High Technology Industry and Innovative Environments: The European Experience*, London: Routledge.

Bagnasco, A. (1977) *Tre Italia. La Problematica Territoriale dello Sviluppo Economico Italiano*, Bologna: Il Mulino.

Batty, M. (1995) 'The computable city', paper presented at the m-squared conference A Multimedia Experience, Cardiff, November 29–30.

References

Becattini, G. (1979) 'Dal settore industriale al distretto industriale. Alcune considerazioni sull' unita di indagine dell'economia industriale' *Rivista di Economia e Politica Industriale*, No. 5, pp. 7–21.

Becattini, G. (1989) 'Le district industriel: milieu creatif', *Espaces et Sociétés, Revue Scientifique Internationale*, No. 66–7, pp. 147–63.

Becattini, G. (1991) 'The industrial district as a creative milieu', in M. Dunford and G. Benko (eds) *Industrial Change and Regional Development*, London: Belhaven Press.

Becker, R. H. and Speltz, L. M. (1986) 'Making more explicit forecasts', *Research Management*, July–August, pp. 31–3.

Benko, G. and Dunford, M. (1991a) 'Structural change and the spatial organisation of the productive system: an introduction', in M. Dunford and G. Benko (eds) *Industrial Change and Regional Development*, London: Belhaven Press.

Benko, G. and Dunford, M. (eds) (1991b) *Industrial Change and Regional Development*, London: Belhaven Press.

Berloznik, R. and Van Langenhove, L. (1998) 'Integration of technology assessment in R&D management practices', *Technological Forecasting and Social Change*, No. 58, pp. 23–33.

Best, M. and Forrant, R. (1998) 'Creating industrial infrastructure' in Ch. Pitelis and N. Antonakakis (eds) *International Competitiveness and Industrial Strategy*, Athens: Typothito Press.

Bianchi, P. and Bellini, N. (1991) 'Public policies for local networks of innovators', *Research Policy*, No. 20, pp. 487–97.

Bierman Jr., H., Bonini, C. P. and Hausman, W. H. (1981) *Quantitative Analysis for Business Decisions*, Irwin: Homewood.

Blind, K. and Grupp, H. (1999) 'Interdependencies between the science and technology infrastructure and innovation activities in German regions: empirical findings and policy consequences', *Research Policy*, Vol. 28, No. 5, pp. 451–68.

Breheny, M., Chesire, P. and Langridge, R. (1985) 'The anatomy of job creation? Industrial change in Britain's M4 corridor', in P. Hall and A. Markusen (eds) *Silicon Landscapes*, Boston: Unwin Hyman.

Britton, J. (1989) 'Innovation policies for small firms', *Regional Studies*, Vol. 23, No. 2, pp. 167–73.

Brusco, S. (1982) 'The Emilian model: productive decentralisation and social integration', *Cambridge Journal of Economics*, No. 6, pp. 167–84.

Calderini, M. and Cantamessa, M. (1997) 'Innovation paths in product development: an empirical research', *International Journal of Production Economics*, Vol. 51, No. 1–2, pp. 1–17.

Camagni, R. (ed.) (1991) *Innovation Networks: Spatial Perspectives*, London: Belhaven.

Camp, R. (2000) 'The path to excellence', *Benchmarking in Europe*, Spring, pp. 14–18.

Cappellin, R. and Tosi, A. (1993) *Politiche Innovative nel Mezzogiorno e Parchi Technologici*, Milano: FrancoAngeli.

Castells, E. and Hall, P. (1994) *Technopoles of the World: The Making of the 21st Century Industrial Complexes*, London: Routledge.

Castells, M. (1989) *The Informational City*, Oxford: Blackwell.

Caves, R. and Walshok, M. (1999) 'Adopting innovations in information technology', *Cities*, Vol. 16, No. 1, pp. 3–12.

Chapman, K. and Walker, D. (1991) *Industrial Location*, Oxford: Basil Blackwell.

Chef, J., Komninos, N., Mercier, D. and Tosi, A. (1995) 'Centro de Innovacion Historico/Ambiental de Parque Tecnologico de Andalucia', report to European Commission, DG XIII, SPRINT Programme.

Chiesa, V. (1996) 'Evolutionary patterns in international research and development', *Integrated Manufacturing Systems*, Vol. 7, No. 2, pp. 5–15.

Cicioti, E. (1998) 'Innovation and regional development in a new perspective: the challenge for action in underdeveloped regions', *Progress in Planning*, Vol. 49, No. 3–4, pp. 133–44.

Club des Technopoles – Association of Science Parks (1988) *Annuaire, Section Francaise*, Ed. Lorraine Contact.

Cohen, M. (1988) 'Des PME de haute technologie – Toulouse: Le Pari du Future', *Annales des Mines*, June, pp. 52–5.

Conceicao, P., Heitor, M., Gibason, D. and Shariq, S. (1998) 'The emerging importance of knowledge for development implications for technology policy and innovation', *Technological Forecasting and Social Change*, Vol. 58, No. 3, pp. 181–202.

Conti, S. and Spriano, G. (1991) 'Urban structure, technological innovation and metropolitan networks', *Ekistcs*, Vol. 58, No. 350–1, pp. 315–23.

Cooke, P. (1988) 'Flexible integration, scope economies and strategic alliances: social and spatial mediations', *Environment and Planning D: Society and Space*, Vol. 6, pp. 281–95.

Cooke, P. and Morgan, K. (1991) 'The network paradigm', paper presented at Conference on Undefended Cities and Regions Facing the New European Order, Lemnos, August, and also (1993) 'The network paradigm', *Environment and Planning* D, Vol. 11.

Cooke, P. and Morgan, K. (1997) *The Associational Economy: Firms Regions and Innovation*, Oxford: Oxford University Press.

Cooke, P., Boekholt, P., Schall, N. and Scienstock, G. (1996) 'Regional Innovation Systems: concepts, analysis and typology', paper presented at RESPOR Conference on Global Comparison of Regional RTD and Innovation Strategies for Development and Cohesion, Brussels, September 19–21.

Cooke, P., Uranga-Gomez, M. and Extebarria, G. (1997) 'Regional innovation systems: institutional and organisational dimensions', *Research Policy*, Vol. 26, pp. 475–91.

Cooke, P., Uranga-Gomez, M. and Extebarria, G. (1998) 'Regional systems of innovation: an evolutionary perspective', *Environment and Planning A*, Vol. 30, No. 9, pp. 1563–84.

Coombs, R., Naranden, P. and Richards, A. (1996) 'A literature-based innovation output indicator', *Research Policy*, Vol. 25, pp. 403–13.

CORDIS (1999) *Fifth Framework Programme 1998–2002*, The European Commission. Online. Available HTTP: <http://www.cordis.lu/fp5>

CORDIS Focus (1997) 'The European Innovation Monitoring System (EIMS), Summaries of studies undertaken by EIMS', *CORDIS Focus*, European Commission, No. 14, December.

Crang, P. and Martin, R. (1989) 'Mrs Thatcher's vision of the new Britain and the other sides of the Cambridge phenomenon', unpublished paper, Department of Geography, University of Cambridge.

CURDS and MERIT (2000) 'Assessment of the RITTS Scheme', report to European Commission, DG Enterprise, The Innovation Programme.

References

Dalton, I. (1985) 'The objectives and development of the Heriot-Watt University Research Park', in J. Gibb (ed.) *Science Parks and Innovation Centres: Their Economic and Social Impact*, Amsterdam: Elsevier.

Dalton, I. (1987) 'Forward', in *Science Parks and the Growth of Technology-Based Enterprises*, West Midlands: UKSPA – Peat Marwick McLintock.

Dalton, I. (1992) 'Science parks: a mechanism for technology transfer', *Topos – Urban and Regional Studies Revue*, No. 5, pp. 55–70.

DATAR (1988) *Atlas de l'Amenagement du Territoire*, Paris: La Documentation Francaise.

DDS (2000) Online available HTTP: <http://dds.nl>

De Toni, A., Nassimbeni, G. and Tonchia, S. (1998) 'Innovation in product development within the electronics industry', *Technovation*, Vol. 19, No. 2, pp. 71–80.

Debresson, C. and Amesse, F. (1991) 'Networks of innovators: a review and introduction to the issue', *Research Policy*, Vol. 20, No. 5, pp. 363–79.

Demachak, C., Friis, C. and La Porte, T. (2000) 'Configuring public agencies in cyberspace: Openness and effectiveness', Cyberspace Policy Research Group.

Deog-Seong, O. (1995) 'High-technology and regional development policy: an evaluation of Korea's Technopolis programme', *Habitat International*, Vol. 19, No. 3, pp. 253–67.

Derwent (1986) *The Derwent Guide to Patents*, London: Derwent Publications.

District de Montpellier (1989) *Montpellier L.R. Technopole*, Montpellier: Municipality of Montpellier.

Douglass, M. (1988) 'The transnationalisation of urbanization in Japan', *International Journal of Urban and Regional Research*, Vol. 12.3, pp. 424–54.

Downey, J. and McGuigan, J. (eds) (1999) *Technocities*, London: Sage.

Drejer, A. (1996) 'Frameworks for the management of technology: towards a contingent approach', *Technology Analysis and Strategic Management*, Vol. 8, No. 1, pp. 9–21.

Drucker, P. (1985) *Innovation and Entrepreneurship: Practice and Principles*, New York: Harper and Row.

Dunford, M. (1991) 'Industrial trajectories and social relations in areas of new industrial growth', in M. Dunford and G. Benko (eds) *Industrial Change and Regional Development*, London: Belhaven Press.

Dunford, M. (1992) 'Technopoles: research, innovation and skills in comparative perspective', *Topos – Urban and Regional Studies Revue*, No. 5, pp. 29–54.

Dunford, M. and Kafkalas, G. (eds) (1992) *Cities and Regions in the New Europe*, London: Belhaven.

Edquist, C. (ed.) (1998) *Systems of Innovation: Technologies, Institutions and Organisations*, London: Pinter.

Edquist, C. and Lundvall, B. A. (1993) 'Comparing the Danish and Swedish systems of innovation' in R. Nelson (ed.) *National Innovation Systems: A Comparative Analysis*, New York: Oxford University Press.

Edquist, C. and Hommen, L. (1999) 'Systems of innovation: theory and policy for the demand side', *Technology in Society*, No. 21, pp. 63–79.

Enright, M. (2000) 'The globalization of competition and the localization of competitive advantage: policies toward regional clustering', in N. Hood and S. Young (eds) *Globalization of Multinational Enterprise Activity and Economic Development*, London: Macmillan.

EPAMARNE (1989) *Cité Descartes*, Marne La Vallée: EPAMARNE.

Escorsa, P. (1988) 'Los futuros parques technologicos espanoles', *Economia Industrial*, March–April.

European Commission (1991) 'Science Park Consultancy Scheme', Directorate General Telecommunications, Information Industries and Innovation, DG XIII.

European Commission (1993a) 'Fourth R&D Framework Programme budget', *I&T Magazine*, DG XIII, Winter.

European Commission (1993b) *Methodological Definition and Feasibility Study for Setting-up a Local Venture Capital Company*, CGF Enterprises, DG XVI.

European Commission (1994a) *Good Practice in Managing Transnational Technology Transfer Networks. Ten years of experience in the SPRINT programme*, Luxembourg: DG XIII & Coopers-Lybrand.

European Commission (1994b) *Regional Technology Plans Guide Book*, 2nd Edition, Brussels: DG XVI/DG XIII.

European Commission (1994c) *Competitiveness and Cohesion: Trends in the Regions, Fifth Periodic Report on the Social and Economic Situation and Development of the Regions in the Community*, Luxembourg: Office for Official Publications of the European Communities.

European Commission (1994d) 'Science Park Consultancy Scheme. Evaluation', Strategic Community Programme for Innovation and Technology Transfer, Call for Proposals (93C – 328/13).

European Commission (1994e) 'Science Park Consultancy Scheme. Core specifications and application forms', Strategic Community Programme for Innovation and Technology Transfer, Call for Proposals (93C – 328/13).

European Commission (1994f) *Europe 2000+: Cooperation for European territorial development*, Luxembourg: Office for Official Publications of the European Communities.

European Commission (1995a) *Capital d'Amorcage*, Luxembourg: DG XIII/B3.

European Commission (1995b) *Towards the Knowledge-Based Society*, White Paper on education and training, Brussels: Directorate General XXII.

European Commission (1995c) *Good Practice in Technology Transfer*, Luxembourg: DG XIII/D.

European Commission (1996a) *Green Paper on Innovation*, Luxembourg: DG XIII, The Innovation Programme.

European Commission (1996b) *Comparative Study of Science Parks in Europe: Keys to a Community Innovation Policy*, European Commission, Luxembourg; DG XIII, EIMS Publication No. 29.

European Commission (1997a) *Innovation Management Tools: A Review of Selected Methodologies*, DG XIII, Telecommunications, Information Market and Exploitation of Research, Luxembourg: Official Publications of the European Communities.

European Commission (1997b) *Innovation Measurement and Policies*, Conference Proceedings, 20–21 May 1996, Eurostat and DG XIII, The Innovation Programme, Luxembourg: Official Publications of the European Communities.

European Commission (1998a) *Innovation for Growth and Employment*, Luxembourg: DG XIII, The Innovation Programme.

European Commission (1998b) 'Reinforcing cohesion and competitiveness through research, technological development and innovation', Communication from the Commission, COM (1998) 275.

References

European Commission (1998c) *Innovation Management Techniques in Operation*, SOCINTEC, DG XIII, Telecommunications, Information Market and Exploitation of Research, Luxembourg: Official Publications of the European Communities.

European Commission (1998d) 'Innovation Management Techniques: Synopsis of Projects', DG XIII, The Innovation Programme.

European Commission (1999a) *Sixth Periodic Report on the Social and Economic Conditions of the European Regions*, Luxembourg: Official Publications of the European Communities.

European Commission (1999b) 'Research and Technological Development Activities of the European Union', 1999 Annual Report by the Commission, COM (99) 284.

European Commission (2000) *The Regions in the New Economy: Guidelines for Innovative Measures under the ERDF in the Period 2000–06*, Communication from the Commission to the member states, Online: HTTP: <http://www.innovating-regions.org>

European Digital Cities (2001) Online available HTTP: <http://www.edc.eu.int>

Evangelista, R., Sandven, T., Sirilli, G. and Smith, K. (1997) 'Measuring the cost of innovation in European industry', in A. Arundel and R. Garrelfs (eds) *Innovation Measurement and Policies*, Luxembourg: Official Publications of the European Communities.

Fache, D. (1993) 'Parc Technologique de Hania – Crete', Report to Technical University of Crete, Stratech.

Felsenstein, D. (1994) 'University-related science parks. "Seedbeds" or "enclaves" of innovation?', *Technovation*, Vol. 14, No. 2, pp. 93–102.

Fernandez-Ranada, W., Gurolla-Gal, F. X. and Lopez-Tello, E. (eds) (1999) *3C: A Proven Alternative to MRPII for Optimizing Supply Chain Performance*, Portland: Book News.

Florida, R. and Kenney, M. (1990a) 'High technology restructuring in the USA and Japan', *Environment and Planning A*, Vol. 22, pp. 233–52.

Florida, R. and Kenney, M. (1990b) 'Silicon Valley and Route 128 won't save US', *California Management Review*, Fall, pp. 68–87.

Forrest, J. (1999) 'Models of the process of technological innovation', *Technology Analysis and Strategic Management*, Vol. 3, No. 4.

Foster, R. N. (1986) *Innovation: The Attacker's Advance*, New York: Summit Books.

Freeman, C. (1987) *Technology Policy and Economic Performance. Lessons from Japan*, London: Pinter Publishers.

Freeman, C. (1990) 'Networks of innovators', paper presented at the International Workshop on Networks of Innovators, Montreal, May.

Freeman, C. (1995) 'The national system of innovation in historical perspective', *Cambridge Journal of Economics*, Vol. 19, No. 1, pp. 5–24.

Gamella, M. (1988) *Parques Tecnologicos e Innovacion Empresarial*, Madrid: Los Libros de Fundesco.

Garofoli, G. (ed.) (1992) *Endogenous Development and Southern Europe*, Avebury: Aldershot.

Gavigan, J. and Scapolo, F. (2001) 'Foresight and the long-term view for regional development', *IPTS-JRC Seville*, No. 56, pp. 19–29.

General Secretariat for Research and Technology (1996) *Innovation of Companies in Greece*, Athens: GSRT and Ministry of Development.

Gentler, M. (1996) 'Barriers to technology transfer: culture and the limits to regional systems of innovation', paper presented at the Conference RESTPOR 96, Brussels, 19–21 September.

Gibb, J. (ed.) (1985) *Science Parks and Innovation Centres: Their Economic and Social Impact*, Amsterdam: Elsevier.

Gilly, J. P. (1992) 'Groups and new productive spaces: the case of Matra at Toulouse' in M. Dunford and G. Kafkalas (eds) *Cities and Regions in the New Europe*, London: Belhaven.

Girard, B. and Poncet, D. (1982) 'L'atelier automatise flexible de Citroën a Meudon', *Annales des Mines*, May–June, pp. 103–14.

Giunta, A. and Martinelli, F. (1993) 'The impact of corporate restructuring in a peripheral region: a case study in the Mezzogiorno of Italy', paper presented at Conference on Conflict and Cohesion in the Single Market, Newcastle Upon Tyne, November.

Glasmeier, A. (1987) 'Factors governing the development of high tech industry agglomerations: a tale of three cities', *Regional Studies*, Vol. 22, No. 4, pp. 287–301.

Global Affairs Institute (1999) 'The intelligent cities project report', Online available: HTTP: <www.maxwell.syr.edu/gai/Research/Groups/Governance/Projects/Cities/report.htm

Goel, P. and Singh, N. (1998) 'Creativity and innovation in durable product development', *Computers and Industrial Engineering*, Vol. 35, No. 1–2, pp. 5–8.

Goldman, J. E. (1969) 'Basic research in industry', in D. Alison (ed.) *The R&D Game*, Cambridge, Massachusetts, and London, England: The MIT Press.

Gottdiener, M. and Komninos, N. (eds) (1989) *Capitalist Development and Crisis Theory: Accumulation, Regulation and Spatial Restructuring*, London: Macmillan Press.

Gottdiener, M., Collins, C. and Dickens, D. (1999) *Las Vegas. The Social Production of an All-American City*, Malden MA: Blackwell.

Graham, S. (1997) 'Telecommunications and the future of cities: debunking the myths', *Cities*, Vol. 14, No. 1, pp. 21–9.

Grasland, L. (1992) 'The search for an international position in the creation of a regional technological space: the example of Montpellier', *Urban Studies*, Vol. 29, No. 6, pp. 1003–10.

Grupp, H. (1994) 'Technology at the beginning of the 21st century', *Technology Analysis and Strategic Management*, Vol. 6, No. 4, pp. 379–410.

Grupp, H. and Linstone, H. (1998) 'National foresight activities around the globe: resurrection and new paradigms', *Technological Forecasting and Social Change*, Vol. 60, pp. 85–94.

Halal, W., Kull, M. and Leffman, A. (1998) 'The George Washington University Forecast of Emerging Technologies: A continuous assessment of the technology revolution', *Technological Forecasting and Social Change*, Vol. 59, No. 1, pp. 89–110.

Hall, P. (1988) *Cities of Tomorrow: An Intellectual History of Urban Planning and Design in the Twentieth Century*, London: Basil Blackwell.

Hall, P. (1994) *Innovation, Economics and Evolution: Theoretical Perspectives on Changing Technology in Economic Systems*, New York: Harvester Wheatsheaf.

Hall, P. and Markusen, A. (eds) (1983) *Silicon Landscapes*, Boston: Unwin Hyman.

References

Hall, P., Brehemy, M., McQuaid, R. and Hart, D. (1987) *Western Sunrise: The Genesis and Growth of Britain's Major High Tech Corridor*, London: Allen and Unwin.

Hamel, G. and Prahalad, C. K. (1994) *Competing for the Future*, Cambridge, MA: Harvard Business School Press.

Hamidi, A., Beck, N., Thomas, K. and Herr, E. (1999) 'Reliability and lifetime evaluation of different wire bonding technologies for high power IGBT modules', *Microelectronics Reliability*, No. 39, pp. 1153–8.

Hammond, K., Franklin, D., Flachsbar, J. and Firby, J. (1998) 'The intelligent classroom'. Online available HTTP: <http://www.ils.nwu.edu/~franklin/iClassroom/>

Harvey, D. (1989) *The Condition of Postmodernity*, London: Basil Blackwell.

Harvey, D. (1998) *The Urban Experience*, Oxford: Basil Blackwell.

Hassink, R. (1993) 'Regional innovation policies compared', *Urban Studies*, Vol. 30, No. 6, pp. 1009–24.

Hennebery, J. (1992) 'Science parks: a property-based initiative for urban regeneration', *Local Economy*, pp. 326–35.

Heraud, J. A. and Cuhls, K. (1998) 'Current foresight activities in France, Spain, and Italy', *Technological Forecasting and Social Change*, Vol. 60, pp. 55–70.

Herdman, R. C. and Jensen, J. E. (1997) 'The OTA story: the agency perspective', *Technology Forecasting and Social Change*, No. 54, pp. 131–43.

Hill, C. (1997) 'The Congressional Office of Technology Assessment: a retrospective and prospects for the post-OTA world', *Technology Forecasting and Social Change*, No. 54, pp. 191–8.

Hirtzman, P. and Cohen, M. (1988) 'La technopole de l'agglomeration toulousaine et la region Midi-Pyrenees', *Les Annales des Mines*, June, pp. 18–20.

Howells, J. (1996) 'Tacit knowledge, innovation and technology transfer', *Technology Analysis and Strategic Management*, Vol. 8, No. 2, pp. 91–107.

Hudson, R. (1996) 'The learning economy, the learning firm and the learning region: a sympathetic critique of the limits to learning', paper presented at Conference on Space, Inequality and Difference, Milos.

Hugeland, J. (1989) *Artificial Intelligence: The Very Idea*, Cambridge MA: MIT Press.

Hull, J. C. (1980) *The Evaluation of Risk in Business Investment*, Oxford: Pergamon Press.

Hustler, M. (1988) 'Problems of venture capital and some existing schemes', in *Science Parks as Opportunity for Property and Venture Capital Investment*, UKSPA – Peat Marwick McLintock.

IASP (1998) *Directory of Science Parks*, Valencia: International Association of Science Parks.

IBM (2000) 'Knowledge management and intelligent agent technologies'. Online available HTTP: <http://www.ibm.com>

IDEA (1995) 'Editorial', *Revista de Informacion Tecnologica*, No. 4, p. 5.

IDEA (1997) 'Convenio entre el PTA y el Banco Sabadell', *Revista de Informacion Tecnologica*, No. 9, p. 17.

Ifo Institut (1989) 'An Empirical Assessment of Factors Shaping Regional Competitiveness in Problem Regions', report to the Ministry of Development.

Irvine, J. and Martin, B. (1984) *Foresight is Science: Picking the Winners*, London: Pinter Publishers.

Isarken, A. (1999) 'Evaluation of a regional innovation programme: the Innovation and New Technology Programme in Northern Norway', *Evaluation and Program Planning*, Vol. 22, No. 1, pp. 83–90.

Jessop, B. (1989) 'Conservative regimes and the transition to post-Fordism: the cases of Great Britain and West Germany', in M. Gottdiener and N. Komninos (eds) *Capitalist Development and Crisis Theory. Accumulation, Regulation and Spatial Restructuring*, London: Macmillan.

Joint Research Centre (1998) 'Catalytic Conversion', *Innovation and Technology Transfer*, Vol. 3, pp. 5–6.

Kafkalas, G. *et al.* (1998) 'The making of the intelligent region: The role of structural funds and regional firms in Central Macedonia', Report to European Commission, DG XII, Leonardo da Vinci Programme, and *Gateway Europe*, Spring, pp. 8–9.

Kafkalas, G. and Komninos, N. (1999) 'The Innovative region strategy: lessons from the C. Macedonia regional technology plan', in K. Morgan and C. Neuwelaers (eds) *Regional Innovation Strategies. The Challenge of Less-Favoured Regions*, London: The Stationery Office.

Keeny, R. L. and Raiffa, H. (1976) *Decisions with Multiple Objectives: Preferences and Value Tradeoffs*, New York: Wiley.

Kodama, F. (1995) *Emerging Patterns of Innovation: Sources of Japan's Technological Edge*, Cambridge, MA: Harvard Business School.

Komninos, N. (1986) *Theory of Urbanity*, Athens: Synchrona Themata.

Komninos, N. (1992a) 'Les nouveaux espaces de croissance: La naissance des centres du developpement post-Fordiste', *Espaces et Sociétés*, No. 66–7, pp. 217–32.

Komninos, N. (1992b) Science parks in Europe: flexible production, disintegration and technology transfer, in M. Dunford and G. Kafkalas (eds) *Cities and Regions in the New Europe*, London: Belhaven.

Komninos, N. (1993) *Technocities and Development Strategies in Europe*, Athens, Gutenberg.

Komninos, N. (1998) *The Innovative Region: The Regional Technology Plan of Central Macedonia*, Athens: Gutenberg.

Komninos, N. and Hatzipandelis, T. (1992) 'Flexible production, technology transfer, and the development of science parks', *Synchrona Themata*, September, pp. 81–92.

Komninos, N. and Sefertzi, E. (1992) 'Science Parks and the development of the post-Fordist industry', *Topos – Urban and Regional Studies Revue*, No. 5, pp. 7–29.

Komninos, N. and Sefertzi, E. (1998) 'Neo-industrialisation and peripherality: evidence from regions of Northern Greece', *Geoforum*, Vol. 29, No. 1, pp. 37–50.

Komninos, N., Kyrgiafini, L. and Sefertzi, E. (eds) (2001) *Innovation Development Technologies in Regions and Production Complexes*, Athens: Gutenberg.

Komninos, N., Mercier, D. and Tosi, A. (1996) 'Science Park of Technical University of Crete', report to European Commission, DG XIII, SPRINT Programme.

Komninos, N., Sefertzi, E., Xastaoglou, V. and Xatzipandelis, T. (1990) 'Technopoles and Science Parks: European experience and applications in Greece', report to the General Secretary of Research and Technology, Athens.

Kratke, S. (1992) 'Cities in transformation: the case of West Germany', in G. Benko and M. Dunford (eds) *Industrial Change and Regional Development*, London and New York: Belhaven Press.

Krugman, P. (1997) *Geography and Trade*, Leuven and Cambridge MA: MIT Press.

Kuwahara, T. (1998) 'Technology forecasting activities in Japan', *Technological Forecasting and Social Change*, Vol. 60, pp. 5–14.

Kyoto (2000) 'Intelligent Kyoto'. Online available HTTP: <http://www.kyoto.org>

Landabaso, M. (1995) 'The promotion of innovation in regional Community policy: Lessons and proposals for a regional innovation strategy', International workshop on regional science and technology policy, Himeji, 13–16 February.

Landabaso, M. (1999) 'EU policy on innovation and regional development' in F. Boekema, K. Morgan, S. Bakkers and R. Rutten (eds) *Knowledge, Innovation and Economic Growth: The Theory and Practice of Learning Regions*, London: Edward Elgar Publishing.

Landabaso, M., Oughton, C. and Morgan, K. (1999) 'Learning regions in Europe: theory, policy and practice through the RIS experience', paper presented at the 3rd International Conference on Technology and Innovation Policy: Global knowledge Partnerships, Creating value for the 21st Century, Austin, USA, 30 August–2 September.

Landry, C., Bianchi, F., Ebert, R., Gnad, F. and Kunzmann, K. (1994) 'The creative city in Britain and Germany', Anglo-German Foundation for the Study of Industrial Society, The Creative City Workshop, Glasgow, May.

Larsen, J. and Rogers, E. (1984) *Silicon Valley Fever. Growth of High-Technology Culture*, London: Counterpoint.

Lawson, C. and Lorenz, E. (1999) 'Collective learning, tacit knowledge and regional innovative capacity', *Regional Studies*, Vol. 33.4, pp. 305–17.

Leborgne, D. and Lipietz, A. (1990) 'Fallacies and open issues about post-Fordism', CEPREMAP, Orange Cover, No. 9009.

Lee, T. H. and Nakicenovic, N. (1988) 'Technology life-cycles and business decisions', *International Journal of Technology Management*, No. 3, pp. 411–26.

Lindhom Dalhstrand, A. (1999) 'Technology-based SMEs in the Goteborg region: their origin and interaction with universities and large firms', *Regional Studies*, Vol. 33.4, pp. 379–89.

Lipietz, A. (1984) 'Accumulation, crises et sorties de crise: quelques réflexions méthodologiques autour de la notion de régulation', CEPREMAP, Orange Cover, No. 8409.

Lundvall, B. (1988) 'Innovation as an interactive process: from user-producer interaction to national systems of innovation', in Dosi *et al.*, *Technical Change and Economic Theory*, London: Pinter Publishers.

Lundvall, B. (1992) *National Systems of Innovation: Towards a Theory of Innovation and Interactive Learning*, London: Frances Pinter.

Lundvall, B. and Johnson, B. (1994) 'The learning economy', *Journal of Industry Studies*, No. 1, pp. 23–41.

Luger, M. and Goldstein, H. (1991) *Technology in the Gardens. Research Parks and Regional Economic Development*, Chapel Hill and London: The University of North Carolina Press.

Lymberaki, A. (1991) *Flexible Specialisation. Crisis and Restructuring in Small Industry*, Athens: Gutenberg.

Mahizhnan, A. (1999) 'Smart cities: The Singapore case', *Cities*, Vol. 16, No. 1, pp. 13–18.

Mansel, R. (1991) 'Information, organisation and competitiveness: networking strategies in the 1990s', unpublished paper, University of Sussex, SPRU.

Marshall, A. (1920) *Industry and Trade*, London: Macmillan.

Maskell, P. and Malmberg, A. (1995) 'Localised learning and industrial competitiveness', paper presented at the Regional Studies Association European Conference on Regional Futures, Gothenburg, 6–9 May.

Masser, I. (1990) 'Technology and regional development policy: a review of Japan's technopolis programme', *Regional Studies*, Vol. 24.1, pp. 41–53.

Massey, D. and Wield, D. (1992) 'Science parks: a concept in science, society, and space', *Environment and Planning D: Society and Space*, Vol. 10, pp. 411–22.

Massey, D., Quintas, P. and Wield, D. (1992) *High Tech Fantasies: Science Parks in Society, Science and Space*, London: Routledge, Chapman and Hall.

Mercier, D. (1985) 'The Louvain-la-Neuve science park, part of an innovation centre' in J. Gibb (ed.) *Science Parks and Innovation Centres: Their Economic and Social Impact*, Amsterdam: Elsevier.

Metcalfe, S. (1995) 'The economic foundations of technology policy: Equilibriums and evolutionary perspectives', in P. Stoneman (ed.) *Handbook of the Economics of Innovation and Technological Change*, Oxford: Blackwell.

Miège, R. (1992) 'Les parcs scientifiques et la Communauté Européenne', paper presented at Conference on Science Parks, Luxembourg, May 5–6.

Mimos, B. (2001) 'Intelligent City Management'. Online available HTTP: <http://www.icities.com>

Mintzberg, H. (1990) 'Crafting strategy' in A. Thompson, W. Fulmer and A. Strickland (eds) *Readings in Strategic Planning*, Boston: Irwin.

Mitchell, W. (1995) *The City of Bits: Space, Place, and the Infobahn*, Cambridge, MA: MIT Press.

Monck, C. (ed.) (1987a) *Science Parks and the Growth of Technology-Based Enterprises*, West Midlands: UKSPA – Peat Marwick, McLintock.

Monck, C. (1987b) 'Science parks tenants and their growth potential. Policy implications', in *Science Parks and the Growth of Technology-Based Enterprises*, West Midlands: UKSPA – Peat Marwick McLintock.

Monck, C. (1988) 'Harnessing the growth potential of new technology', in *Science Parks as Opportunity for Property and Venture Capital Investment*, West Midlands: UKSPA – Peat Marwick McLintock.

Monck, C., Quintas, P., Porter, R., Storey, D. and Wynarczyk, P. (1988) *Science Parks and the Growth of High Technology Firms*, London: Croom Helm.

Morgan, K. (1996) 'Institutions, innovation and regional renewal. The development agency as animateur', paper presented at Conference on Regional Futures: Past and Present, East and West, Gothenburg, Sweden 6–9 May.

Morgan, K. (1997) 'The learning region: institutions, innovation, and regional renewal', *Regional Studies*, Vol. 31, pp. 491–503.

Morgan, K. (1998) 'The Intelligent Region Project', Report to the European Commission, DG XII.

Muller, A. (1985) 'Les mutants de Sophia Antipolis', in Y. Kerorguen and P. Merlan (eds) Technopolis, Paris, *Autrement*, No. 74, pp. 150–6.

Murray, R. (1987) 'Flexible specialisation in the Third Italy', *Capital and Class*, No. 33, Winter.

References

Murray, R. (1991) 'Local Space: Europe and the new regionalism', Manchester: The Centre for Local Economic Strategies.

Nelson, R. (ed.) (1993) *National Innovation Systems: A Comparative Analysis*, Oxford: Oxford University Press.

Nelson, R. and Winters, S. (1982) *An Evolutionary Theory of Economic Change*, Cambridge MA: Harvard University Press.

Nelson, R. and Rosenberg, N. (1993) 'Technical innovation and national systems', in R. Nelson (ed.) *National Innovation Systems: A Comparative Analysis*, New York: Oxford University Press.

Nieto, M., Lopez, F. and Cruz, F. (1998) 'Performance analysis of technology using the S curve model: the case of digital signal processing (PDS) technologies', *Technovation*, Vol. 18, No. 6/7, pp. 439–57.

O'Farrel, P. and Oakey, R. (1993) 'The employment and skill implications of the adoption of a new technology: a comparison of small engineering firms in core and peripheral regions', *Urban Studies*, Vol. 30, No. 3, pp. 507–26.

O'Reagain, S. and Keegan, R. (2000) 'Benchmarking Explained', *Benchmarking in Europe*, Spring 2000, pp. 8–11.

Oakey, R. and Cooper, S. (1989) 'High technology industry, agglomeration and the potential for peripherally sited small firms', *Regional Studies*, Vol. 23.4, pp. 347–60.

OECD (1997) *National Innovation Systems*, Paris: OECD Publications.

OECD (1998) *21st Century Technologies: Promises and Perils of a Dynamic Future*, Paris: OECD Publications.

Ohmae, K. (1982) *The Mind of a Strategist: The Art of Japanese Business*, New York: McGraw Hill.

PACE-Telecities (2000) Papers presented at conference on public administrations and business in the new economy, Rome, 6–7 December. Online available HTTP: <http://www.microsoft.com/europe/public_sector/Gov_People/173.htm>

Padrmore, T. and Gibson, H. (1998) 'Modelling systems of innovation. A framework for industrial cluster analysis', *Research Policy*, Vol. 26, No. 6, pp. 625–41.

Parque Tecnologico de Andalusia (1994) *Prospectus*, Malaga: PTA.

Patchell, J. (1993) 'From production systems to learning systems: lessons from Japan', *Environment and Planning A*, Vol. 5, pp. 797–815.

Patel, P. and Pavit, K. (1994) 'The nature and economic importance of national innovation systems', *STI Review*, No. 14, Paris, OECD.

Phillimore, J. (1999) 'Beyond the linear view of innovation in science park evaluation. An analysis of Western Australian Technology Park', *Technovation*, Vol. 19, No. 11, pp. 673–80.

Phillips, J. J. (1983) *Handbook of Training Evaluation and Measurement Methods*, Houston: Gulf Publishers.

Piore, M. (1986) 'Perspectives on labour market flexibility', *Industrial Relations*, Vol. 25, No. 2.

Piore, M. and Sabel, C. (1984) *The Second Industrial Divide: Possibilities for Prosperity*, New York: Basic Books.

Porter, M. (1990) *The Competitive Advantage of Nations*, New York: Free Press.

Poulit, J. (1989) 'Création d'un espace économique nouveau. L'exemple de Marne La Vallée', paper presented at the 13th Conference of INTA.

Pyke, F., Becattini, G. and Sengenberger, N. (1990) *Industrial Districts and Inter-firm Cooperation in Italy*, Geneva: International Institute for Labour Studies.

Radke, M. (1987) 'The development in the United States of strategic partnering between large and small firms', in H. Summan (ed.) *Science Parks and the Growth of Technology-Based Enterprises*, West Midlands: UKSPA – Peat Marwick McLintock.

Radovic, S. and Auriol, L. (1999) 'Patterns of restructuring in research, development and innovation activities in central and eastern European countries: an analysis based on S&T indicators', *Research Policy*, Vol. 28, No. 4, pp. 351–76.

Rafaelidis, V. (1996) *The Peoples of Europe. Origins and Features*, Athens: Eikostou Protou Press.

Regional Studies (1999) *Regional Networking, Collective Learning and Innovation in High Technology SMEs in Europe*, Special Issue, Vol. 33, No. 4.

Ribeiro, C. (1998) 'Innovation and regional development: a regression through the literature', *Progress in Planning*, Vol. 49, No. 3–4, pp. 117–31.

Roberts, R. (1998) 'Managing innovation: The pursuit of competitive advantage and the design of innovation intense environments', *Research Policy*, No. 27, pp. 159–75.

Romano, A. and Bozzo, U. (1985) 'Tecnopolis Novus Ortus: the participation of Southern Italy in the European technological challenge', in J. Gibb (ed.) *Science Parks and Innovation Centres: Their Economic and Social Impact*, Amsterdam: Elsevier.

Rothwell, R. (1992) 'Developments towards the fifth generation model of innovation', *Technology Analysis and Strategic Management*, Vol. 1, No. 4.

Roussel, P. A. (1984) 'Technological maturity proves a valid and important concept', *Research Management*, January–February, pp. 29–34.

Roussel, P., Saad, K. and Erickson, T. (1991) *Third Generation R&D*, Cambridge MA: Harvard Business School Press.

Rowe, D. (1988) 'Achievement from enterprise', in *Science Parks as an Opportunity for Property and Venture Capital Investment*, West Midlands: UKSPA – Peat Marwick McLintock.

RTP C. Macedonia (1996) 'Regional Technology Plan of C. Macedonia', report to European Commission, DG XVI and DG XIII.

Salais, R. and Storper, M. (1993) *Les Mondes de Production*, Paris: Editions de l'EHESS.

Saxenian, A. (1990) 'Regional networks and the resurgence of Silicon Valley', *California Management Review*, Fall, pp. 89–111.

Schon, D. (1969) 'The fear of innovation', in D. Alison (ed.) *The R&D Game: Technical Men, Technical Managers, and Research Productivity*, Cambridge MA: MIT Press.

Schonberger, R. J. (1986) *World Class Manufacturing – The Lessons of Simplicity Applied*, New York: The Free Press.

Scott, A. (1987) 'The semiconductor industry in south-east Asia: Organisation, location and the international division of labour', *Regional Studies*, Vol. 21.2, pp. 143–60.

Scott, A. (1988a) *New Industrial Spaces. Flexible Production, Organisation and Regional Development in North America and Western Europe*, London: Pion.

Scott, A. (1988b) 'Flexible production systems and regional development: the rise of new industrial spaces in North America and Western Europe', *International Journal of Urban and Regional Research*, Vol. 12–2, pp. 171–86.

References

Scott, A. (2000) *Cultural Industry and the Cities*, New York: Wiley.

Scott, A. and Soja, E. (eds) (1998) *The City. Los Angeles and Urban Theory at the End of the Twentieth Century*, Berkeley, Los Angeles and London: University of California Press.

Sefertzi, E. (1996) 'Flexibility and alternative corporate strategies', *Industrial Relations*, Vol. 51, No. 1, pp. 97–119.

Sefertzi, E. (ed.) (1998) *Innovation and System-areas in Greece*, Athens: Gutenberg.

Segal, N. S. and Quince, R. E. (1985) 'The Cambridge Phenomenon and the role of the Cambridge Science Park', in J. Gibb (ed.) *Science Parks and Innovation Centres: Their Economic and Social Impact*, Amsterdam: Elsevier.

Segal Quince Wicksteed Limited (1995) 'Review of Funding Proposals for Greek Science Parks, report to the Ministry of Industry, Energy and Technology, Greece.

Sfortzi, F. (1989) 'The geography of industrial districts in Italy', in E. Goodman (ed.) *Small Firms and Industrial Districts in Italy*, London: Routledge.

Shearmur, R. and Doloreux, D. (2000) 'Science parks: Actors or reactors? Canadian science parks in their urban context', *Environment and Planning A*, Vol. 32, No. 6, pp. 1065–82.

Sigismund, C. (2000) *Champions of Silicon Valley. Visionary Thinking from Today's Technology Pioneers*, New York: John Wiley and Sons.

Simmie, J. (ed.) (1997a) *Innovation, Networks, and Learning Regions?*, London: J. Kingsley Publishers.

Simmie, J. (1997b) 'The origins and characteristics of innovation in highly innovative areas', in J. Simmie (ed.) *Innovation, Networks and Learning Regions?*, London: J. Kingsley Publishers.

Simmie, J. (1998) 'Reasons for the development of islands of innovation: evidence from Hertfordshire', *Urban Studies*, Vol. 35, No. 8, pp. 1261–89.

Small Business Service (2000) 'The Performance of SMEs within the Benchmark Index', Stoke-on-Trent, Department of Trade and Industry.

Smart Cities Guide Book (2001) Online available HTTP: <http://www.smartcommunities.org>

Smilor, R., Kozmentsky, G. and Gibson, D. (1988) *Creating the Technopolis*, Cambridge MA: Ballinger Publishing Company.

Smith, K. (1997) 'Innovation measurement and the CIS approach', Eurostat (ed.) *Innovation Measurement and Policies*, Luxembourg: Official Publications of the European Commission.

Soja, E. (1992) 'Inside Exopolis: Scenes from Orange County', in M. Sorkin (ed.) *Variations on a Theme Park. The New American City and the End of Public Space*, New York: Hill and Wang.

Sorkin, M. (ed.) (1992) *Variations on a Theme Park*, New York: Hill and Wang.

Starkey, K. and Barnatt, C. (1997) 'Flexible specialisation and the reconfiguration of television production in the UK', *Technology Analysis and Strategic Management*, Vol. 9, No. 3, pp. 271–86.

Steffensen, M., Rogers, E. and Speakman, K. (2000) 'Spin-offs from research centers at a research university', *Journal of Business Venturing*, Vol. 15, No. 1, pp. 93–111.

Storper, M. (1993) 'Regional worlds of production: learning and innovation in the technology districts of France, Italy and the USA', *Regional Studies*, Vol. 7, pp. 433–55.

Storper, M. (1994) 'The resurgence of regional economies. Ten Years Later: The region as nexus of untraded interdependencies' paper presented at the conference on Cities, Enterprises and Society at the Eve of the XXIst Century, Lille, 16–18 May.

Storper, M. (1997) *The Regional World*, London and New York: The Guilford Press.

Storper, M. and Scott, A. (1988) 'The geographical foundations and social reproduction of flexible production complexes', in J. Wolch and M. Dear (eds) *Territory and Social Reproduction*, London: Allen & Unwin.

Sunman, H. (1987) 'The growth of science parks in Europe', in H. Summan (ed.) *Science Parks and the Growth of Technology-Based Enterprises*, West Midlands: UKSPA – Peat Marwick, McLintock.

Takikonda, M. and Rosental, S. (2000) 'Successful execution of product development projects: Balancing firmness and flexibility in the innovation process', *Journal of Operations Management*, Vol. 18, No. 4, pp. 401–25.

Tatsumo, S. (1986) *The Technopolis Strategy: Japan, High Technology and the Control of the Twenty-First Century*, New York: Prentice Hall.

Technopolis (1998) 'Regional Technology Plan Central Macedonia', Evaluation report to the European Commission, DG XVI.

Technopolis International (1992) *Archipel Europe: Islands of Innovation*, No. 8, June 1992.

The Index of the Massachusetts Innovation Economy. Online, HTTP: <http://www.mtpc.org/theindex/index_99.htm>

Toedtling, F. (1994) 'Regional networks of high-technology firms. The case of the greater Boston region', *Technovation*, Vol. 14, No. 5, pp. 323–37.

Tolomelli, C. (1990) 'Policies to support innovation in Emiglia-Romana: experiences, prospects and theoretical aspects', in E. Cicioti, N. Alderman and A. Twaites (eds) *Technological Change in a Spatial Context: Theory, Empirical Evidence, and Policy*, Berlin: Springer Verlag.

Tomas, E. (1985) 'The free University of Brussels and its science parks', in J. Gibb (ed.) *Science Parks and Innovation Centres: Their Economic and Social Impact*, Amsterdam: Elsevier.

Tosi, A., Komninos, N. and Mercier, D. (1998) 'Stratégie de mise en valeur de la vallée du Belice', report to the European Commission, DG XIII.

Tsagaris, M. (2001) 'South East Europe: Central Macedonia', Motor Region Report, Tsagaris Consultants, European Commission, DG Research.

URENIO (1999) 'InnoRegio: feasibility-verification study', report to the European Commission, DG Regional policy, Recite II Programme.

Utterback, J. (1986) 'Innovation and corporate strategy', *International Journal of Technology*, Vol. 1, No. 1–2, pp. 119–32.

Van den Ende, J., Mulder, K., Knot, M., Moors, E. and Vergragt, P. (1998) 'Traditional and modern technology assessment: toward a toolkit', *Technology Forecasting and Social Change*, No. 58, pp. 5–21.

Van Dierdonck, R., Debackere, K. and Rappa, M. (1991) 'An assessment of science parks: towards a better understanding of their role in the diffusion of technological knowledge', *R&D Management*, Vol. 21, No. 2, pp. 109–23.

Van Dierdonck, R. and Huysman, F. (1992) 'Science parks, their evolution and their evaluation', paper presented at Conference on Science Parks, Luxembourg, May 5–6.

References

Van Wyk, R. J. (1997) 'Strategic technology scanning', *Technological Forecasting and Social Change*, No. 55, pp. 21–38.

Vedovello, C. (1997) 'Science parks and university–industry interaction: geographical proximity between agents as a driving force', *Technovation*, Vol. 17, No. 9, pp. 491–502.

Veryzer, R. (1998) 'Discontinuous innovation and the new product development process', *Journal of Product Innovation Management*, Vol. 15, No. 4, pp. 304–21.

VIPETVA (1993) 'Technopolis of Hania', report to the Technical University of Crete, Athens.

Warwick, K. (1998) *March of the Machines: Why the New Race of Robots will Rule the World*, London: Century.

Watts, R. J. and Porter, A. L. (1997) 'Innovation forecasting', *Technological Forecasting and Social Change*, Vol. 56, pp. 25–47.

Weber, M. (1960) *The City*, London and Edinburgh: Heinemann.

Westhead, P. and Bastone, S. (1998) 'Independent technology-based firms: the perceived benefit of a science park location', *Urban Studies*, Vol. 35, No. 12, pp. 2197–219.

Winner, L. (1992) 'Silicon Valley mystery house', in M. Sorkin (ed.) *Variations on a Theme Park. The New American City and the End of Public Space*, New York: Hill and Wang.

Witholt, B. (1985) 'Science parks and innovation centres in the Netherlands', in J. Gibb (ed.) *Science Parks and Innovation Centres: Their Economic and Social Impact*, Amsterdam: Elsevier.

Worral, B. (ed.) (1988) *Science Park Directory*, West Midlands: UKSPA – Peat Marwick McLintock.

Zitt, M., Barre, R., Sigogneau, A. and Laville, F. (1999) 'Territorial concentration and evolution of science and technology activities in the European Union: a descriptive analysis', *Research Policy*, No. 28, pp. 545–62.

Index

Note: page numbers in *italics* refer to tables or figures

Index

Britain *continued*
    Regional Innovation and
        Technology Transfer Strategy and
        Infrastructure projects 106;
        technology parks 25, 56–7, *64–5*;
        UK Science Park Association 54–5,
        59, 209; university strategy 62;
        Wales 179–80, 237
Britton, J. 51, 98
Broadacre City 186
Brusco, S. 42
business expenditure 110, 141
business incubator 55, 62, 66, 79, 88
business networking 25
business process re-engineering 256,
    260

Calderini, M. 248
California Smart Communities Institute
    188
Camagni, R. 10, 133, 235
Cambridge Econometrics 4
Cambridge science park 3, 25, 56, 88
Camp, R. 219
Cantamessa, M. 248
capital accumulation 184
capitalism 3, 152
CAPITALS project 194
Cappellin, R. 82
Car Free Cities Network 192
Casa, Bath University 229–30
Castells, M. 23, 47, 185
Caves, R. 11, 189, 192
Cederschoid, Carl 197
centres of advanced technological
    services 98–9
certification for production 119, 123
Chapman, K. 41, 69
Chef, J. 70
Chiesa, V. 142
CIAM 186
Cicioti, E. 235
cities: competitiveness 139; growth
    patterns 185; informatization 183;
    planning 184–5; virtual 230; *see also*
    digital cities; intelligent cities; urban
    and regional development
Citroën plant 223
'City of Tomorrow' 160
Club des Technopoles 57
clusters 88: flexible specialization 24;
    high-technology industries 5, 8, 45;
    knowledge-intensive activities 30;
    Macedonia, Central 132–3; small
    and medium-sized enterprises 52

Cohen, M. 22, 66
cohesion policy 168
collaboration: inter-firm 8, 42, 122,
    124; Italy 23–4; networks 126;
    production 7; research and
    development 7, 27–8, 121; small
    firms 22; university/industry 25–6,
    63–4, 89, 101, 122
collective learning 9–10, 229
command centres 101
Community Initiatives 107
Community Innovation Survey 25,
    33–8, 235
Community Support Frameworks 107
company networks 25, 66–7
competitiveness: cities 139; European
    Commission 3–4, 12, 168; European
    Union 12; flexible production
    systems 49–50, *51*; GDP per head
    3–4; global 52–3; innovation 136;
    knowledge 135–6; learning 31–2;
    quality 43; regional variations 4–5,
    270; small and medium-sized
    enterprises 48
computer integrated manufacturing 247
computer-aided design 257
computerized information tools 250–1
Conceicao, P. 235, 236
CONCERT project 194
conservation of environment 166
Construct, *Siena* 230
Conti, S. 29
control theory 249
Cooke, P. 10, 47, 97, 133, 134, 144–5,
    236
Coombs, R. 34
Cooper, S. 50
cooperation: agglomeration 63;
    environment 33; intra-regional *241*;
    Prato 199; technology 98;
    technology parks 54–5
cooperatives 81–3
Le Corbusier 186
CORDIS 157
CORDIS Focus 20
corporatism 49
cost–benefit analysis: online 226–8;
    technology evaluation 222–4
CPERI 59
Crang, P. 49
creative milieu 42
creativity 253, 262
Crete: *Dissemination of Innovation and
    Knowledge Management Technique*
    179–80; Heraklion Park 76;

Index

62; suppliers 45; technology learning 31–2; technology parks 74–5; technology transfer 97–8, 212; urban and regional development 134; virtual 211–17
New Delhi 186
new industrial spaces 44–6
new technology based firms 59–60, 89, 100
Newly Associated Countries, European Union 107–8
niche markets 51
Nieto, M. 170, 221
Norte 179–80, 237
nylon 21

Oakey, R. 50, 86
observatories for innovation 96–7
OECD 34, 141, 143
O'Farrel, P. 86
Office for Technology Assessment 175
Official Journal, European Commission 55
Ohmae, K. 245
OnLi 211–17: virtual system 214–15; virtual toolbox 215, 216, 217
optimized production technique 248
O'Reagain, S. 218
organizations: innovation 19
Organizations of Industrial Property 96–7
Ostfalen Technology Park 212–13
Ottawa, Wizard Solutions 230
OuluTech Ltd 212
outsourcing 259

PACE-Telecities conference 195, 197
Padrmore, T. 143
Palermo 80
Palermo University 81–2
Paris Convention 97
Patchell, J. 136
Patel, P. 143
patents 37, 96–7, 141, 254–5
Pavitt, K. 143
performance 36, 170, 171
PERIPHERA project 194
PH-NE project 194
Phillimore, J. 59
Phillips, J. J. 223
photonics 163
Piore, M. 42–3, 184
planning: cities 184–5; industrial district theory 9; smart communities 190–2; technology parks 61–2, 90–5

POLIS Network 192
Poncet, D. 223
Porter, A. L. 171, 172
Porter, M. E. 29, 245
Portugal: business expenditure 110; InnoRegio 237; islands of innovation 3, 110; national innovation association 145–6; Regional Innovation and Technology Transfer Strategy and Infrastructure projects 106; research and development expenditure 110; Taguspark 212; technology parks *64–5*
post-Fordism 41–2, 133, 187–8
post-modernism 187
Poulit, J. 57
power/knowledge 136–7
Prahalad, C. K. 169
Prato 11, 185, 199, 269
Prieto, H. 86
production: certification 119, 123; collaboration 7; Crete Technical University 77; development stages 19–20; firm size 50; flexibility 3, 49–50, *51*, 52; fragmentation 50; mass 48; networks 62; quality/price 43; renewal/innovation 18; research 7; scheduling/planning 248–9
production engineering 163, 165
products: design and development 255–6; life cycles 256; value analysis 258
property 89–90
public spending, urban renewal 47
Pyke, F. 49, 84

quality/competitiveness 43
quality control 121–2, 123
quality improvement 119, 120
quality management 249–50, 256–7, 261
Quince, R. E. 56

Radke, M. 67
Radovic, S. 23
Rafaelidis, V. 80
Raiffa, H. 223
RAND Organization 175
R&D: *see* research and development
R&D Framework Programmes: European Commission 1, 157–62; Innovation Programme 28, 69, 107; Macedonia, Central 129; technology transfer 87, 97;